The two hands clutched Lovecraft's with desperate strength. From close range he could see the third, larger blob deeper in the water. It was a man's face, a grotesque expression of panic etched upon its features, dark hair waving. Howard tugged harder at the hands. He thought he felt the man rise a trifle. The eyes in the pallid face were wider than seemed possible. The mouth dropped open and air bubbled upward. Lovecraft wondered if the victim was bound by supernatural forces to the riverbed . . .

D0779719

By the same author

Sun's End
Galaxy's End
Time's End
Fool's Hill
Sword of the Demon
Circumpolar!
Countersolar!

Lovecraft's Book

Compiled by
RICHARD A. LUPOFF

GRAFTON BOOKS
A Division of the Collins Publishing Group

LONDON GLASGOW
TORONTO SYDNEY AUCKLAND

Grafton Books
A Division of the Collins Publishing Group
8 Grafton Street, London W1X 3LA

A Grafton UK Paperback Original 1987

ISBN 0-586-07209-8

Printed and bound in Great Britain by
Collins, Glasgow

Set in Times

For Belknap living . . .
. . . and Vincent dead

Compiler's Note

In a sense, my work on *Lovecraft's Book* commenced in 1943 when I first encountered one of Lovecraft's stories and was at once captivated by it. My interest in the man, his work, and his life has thus persisted for more than forty years.

My interest in Lovecraft remained purely literary, however, until the publication of his selected letters beginning in 1965. The connections between Lovecraft and other personages of his era, and his comments on various events and organizations, struck me as covering relationships and occurrences far beyond what was overtly revealed.

This led me to the investigation of a sequence of events, in which undertaking I have had invaluable assistance from many individuals and organizations. To list them all would be impossible, but I will mention at least the most noteworthy:

John Stanley, of the *San Francisco Chronicle,* for access to his priceless collection of tapes, including rare recordings of Father Charles Coughlin's radio broadcasts.

The *other* John Stanley, of the John Hay Library at Brown University, for access to the library's Lovecraft collection and for assistance in its use.

The late Vincent Starrett, for information and advice contained in numerous unpublished letters, as well as the material found in Chapter Ten of *Lovecraft's Book.*

Dr Fred Stripp, of Berkeley, California, for insightful information and anecdotes regarding extremist movements in the San Francisco area from the 1920s to the 1960s.

The late Larry Brown, for technical information and historical data concerning the early installation of radios in cars, as well as his personal reminiscences of social and cultural life in Brooklyn during the 1920s.

Frank Belknap Long, for his generous reminiscences of his legendary friendship with H. P. Lovecraft, and in particular for information concerning the relationship between Lovecraft and George Sylvester Viereck.

Dr Kenneth Sterling, Lovecraft's onetime literary collaborator; Donald A. Wollheim, Lovecraft's onetime editor and publisher; Julius Schwartz, Lovecraft's onetime literary agent; and E. Hoffmann Price, Lovecraft's collaborator and host; all of them, for their recollections of Lovecraft, his life and times.

My high school acquaintance Mike Morelli, for information and insight into his family background in Providence.

My son Kenneth Lupoff, for information concerning Theodore Weiss (Hardeen the Mysterious) and for important suggestions on further areas of investigation.

The folklorist 'Uncle Wash', now of Oakland, California, for his recollections of conditions in rural Texas in the 1920s, most notably regarding the activities of the Ku Klux Klan and 'the Germans'.

Cedric Klute for information regarding the history of the Thor Hotel in San Francisco; and Cedric Klute and Walter B. Gibson for further information regarding Hardeen.

Joe Gores, for examples and advice as to technique and for encouragement in the present project.

The staff of the *Providence Journal-Bulletin* archives, and of the newspaper room of the library of the University of California at Berkeley, for their courtesy, patience, and assistance.

The numerous bookmen (and women) who assisted in

identifying and obtaining needed materials. These included Jack Biblo, Jack Tannen, Alice Ryter, Howard Cherniak, Nikki St Onge, Marcia S. Wright, Stuart Teitler, Michael Kurland, Daryl van Fleet, and Thomas Whitmore.

Brunhilde Gisela Pronzini, for indispensable assistance with non-English-language documents; my own knowledge of languages is limited, and of German in particular, almost nonexistent.

My agent Henry Morrison and the several editors who provided advice and assistance with *Lovecraft's Book*. These included Clyde Taylor, formerly of G. P. Putnam's Sons, who taught me more of textual structure and discipline in one grueling battle than all my composition teachers from kindergarten through university; David G. Hartwell, most peripatetic of redactors; and James Turner, of Arkham House, whose patience, encouragement, assistance, and support have been little short of saintly.

And especially my wife Patricia, who spent weeks tramping with me through Lovecraft country, and our sons and daughter, Kenneth, Katherine, and Thomas, who spent an unforgettable summer reliving with me the daily installments of a serial that included Babe Ruth's sixty home runs, Charles A. Lindbergh's transatlantic flight, the wedding of Chiang Kai-shek, the climactic struggle between Stalin and Trotzky for leadership of the Soviet Union, the plan of Treasury Secretary Mellon to make Prohibition self-enforcing by simply providing poisoned alcohol to those who wished to drink it, the nearly simultaneous Broadway openings of Al Jolson in *The Jazz Singer*, Bela Lugosi in *Dracula*, Jimmy Durante's latest production, Texas Guinan's newest speakeasy, and an obscure but promising hoofer-comedian named Humphrey Bogart – to name just a few of the incidents in that year.

In addition I feel obligated to acknowledge the assistance of the United States Department of Justice for materials provided, however grudgingly, under the provisions of the Freedom of Information Act (DJ file number 146–7–51–1538). And finally, special thanks must be extended to Dr Hans Werner Büchner, director of the Bibliothek für Militärgeschichte in Koblenz, West Germany, for furnishing a microfilm copy of the previously unpublished blueprint of the *Unterwasserprojekt Elf*.

RICHARD A. LUPOFF

1

Providence

The December air was wintry and moist with falling snow. Howard Phillips Lovecraft lifted his long lantern-jawed face toward the midnight sky, scanning the heavy clouds for a break, then shuddered once against the cold, pulled down the brim of his dark fedora, and turned up the collar of his heavy overcoat.

He was troubled by cold weather, a sensitivity that could render him almost paralyzed if he didn't bundle up properly, but for a magical moment he forgot the December chill and stood gazing down dark Angell Street toward the Seekonk River. His ears strained for the creak of ghostly carriage wheels and the soft *clop-clop* of horses' hooves in fresh, soft snow.

Briefly he surrendered to his yearning for the vanished past, the days of comfort and grace when he was himself a small child and could ride between his Grandfather Phillips and his pretty mother Susie while the coachman whipped up the splendid team.

But the spell popped like a bubble. Instead of a carriage he heard the growl of an automobile's engine. A yellow glow swept along the white-coated roadway. The motor car roared up, a heavy high-bodied model casting twin shafts of light in its path. It swept past him, then disappeared onto River Drive where the snow-dusted road curved northward toward Swan Point.

Lovecraft stamped his feet to restore circulation and continued his interrupted walk. He reached River Drive just at the Narragansett Yacht Club. The club's lights were ablaze, and inside he could hear a society orchestra playing some popular tune; a few senseless lyrics drifted across the white-coated lawns, lines about mountain greenery where God painted scenery. Howard Lovecraft kept to the opposite side of River Drive until he was past the lights of the club. His feet and legs were growing chilled despite his thick woolen socks and long underwear. He was ready to turn back toward home when he heard the sounds of a struggle from the river's edge.

There were shouts, curses, the thump of blows being struck. There was a final heavy crunch, a moment of silence, a splash. Lovecraft started forward, toward the source of the sounds, but he was halted by the shrill grinding of an automobile's self-starter. Two lights sprang into life. With a screech and a roar the heavy car Lovecraft had seen on Angell Street spun through a U-turn on River Drive and sped past him, headed back the way it had come.

Lovecraft paced uncertainly for a few strides, then ran at top speed toward the Seekonk. He was a sedentary man, approaching forty years of age, yet he reached the riverbank in seconds. He peered down into the water. A few lights reflected on its surface from East Providence – the Seekonk was relatively narrow at this point – and an occasional sliver of moonlight penetrated the clouds.

Three white blobs wavered a foot or so beneath the surface of the river. For a moment Lovecraft wished for the reading glasses he'd left at home at Barnes Street. He leaned over the bank, trying to identify the blobs. Startled, he realized what they were. He stiffened with sudden resolve. He pulled his overcoat and suit jacket off with a single movement, dropping them onto the snowy grass.

He flopped onto his belly and stretched as far as he could over the water, but was unable to reach the objects. He drew a deep breath, inched forward, and slipped from the riverbank into the water, striving for the two hands just below the surface, grasping them and kicking with his feet to stay afloat.

The two hands clutched Lovecraft's with desperate strength. From close range he could see the third, larger blob deeper in the water. It was a man's face, a grotesque expression of panic etched upon its features, dark hair waving. Howard tugged harder at the hands. He thought he felt the man rise a trifle. The eyes in the pallid face were wider than seemed possible. The mouth dropped open and air bubbled upward. Lovecraft wondered if the victim was bound by supernatural forces to the riverbed.

Lovecraft tugged again at the hands, felt them pull back convulsively. He was drawn deeper into the water, his hands on the sides of the man's head straining to raise him. Instead he felt himself being drawn down, deeper into the dark icy river. He released his grip on the head and shoved against the shoulders to get his own face above water.

He succeeded in snapping his face upward, gasping icy air into straining lungs. He hardly noticed that the man had released his hands as well, had grabbed frantically at Lovecraft's legs as he pushed the other away. Lovecraft lowered his face once more. The man held his ankles in a desperate convulsive grip. He reached towards the man's head. All he could see now was the dark, floating hair. He tilted back the head and saw the face staring blankly at him. The mouth was still open, fixed in a silent scream; the eyes betrayed the dull emptiness of death.

Lovecraft shuddered, suddenly aware of the icelike chill of the Seekonk. He turned to swim back the short distance to shore. He was not an expert swimmer, had only enjoyed an occasional dog paddle at summer shore resorts. Now he reached out for the bank and found himself held back by the drowned man's unyielding grasp on his ankles.

He turned and drew a deep breath, reached back to dislodge that icy clutch. He managed to loosen the fingers of one hand completely before they snappped shut again in chilly convulsion. Lovecraft drew another breath and pried at the dead man's other hand. The fingers resisted, then yielded, then clenched again. Lovecraft's ankle was free. The fingers had closed in the heavy cloth of his trouser cuff. He tried again and again to pry open the fingers.

Finally, shuddering with despair from his grisly exertions, Lovecraft opened his metal belt buckle, unbuttoned his trousers, and squirmed free of them. Panting and sobbing, he fought his feet clear, pulled himself onto the bank, and struggled upright. He stood dazed, unable to collect his thoughts. He had not faced death since his mother had expired six years earlier, and hers had been a quiet death in a hospital ward. This –

Through some vagary of night air the strains of 'Auld Lang Syne' drifted along the river from the Narragansett Club to jar Lovecraft from his reverie. He was shivering violently, and his feet and his fingers were growing numb. He cast about him in the thin snow and found his suit jacket and overcoat, the one garment still nested neatly within the other.

He struggled back into the dry coats and started to jog towards home. Within seconds he realized that he had not the stamina to make it. He slowed to a dogtrot, then to a walk. He wished for a car on River Drive, but there was no traffic. He could still hear the faint wisps of melody from the yacht club, and the still fainter clangor of distant church bells heralding the New Year.

The glittering facade of the Narragansett Club appeared. He turned and stumbled through the ornate iron gate. The front courtyard of the club was filled with parked automobiles, and the lights of the clubhouse were ablaze. He staggered up the driveway, slumped against the huge main doorway of the clubhouse, and pounded desperately.

After an eternity the door swung open and Lovecraft stumbled into the hall. He was caught by a liveried doorman. In a dazzle he saw dozens of celebrants, men in formal black and white, women in highly colored gowns, rushing to cluster around him. He was half carried to a sitting room and placed on a heavy stuffed divan.

Faces appeared, voices buzzed and mumbled, hands worked over him.

There came a period of half-heard voices and half-sensed movement. Then Lovecraft felt himself supported to an upright posture, something was pressed against his lips, and an unfamiliar burning sensation entered his mouth. He sputtered and gasped for breath, then was fully conscious.

A stocky man in formal dress was bending beside the divan, holding Lovecraft upright. Howard looked down and saw that a heavy car-blanket had been drawn over him; his soaked clothing had been thrown in a dripping pile near the divan. 'I – there was a man – ' Lovecraft began to say.

'What happened to you?' the stocky figure interrupted.

Lovecraft shook his head, gathering his thoughts. 'There was a man. In the Seekonk. I tried to pull him out. He grabbed me and we both nearly drowned. I barely managed to escape.'

The stocky man said, 'Are you certain? Maybe you've celebrated the New Year too much. Mightn't you have fallen in the river?'

'No, no,' Lovecraft protested. If only this person would take him seriously – murder had been done!

The stocky man grinned. 'Well, it's a little odd, don't you agree? The way you arrived here, I mean. Thumping at the door of the clubhouse at midnight on New Year's Eve, drenched in cold water. Maybe you decided to have a little dip on your way home from a party.

'But there's no harm done.' The stocky man patted Lovecraft on the back. 'One little snort of brandy seems to've fixed you up, sir. And you provided some fine excitement for us all. I'm the manager here, and our New Year's gala was getting a trifle tired until you arrived!' He smiled at his companions.

'Well, if you'd like to use our telephone to summon a taxicab. Or is there someone who can come fetch you home?'

'But there really *was* a man!' Lovecraft pounded his fist on the plump divan. 'We need to summon the police!'

The stocky man laughed. For the first time genuine concern registered in his expression. 'Don't you think you'd just be embarrassed in the morning? If you really insist, of course, I can place a call. It's your responsibility, sir.'

Now Lovecraft was determined. 'Yes!'

'But then how will you explain your odd state of costume?' The manager nodded towards Lovecraft's lower extremities. 'Where are your trousers?'

By the time the Providence police arrived, Lovecraft was sitting in the manager's office, outfitted with a set of nondescript borrowed garments. He had telephoned his two aunts and assured them that he was all right. They'd been worried by his long absence from home on a cold winter's night. He told them he would be some while longer but that he was safe and warm.

The manager of the yacht club left the office to meet the police, returned chatting familiarly with a jowly plainclothesman. Howard Lovecraft rose and shook hands with the officer, who introduced himself as a lieutenant of the homicide detail. A uniformed sergeant and a patrolman stood behind the lieutenant.

Lovecraft told the lieutenant all that had happened, from the first passage of the heavy car on Angell Street to his arrival at the yacht club. The plainclothesman asked questions throughout Lovecraft's story while the patrolman unobtrusively jotted notes. At the completion of Lovecraft's recital the lieutenant said, 'There's only one way to find out if this all really happened. Will you take us there and show us the drowned man?'

Lovecraft assented. The evidence would prove him to be a sober and reliable reporter. He had acted properly, despite the manager's jocular implications.

They clambered into the Providence police car, the patrolman driving and the plainclothesman beside him, Lovecraft seated uneasily with the officer in the rear seat. He directed them to the location on River Drive, where they climbed from the patrol car and permitted Lovecraft to lead them to the edge of the Seekonk. Thick flakes still sifted down from heavy clouds, but the reflected lights of East Providence had diminished during these postmidnight hours.

The patrolman produced a large electric torch and played its light over the water at Lovecraft's direction. 'There!' Lovecraft exclaimed. 'You see? There are my trousers!'

He pointed at the spot. Beside the trousers, unmoving under dark, rippling water, the dead face seemed almost to glow.

'Okay,' the lieutenant grunted. 'I gotta believe you now, Mr Lovecraft.' He turned to the patrolman. 'You stay here and stand guard. We'll get back to the yacht club and call for the coroner's wagon.

'Mr Lovecraft, you'll have to come down to Elbow Street and give us your full statement.'

Lovecraft blanched. Must he face interrogation like some mongrel thug? 'I told you everything at the yacht club. Won't that do, sir?'

The officer shook his head. 'I'm afraid that was just a preliminary statement, Mr Lovecraft. What we call an incident report. Now that we know there's been a homicide, we'll need a full statement. We'll ask you to sign it before a notary. You have no objection?'

Lovecraft shook his head. As long as he himself was not under suspicion, he was pleased to provide assistance.

'Unless you'd rather do it in the morning?'

'No. I – but if I could get my own clothing back. I don't see my fedora anywhere. I suppose it's down in the harbor by now. One doesn't find a good hat easily these days.'

'No, sir,' the lieutenant said. 'But we can pick up your other clothes at the club, and you'll have these trousers back in a day or two. Once we pull that poor simp out of the drink and check everything for clues.'

Lovecraft grinned inwardly at the word *clues*. 'I was a devoted follower of the great Sherlock Holmes as a child, but I never dreamed that I would be involved in a homicide investigation!'

At Elbow Street, Lovecraft sat in the lieutenant's stuffy green-walled office and answered question after question, working his way through the night once again. No, he couldn't identify the heavy car. He hadn't noticed its license tags. He wasn't certain of the make – some large model, a Packard or Pierce. Maybe even a foreign design. He didn't know.

And, no, he hadn't seen inside the passenger compartment. The only light had come from the headlamps of the car.

He'd heard voices and a struggle before the splash, but he hadn't made out any words except a few profanities. Were they speaking English? He wasn't sure. It might have been some lingo like Portuguese. And the man in the river hadn't been able to say anything during the minute or so – that was as long as the whole incident could have taken – of Lovecraft's futile attempt at rescue.

To Lovecraft's own ear the statement was unsatisfying. The narration was bald, vital details were absent. There were merely events without pattern or meaning.

When he was finished, Lovecraft asked the lieutenant if he knew the identity of the drowned man. The officer shook his head. He opened the door of his office and queried a desk sergeant whether identification had been made. He returned to the green room and told Howard Lovecraft that he could drink a cup of coffee while his statement was typed for signature and notarization.

Lovecraft followed the officer to a corner where a pot of black sludge simmered over a chipped porcelain hot plate. Vaguely from the other end of the long room he could hear the arhythmic clicking of an upright typewriter. A sudden worry flickered across his mind, and Lovecraft patted the breast pocket of his recovered suit jacket. The rustle of papers assured him that his letters had not been lost in the excitement and activity of the night.

He pulled the three envelopes from the pocket and examined them. The letters from Viereck and Starrett were typewritten and relatively unharmed by their adventure. Sonia's was inscribed in her familiar hand, in her favorite odd shade of Waterman's ink. The suit jacket had never got drenched but the envelope was damp, the address blurred. He extracted the folded sheets of stationery and opened them: he found the ink still legible and returned the letter to his pocket.

The plainclothes lieutenant had disappeared from the

room, but now he returned holding a slim sheaf of
notepaper and report forms. He took Lovecraft by the
elbow and steered him back to the office where his
statement had been taken.

'Mr Lovecraft, we have a tentative identification now,
and of course the cause of death. He'd been battered
pretty well and there was a good blow to the skull, but
death was caused by drowning.'

Lovecraft nodded. They both took seats in the lieutenant's office.

'Standard technique. The perpetrators put the victim's
feet in a bucket of wet cement. Kept him there until the
cement was hard, dumped him in the river and let nature
take its course.'

Lovecraft nodded but said nothing. His intimation of a
supernatural weight had been close to actuality.

'You were very lucky, in fact,' the lieutenant said.
'They must not have seen you, in the snow. And they
passed you twice, eh? On their way to the river and again
on their way back to Federal Hill.'

Lovecraft jerked in astonishment. 'How do you know
they came from Federal Hill? Do you know who the
killers are?'

The lieutenant leaned forward. 'Let me put it this way,
sir. Knowing the identity of the victim, it becomes obvious
who the perpetrators must be. That doesn't mean we
know by name each person in that car tonight. And I
doubt that we'll ever be able to prove it on them, unless
we can crack the mobsters' code of silence.

'But, off the record, Mr Lovecraft, have you ever heard
of the Morelli gang?'

Lovecraft shook his head.

The lieutenant sighed. 'I don't suppose they have much
impact on you, over on College Hill. They generally keep
their noses away from there and don't stir up the more

respectable elements in town. The Morellis are the main underworld mob in Providence. In fact, they control most of the crime between here and Boston.

'The victim tonight was a mug named Constantine Madeiros, and his killing – we think – was a warning.'

Lovecraft frowned and shook his head. What sordid deeds transpired beneath those white steeples visible from his own parlor window! 'You're away beyond me, Lieutenant. This Madeiros, is he a member of the Morelli gang? If so, why would his own associates drown him? As a warning to whom? The murder makes no sense to me.'

The officer stood up and walked to his desk. He looked at a few papers abstractedly, then turned back to Lovecraft. 'Do you know who Nicola Sacco and Bartolomeo Vanzetti are, Mr Lovecraft?'

'Of course! Those two wops who murdered the payroll guard over at Braintree. They should have been executed years ago. I cannot see why they weren't.'

The officer grimaced. 'The chief reason for their still being alive is a jailbird named Celestine or Celestino F. Madeiros. He's in Dedham prison with Sacco and Vanzetti, and he's slated for the chair, too.'

'I did not know there was a third associate,' Lovecraft muttered.

'There wasn't. Madeiros – Celestino Madeiros – was convicted in a different killing altogether. He's a common hoodlum. But he confessed to being present at the Braintree holdup. He's a member of the Morelli gang, and he says the Morellis pulled that crime. Sacco and Vanzetti, he claims, weren't even there!'

'Well, I don't see what all of this has to do with – what was this other fellow's name? Constantine?'

The lieutenant gestured broadly. 'You see, the Madeiroses are a big family, and they're all tied with the

Morelli gang here in Providence. The Morellis are getting more and more nervous about Celestino talking, if the Commonwealth of Massachusetts ever gives Sacco and Vanzetti the new trial they keep demanding.

'The authorities in Massachusetts have Celestino under close guard to make sure he stays alive. So the Morellis are sending him a message. These are ruthless men, Mr Lovecraft. Killing Constantine was a warning to Celestino, that the Morellis will wipe out the rest of the Madeiros family if Celestino talks.'

'What barbarism!' Lovecraft lowered his coffee cup. 'The city should be cleansed of these Morellis. In fact, our English nation must rid itself of these Mediterranean mongrels and restore the old New England identity.'

The lieutenant exhaled loudly and crossed the room. He opened the door, looked into the station, and nodded. 'Your statement is ready, Mr Lovecraft. I think we can close this off for now, once it's signed and notarized.'

'You will not need me anymore, Lieutenant?'

'We'll get you a ride home, sir.'

'How long until you round up these Morellis?'

'I'm afraid it isn't that simple, Mr Lovecraft.' The officer smiled through his teeth. 'I mentioned the code of the mobsters. We know pretty well who killed the man tonight. But I doubt that we can prove it.'

He accepted a typewritten document from a uniformed officer. 'And very frankly, Mister, and strictly off the record, we don't really mind too much these hoodlums putting each other out of the way. As long as they leave respectable citizens alone, we don't interfere a whole lot in their dealings with one another.'

2
Manhattan

The elevated train carrying Joseph Carisi and Nicholas Amoroso crossed over the East River and screamed to a halt as it entered the dingy station above Third Avenue. Joseph and Nicholas were dressed in similar outfits: dark suits and soft hats, white shirts and dark ties. The fascisti had discussed appearing in uniform for their demonstrations, but the president of the Fascist League of North America, Count di Revel, had ordered them to keep to civilian garb, at least for the time.

Other organizations could outfit themselves in ceremonial attire. The Ku Klux Klan had garnered headlines and photographs in the newspapers and newsreels with their spectacular robes and hoods. And they had almost certainly attracted members by their flamboyance.

But Count di Revel held that such demonstrations were undesirable, or at least premature. Il Duce had come to power in Italy, but he had not fully consolidated his position as yet. While there remained opposition to fascism in the old country, followers of the movement in the new country should hold back from excesses of controversy. At least, so Count di Revel counseled, and the count was to be respected and obeyed.

Today's demonstrations and parade were to be orderly and dignified. Loyal fascisti had been instructed to appear in quiet clothing, to be sober, and to comport themselves with decorum.

The train pulled out of its station and moved southward, toward midtown. Joseph and Nicholas chatted, partially in Italian, mostly in English. Although they had been born in the old country they took pride in their skill with the language of the New World. Immigrants and the sons of immigrants like the spectacular Chicago gangsters Colosimo and Caponi – now he was calling himself Capone, but former acquaintances from Five Points remembered the old pronunciation – were giving a bad name to all *paesanos*.

As the lights in the car flickered, Joseph Carisi unfolded an Italian-language newspaper and held it so both he and his friend could read the headline story, all the while he clutched a swaying strap with his free hand. The newspaper had a large photograph of Il Duce on the front page, and beside it a report of the leader's latest speech.

With Victor Emmanuel at his side, he had celebrated his fifth anniversary as leader of the country with the announcement of his plans for the next five years. All political opposition was to be banned. Complaints that women were oppressed by being denied the right to vote while their husbands were free to cast ballots would be met by the simple abolition of all elections. With no opposition parties permitted there would be no need for elections anyway.

Il Duce would raise the level of Italy's army to five million men. The recognition of the nation's rights in the world would be assured, and the rule of Il Duce himself would continue indefinitely. 'My successor,' the leader was quoted, 'has not yet been born.'

Nicholas and Joseph grinned at each other as Joseph folded the newspaper again and tucked it under his arm. The only problem with bringing fascism to the New World was some dissension among the followers of the Duce. One branch of the movement wished to move ahead now. They had organized into paramilitary Blackshirt units and planned a parade for this very day. The count advised against participation. If for no other reason, it would place them in a position of competing with the Ku Klux Klan, and the Klan far outnumbered the fascisti in New York. Di Revel did not wish the fascisti to appear in second place to anyone, not even the Klan for whom he had quietly expressed his admiration many times.

And there were the enemies of fascism, the socialist and communist radicals whose opposition had, ironically, helped to bring fascism to power in Italy. The count did not wish to face the bolshevists yet, either. Not until the fascisti were prepared to smash their opponents as the Duce had smashed the bolshevists in the old country.

Again the elevated train pulled to a stop. The headquarters of the Fascist League of North America was a short walk from the station. Nicholas and Joseph left the train.

From Turin's Chop House facing onto Third Avenue just beneath the elevated tracks, two men strode onto the sidewalk. One of them was tall, slightly heavyset, wearing well-made clothing of a soft, casual design. He raised his face towards the elevated platform and nodded to the companion at his side.

The second man was shorter and stockier than his tall companion. His bearing was stiff and the cut of his clothing more severe, almost military in appearance.

The taller man wore spectacles with broad dark circular rims that made them stand out prominently from his face. Beneath the shorter man's hat his light-colored, close-cropped hair gave an appearance that might fool a casual observer into thinking that he was bald.

As Nicholas Amoroso and Joseph Carisi left the platform and started down the echoing iron stairway toward the sidewalk, the two men from Turin's Chop House, walking side by side, began to climb the same stairway. Halfway between elevated platform and sidewalk the four came face to face.

The two men from the chop house stopped in their tracks. Simultaneously they drew back their overcoats and reached inside. Nicholas and Joseph saw for the first time that both of them wore flaring red neckties. Nicholas grabbed Joseph by the elbow and shouted, 'Bolshevists!'

Joseph shouted, 'Rosso!' and clenched his fists, preparing for a tussle with the two men. That he and Nicholas stood on higher treads of the stairway would give them an advantage. And in this neighborhood, if not throughout the city, there should be many fascisti to come to the aid of a threatened comrade.

But before a blow could be struck the shorter man's hand flashed from inside his overcoat. In it was a flat, ugly revolver. Without a word the short man shoved the revolver against Joseph's ribs. Nicholas heard an explosive roar, saw his comrade flung backward by the force of the bullet entering his body. He crashed against the steps behind Nicholas.

In horror Nicholas turned back to the two strangers. The short man was standing with the revolver still in his hand. Smoke was curling upward into the cold evening air from its stubby barrel. The front of the man's clothing was spattered with Joseph's fresh blood. A blotch of it had stained the short man's cheek, but he did not seem to have noticed.

Beside the short man the other stranger had drawn his own hand from inside his overcoat. There was a long thin-bladed knife in his hand. A stiletto. Before Nicholas could make any move the tall man lunged toward him. In a startling maneuver the knife flashed downward as if aimed at Nicholas's belly, to penetrate his thick overcoat, his jacket and shirt, and then enter his body.

But instead the tall man reversed the movement of his hand, drove the knife blade straight upward, catching Nicholas beneath the jaw and penetrating the soft flesh

behind the chin, piercing his neck and tongue and embed-
ding itself in the hard bony roof of his mouth.

Nicholas toppled backward, sprawling on his back atop
the body of his friend Joseph. Directly overhead he could
make out the grimy electric bulb that served to illuminate
the elevated stairway. For a moment he thought he
perceived the face of the tall stranger bending over him,
the dark-rimmed eyeglasses forming twin circles in his
dying vision. Before he could be certain of what he
was seeing the face withdrew, the grimy electric bulb
reappeared, then faded into blackness.

At the sound of chimes Frank Belknap Long, Jr, put
down his pipe and looked up from his poem. Although
the thick carpets of the apartment muffled any but the
loudest of footsteps, he could count the measured tread
of the colored maid as she crossed the living room and
vestibule to answer the front door. He could hear the
brief, muffled conversation as she welcomed his familiar
visitor and ushered him into the apartment.

Long smiled, slipped his pipe into a pocket of his tweed
jacket, and ran a finger along his narrow young-man's
moustache. He rose to greet his friend as the other stood
diffidently in the doorway to Long's study.

'Well, Grandpa, how are you doing in this new year?'

Howard Lovecraft managed one of his rare smiles, his
long angular face creasing with the expression. 'Well
enough, Belknapius. For a little time I thought there was
no way to escape *la grippe*. But somehow old Dr Leet
pulled me through once again, and here I am, to the
relief of my dear little aunts and the dismay of the rest of
the world!'

Frank Long crossed the study, guiding Lovecraft away
from its clutter of papers and his smoker's implements
and toward the comfort of the living room. At a discreet

signal the maid disappeared into her pantry to emerge again carrying a tray with two cups, a pot of strong coffee, and plenty of sugar to please Howard Lovecraft's taste.

'I can't get over that New Year's incident you described in your letter,' Long ventured. 'It must have been a shattering experience – caught in the clutches of a ghastly revenant, pulled beneath the icy waters of a midnight stream. Ho! Folk such as we think that we can invent the most chilling of grisly events. Reality outstrips us without an effort!'

'It was a terrifying moment, of course. In retrospect.' Lovecraft spooned sugar into his cup, stirred the contents, tried one tentative sip, and added another spoon of sugar. 'But in fact, I was so caught up in the moment of desperation that I had no time to fear. You know how soldiers returned from the Great War with tales of their own phlegmatic response to danger. They're quite right. One is literally too busy and too involved to be afraid.'

Long nibbled at his moustache for a moment, then said, 'Well, and you found that the police knew the identity of the murderers but refused to act in the matter?'

'Not precisely that. They felt they could obtain no evidence. They blame some local mobsters but have not identified the individuals who committed the act. But they show a most admirable attitude towards these murderous mongrels. Let them exterminate one another, so long as they leave honest citizens unmolested! It's a pleasure to see rats wipe out rats, as far as I'm concerned!'

Long smiled. 'Well, as long as you're fully recovered from the grisly experience – '

Lovecraft interrupted. 'I cannot say that I am, as yet, fully recovered from that night's events. Even now I waken, some nights, reliving those cold moments. And then I wonder if there is not some – meaning, I suppose, for want of a better word. Some meaning of a more cosmic nature than the tawdry affairs of an immigrant gang.

'At age ten I was the founder and chief investigator of the Providence Detective Bureau.' He smiled wistfully. 'Violent death in the world of realities, Belknap, is a different matter than it was when I dreamed of Holmes's London.'

He solemnly added a half-teaspoon of sugar to his coffee. 'But this has no connection with my present visit to New York. An array of errands has brought me here. My feelings regarding them are mixed.'

Long nodded encouragement.

'One item that I am sure will please you as it does me. I've had word from Vincent Starrett in Chicago –'

'Ah, the poet and fantasy writer.'

'Indeed. He's thrown down his newspaper job. Taken a year's leave, at any rate. He's got a contract to write a fantasy novel for George Doran, and he's coming to New York to write it. A good decision, I think. Chicago is far too much a part of this world, with its foul smells, its stockyards and speakeasies, its gangsters and its palaces of vice, to offer a congenial nest for the dreamer.

''tany rate, Starrett says he's going to put up temporarily with Alex Laing in Greenwich Village until he has a place of his own. He says he's sent in a deposit against the rental of a cottage in Beechhurst, but it won't be ready for a while and he wishes to come East and start his novel. Something about the fountain of youth. A pretty conceit!'

Long refilled Lovecraft's cup, and the taller man returned to add sugar to the thick mixture. Long commented, 'Then you'll be able to see Starrett. And what other topics are on your agenda?'

Lovecraft gazed at the younger man across the lip of

his coffee cup. 'Do you remember the name George Sylvester Viereck, Belknap?'

'Indeed! What was it you called the man, in your amateur journal? A liar and a thief?'

'"The honest truth poor Viereck ne'er could speak, and Britons hate a liar and a sneak,"' Lovecraft quoted himself.

Long fumbled in his pocket, pulled out his cold pipe, inspected it carefully, and put it back. 'The man had troubles enough, as I recall. Didn't the T-men capture him with some alien funds in his possession?'

Lovecraft nodded vigorously. 'All of that was during the war. He has invited me now to visit his office and discuss the publication of a book. That's what has me thrown for a loss, Belknap. You know, it would be the culmination of a dream, to see my tales gathered between boards. And, not to disparage a gentleman printer like Cook up in Athol – '

'I quite understand.' Long smiled deprecatingly. 'My little volume of poetry is a modest achievement, and Cook's edition is a modest enough production.'

Lovecraft's face showed mild embarrassment. 'Well. Hmph.' There was a silence, then he said, 'In any case, Viereck is presently associated with the Jackson Press.'

'A very substantial firm,' Long supplied.

'Indeed.' Lovecraft drew a business-style envelope from his inner pocket. 'And if he is desirous of issuing a collection of my works, I wonder just how to deal with his somewhat unsavory past. And with my own rather harsh comments about him.'

Long gave a small nervous chuckle. 'I should hope he would have turned his attention away from the war, Howard. After all, nearly a decade has passed. And I should think that your dealings with Mr Viereck would be of a nature other than a political one. Besides, it is a far cry from his Kaiserian propaganda campaign to his interest in collecting your fiction from *Weird Tales*.'

Lovecraft rose and crossed the room. He stood gazing at the dark river and the looming palisades beyond. 'Well, I think you are right, Belknap. At any rate, I have an appointment to meet Mr Viereck at his office tomorrow. Then we shall see how the land lies.'

'Then you'll be staying overnight?'

'If you and your parents are willing to put up with an old codger from New England.'

'Of course! Any time, Howard. You know that. How long do you expect to stay in town?'

'Just a few days. First I shall see Starrett. I've never met the man – or his host Laing. You know, he too is a colleague. His collected verse is amusing. I shall try to reach Laing and arrange a meeting. Then – ' He turned and paced from the window to a tall breakfront, ran his eyes distractedly over the china on display, then turned back to face his young friend.

'I have received one other communication, to which I do not know the proper response.'

'Oh?'

'A note from Sonia, inviting me to visit her while in the city.'

Long remained noncommittal.

'Of course she understands that our marriage is at an end. I am not unwilling to share her companionship on a platonic basis, but marriage is not for me. Friendship is a splendid consolation, and I suppose that the even closer bond of marriage is a great satisfaction to the proper individual. But I dwelt for too many years as a literary recluse in my Providence-Plantations home to make a very good husband.'

'Then I see no problem,' Long ventured.

Lovecraft grinned. 'Would that Sonia were so reasonable.'

'Then what is your concern? What did she write, Howard? If I might pry to such an extent . . .'

Lovecraft spread his hands. 'Domestic trivia, for the most part. She did go on at some length about a new radio set she has purchased for the Parkside Avenue apartment. And she mentioned meeting Theo Weiss in the street, and his sending greetings to me. I wonder if there might not be some potential there for more work.'

'Of the sort you did for Theo's brother, the great magician?'

Lovecraft nodded.

'It was a tragedy when Houdini died,' Long resumed. 'I think his brother has done nobly in keeping his work alive. Not only the stage magic and the escape act, but the work of exposing spiritualist frauds. I wish I'd had the opportunity to meet Houdini. I know he thought the world of you, Howard. Some of the letters that you showed me . . .'

'A paradoxical man, Houdini. He had a good mind, and his work was very admirable. I enjoyed being his ghost, Belknap. And what do you think of sitting in your home, chatting with the ghost of the world's champion ghost-breaker, Harry Houdini?'

Long grinned broadly. 'There are ghosts and there are ghosts.'

'Quite.'

'And Houdini's brother, Theo Weiss – does he intend to take up Houdini's literary crusade as well?'

'Oh, I don't really know that. Sonia merely mentioned having met him on the street, near her place of business. She says he cuts as dashing a figure as ever. Houdini was a wiry, dynamic little fellow, you know, Belknap. His brother Hardeen is a big strapping man. Houdini always seemed slightly rumpled in his clothing. I vow, he could put on a freshly laundered outfit tailored to measure, and inside of thirty seconds he'd look as if he'd slept on a park bench and been caught in a rainstorm.

'Not so Dash Hardeen! I've never seen him looking other than the fashion plate. And as different in manner as in appearance. As good a mind as Houdini's, but Hardeen moves more slowly, thinks more methodically. Ehrich Weiss would leap mentally from premise to conclusion and leave it for others to fill in the logic, *post hoc*. Theo will gather his data, propound a hypothesis, place the evidence in order, make a judgement.

'Houdini would have made an exemplary mystic if he hadn't become such a foe of mystical frauds. Hardeen would be an admirable scientist if he were ever inclined to give up the stage. Not that he's likely to do that.'

Long said, 'Will you phone him?'

Lovecraft shook his head. 'I think not now, at any rate. You know, he lives out in Brooklyn, not very far from Parkside. There might be too much danger of a reentanglement, if you take my meaning.'

Lovecraft rode a local car from the Longs' home, all the way to Forty-second Street. He was early for his appointment and walked to Viereck's East Side office, stopping to browse at booksellers' stalls and to examine theater posters en route. He rode the elevator to the offices of the Jackson Press and sent his name to the inner office by means of a shingle-haired receptionist wearing a too-short flapper skirt.

Through the open door to the inner office he could see the other man engaged in a brief dialogue with the receptionist. Viereck had changed little from the newspaper photographs Lovecraft had seen of him during the scandal of 1915. Then, caught out in his efforts to

influence America's war policies away from proper neu-
trality and toward the side of the Hun, Viereck had
peered owlishly from the front pages of the dailies.

He still preferred the same soft tweeds, Lovecraft
noted. Viereck's hair was graying at the temples, but was
otherwise as thick and romantically curled as in those
days. He favored a low soft collar and lavishly knotted
necktie, and still fancied the round heavy-rimmed spectacles that had given him his owlish appearance in those
old photographs.

The receptionist returned to the outer office and ushered Lovecraft in.

Viereck rose and strode around his desk to clasp his
visitor by the hand. 'I'm most pleased that you could
accept my invitation, Mr Lovecraft. I've seen some of
your work and admired it very much.'

Lovecraft followed Viereck's gesture and took a black
leather chair studded with brass nailheads. 'I have perused
some of your own writings,' he responded. 'I greatly
enjoyed your *House of the Vampire*. If I may say so, I
have wondered at your abandonment of fantasy in recent
years.'

Viereck was slouched into a swivel chair behind his
desk, his elbows propped on the arms of the chair and his
fingers steepled before his dark lips. He laughed loudly.
'Recent years, indeed! When was *House of the Vampire*?
It's been so long – '

'In 1907,' Lovecraft supplied. 'I believe you've done no
fantasy since. Have your interests turned altogether to
other fields?'

Viereck said, 'I've been playing around with some
notions. Considering a little yarn with my friend
Eldridge.' He leaned forward, sliding his elbows on the
desktop. 'But my immediate interest is not in fantasy.

Not in fiction at all, in fact.' He leaned back again, dropping his hands to the arms of his swivel seat.

'One surveys the world, Mr Lovecraft, and one sees a time of great potential. And of grave danger. Without yielding to melodrama, I can still predict apocalyptic turns of events in the next few years. These two Italians murdered by communists – you must have seen it in the papers. Now Mussolini is raising a tempest over the incident, and I suppose if he obtains any satisfaction, the Russians will be heard from next. These signs do not bode well.'

Lovecraft rubbed his jaw with two long bony fingers. 'I can hardly disagree, Mr Viereck. But I must ask why you wrote to me at this time. I had the impression from your letter that the Jackson Press had some interest in my works of fantasy. I had thought, in fact, that your organization might undertake to issue a volume of them.'

Viereck leaned forward. 'I did not mean to mislead you. But let me be more specific about my concern over the developing political situation. I shall make it clear just which project I would hope to engage your talents in.'

Lovecraft nodded dour assent.

'Mr Lovecraft, you will pardon me please if I am somewhat pedantic. It comes of striving for several decades to educate a sadly rigid-minded and not very receptive public.

'I think you will agree, in recollection, that the first decade of this century was an optimistic time. There was peace and order in Europe, progress and economic development in the New World, a spread of enlightenment to the primitive lands of the East. I would say that we seemed on the brink of a Golden Age.' He heaved a sigh dramatically. 'Then began the Great War. I believe that you wrote of it yourself.'

Lovecraft felt a blush creep upward from beneath his collar. 'I did inscribe a little piece on the subject.'

'"The Crime of the Century", was it not?'

Lovecraft nodded.

'Please, I have no mysterious sources,' Viereck said. 'A mutual acquaintance, Mr Rheinhart Kleiner, showed me a copy of your essay. That was a most interesting piece. You know, I do a good deal of reportage for Mr William Randolph Hearst. Reportage and editing. I had reason recently to seek a literary man of certain specific qualifications, and my fellow Hearst employee, Mr Merritt, mentioned your name.'

'Ah!' Lovecraft nodded vigorously. 'I wondered how you had heard of me.'

'Yes. And almost to the day, Kleiner mentioned you also. Almost more than coincidence, eh?'

Viereck leaned forward earnestly. 'Now, what I need is someone of impeccable old American stock. Preferably of English ancestry. To do some articles, perhaps, for my monthly. And definitely to write a volume for the Jackson Press.'

'On a political theme?' Lovecraft asked.

'Yes.' Viereck was altogether open about it. 'Let me return for a moment to my historical thesis. I agree with your contention, Mr Lovecraft, as expressed in "The Crime of the Century". The division of the Nordic races and the enmity between Germanic and Anglo-Saxon cousins was an historic tragedy. And what do we see today, the aftermath of that sorry turn of events?

'Germany – the land of my birth – in a state of confusion and weakness. The darkness of Bolshevism in control of Russia. Waves of anarchy and terror threatening to spill over the borders and sweep across the continent. America falling more and more under the sway of gangsters and bootleggers.'

Lovecraft nodded agreement.

'Speaking of which,' resumed Viereck, 'would you care for a small refreshment?' He walked to the wall and pressed an unobtrusive bit of decorative carving. A half-door swung open to reveal a shelf of bottles and glasses.

Through pursed lips Lovecraft said, 'I do not use alcohol.'

Viereck swung the panel shut. He went on as if the exchange had never occurred. 'It is my firm conviction that the trends toward anarchism and degeneracy are rising, rising, rising.' He held his hands out, palms down, in front of his shoulders, and raised them in stages as if they floated on the surface of a deepening pond.

'A new Dark Age may be upon us,' he said. 'Or, if these trends can be reversed . . . if the course of world politics, world culture, can be set back on the direction that we lost at the time of the World War . . . we might, instead, enter upon a new Golden Age.'

For a moment Lovecraft held his silence. Viereck was obviously awaiting a response. Finally Lovecraft said, 'I can hardly disagree with your basic formulation. But important questions remain unresolved.'

Viereck asked what they were.

'In a very broad sense,' Lovecraft said, 'how do you propose to set the world aright? Utopian schemes are a shilling a shelfload. Any one of them might succeed, one supposes, if all the world could be made to adopt it. Vegetarianism, primitive communalism, even Christianity – for all that I disdain Christianity as the comfort of sheep being led to the slaughter. If everyone could, by some miracle, become a sincere Christian, and if everyone could agree upon what a sincere Christian really was, then utopia might, indeed, be attained.

'But there has never been universal agreement upon any of the innumerable utopian schemes that have been propounded through the ages. All we can do is provide an opportunity for the fortunate few of intelligence, sensitivity, taste, and good breeding, to live the lives of which they are worthy. Lives not dissimilar to those of Elizabethan ladies and gentlemen of leisure. Or perhaps like those of the finest type of Athenian at the height of the Hellenic Age.

'As for my second question – assuming that the first is satisfactorily resolved – what role do you propose for me in your scheme? I am, after all, a humble scribbler of inconsequential horror stories. It had been my impression that you wished to produce a volume containing my collected efforts. If that is not the nature of your interest in me, I am not at all certain what I can do to be of service to the Jackson Press. Or vice versa.'

Viereck flicked a glance at the ornately carven clock that stood on the mantelpiece facing his desk. 'I see it is nearly luncheon time. I've taken the liberty of reserving a table for us. I hope you don't mind – will you join me?'

The early afternoon sun was bright, the winter air crisp and fresh outside the Jackson Press building. Viereck and Lovecraft strolled along Forty-second Street, Lovecraft bundled in his heavy woolen overcoat and new gray fedora, Viereck in loden green and a soft Tyrolean cap.

They walked down Fifth Avenue, past newsboys shouting of war in China, upheaval in Russia, revolution in Mexico, peddling the *Sun,* the *Graphic*, the dignified gray *Post*. At Thirty-fourth Street they crossed to the Waldorf-Astoria, and Viereck ushered Lovecraft to the Turkish Salon. They were greeted by a swarthy character garbed in outlandish costume from red fez to pointed slippers, and then seated on cushions at an inlaid table.

A boy in golden-frogged vest and baggy trousers poured thick, steaming coffee from a brass pot. Lovecraft sniffed at his cup suspiciously, tried a sip, then sighed and slid down into his cushion with pleasure.

He watched Viereck pull a jade-and-gold cigar case from his pocket, offer a belvedere maduro which Lovecraft waved aside, and extract one for himself. 'Now as to your questions,' Viereck muttered around the tip of the belvedere. He struck flame from a pocket lighter, the mate of the cigar case, and brought the belvedere to life. 'Very natural questions, very proper of you to ask.

'Permit me to say, first, that I agree with your rather pessimistic view of utopianism. Man is a selfish and shortsighted beast, Mr Lovecraft. The great German philosopher Kant expressed what he called the Categorical Imperative for proper conduct. He declared that one must determine each act as if all men were to act in that manner, given like circumstances.'

'A mere restatement of the Golden Rule,' Lovecraft interjected.

'As you say,' Viereck nodded. He drew on his belvedere, blew a feather of blue-gray smoke toward the salon's ornate ceiling, then laid the cigar across the lip of a brass-and-velvet smoking stand.

'I raised the point only to demonstrate that philosophers through all time have arrived at similar notions for guiding man's conduct. And through all time people have ignored that imperative and have acted in their own selfish, immediate interests. Often to good results – for themselves, and in the short run.

'But ultimately, the world suffers.

'I am not a utopian, Mr Lovecraft.' He retrieved the smoldering belvedere and used it as a pointer. 'I believe that if world order and progress are to be reestablished, if things are to be set to rights, it will be done by a relatively small, intelligent, thoroughly disciplined movement. A movement of persons who will not stop to debate every decision, who will not trouble themselves with Kant's Imperative or Jesus' Golden Rule. Persons who will follow loyally the instructions they receive from their leaders.'

Suddenly Viereck changed his tack. 'You are, perhaps, aware that I have traveled extensively in the United States and in Europe?'

'I have seen some of your pieces,' Lovecraft said. 'In the Hearst press, in *Liberty* and the *American Monthly*.'

Viereck nodded sharply. 'I have met the political leaders of every nation in Europe and the royalty of most. In Italy, I conducted an interview with Il Duce. In England, I met Baldwin – and the Prince of Wales. In Germany, I spoke with President von Hindenburg and with other men who will shape the future of the Reich and of the Continent.

'Yes, I traveled to Doorn in the Netherlands, where I was the first journalist granted an audience by the Kaiser since his abdication. And in Bavaria I met the leader of the NSDAP, Herr Hitler. You know, Mr Lovecraft, it was not a German but Signor Mussolini who said to me, "Barbarossa will awaken once more," and he was correct, Mr Lovecraft! Once Hindenburg is gone, Barbarossa will indeed awaken.'

Sourly, Lovecraft said, 'I cannot claim any feeling of joy at the prospect of an aggressive Germany. Do you truly believe that the nations of the world would permit a Hohenzollern restoration?'

Viereck made an uncertain gesture. 'I do not know whether a restoration is in the cards. Surely the communists are active in Germany. Someone will have to stop them once the old Marshal goes. Perhaps the National Socialists. Perhaps someone else.' He looked up as the serving boy in Turkish garb approached with menus. 'Let's order some food, at any rate,' he suggested.

3

Greenwich Village

The buzzer sounded. Alex Laing set aside his bourbon-on-rocks and extended a callused hand to open the door. He peered into the face of a tall, almost cadaverously slender figure in funereal black and gray. 'You're Lovecraft,' Laing barked.

'Indeed, sir.' The angular lantern-jawed face tipped and rose again in a courtly nod. 'And I take it that you are Mr Alexander Laing.' He leaned forward, craning his neck to look into the apartment. 'I take it, then, that I have the pleasure of addressing Mr Vincent Starrett as well.'

Starrett had left the couch and advanced with almost imperceptible unsteadiness to stand beside Laing. His broad shoulders and dark pompadour gave him an appearance of slightly tipsy majesty.

Lovecraft entered the apartment, shook hands with both men, and deposited his hat and coat in the vestibule. 'A most admirable building in which to make one's home, Mr Laing. One of the last of the truly classic structures in the neighborhood. Long may it stand!'

Laing led Lovecraft into the living room. 'Vinnie was just telling me about you, Lovecraft. Says you're a real old-fashioned gentleman, or at least you write like one. What do you think, Vin?' He wheeled to face the tall Starrett, now seated on the couch and clutching his own glass once again. 'Does the kid live up to his billing, or does he? Truly classic structures, hey? It's cheap digs in my book!'

Lovecraft, pale, had perched on the edge of a straight-backed chair. 'Perhaps, Vincent, we might discuss some topic of greater interest to Mr Laing, if he cares nothing for the study of architecture. I hope that your patron Doran has made a good, firm commitment regarding your fantasy novel.'

Starrett's expression combined something of a grin with a goodly portion of a wince. 'Doran is in my corner, all right. I've got my contract and the advance is all spent, as I understand is required conduct.'

Lovecraft smiled wanly. Starrett's situation was one he could silently envy.

Alex Laing thumped Starrett on the shoulder. 'Don't let 'em wear you down, Vin!' He swung back to Lovecraft. 'What do you say, Howie? How's about a little snort to warm your belly on a cold night, and then we'll tie on the feedbag?'

Lovecraft declined the invitation. Starrett and Laing emptied their glasses and the three set out toward Tenth Street, then over to an Italian restaurant near Sheridan Square. A scrawny black-and-white cat sidled toward them from a grimy alcove outside the restaurant, and Lovecraft paused to pet the creature and promise it a snack of leftovers.

Inside the restaurant, Laing whispered briefly to the maitre d' and they were led past a room full of diners, through the deliciously odoriferous kitchen, and into a second dining room identical to the first.

At their table Laing signaled for menus. A bottle of red wine appeared with the hot soup, and their waiter poured for all three. Lovecraft started to wave his glass away, but Starrett laid a carefully manicured hand on his cuff. 'A little wine for thy stomach, Howard. It won't do you any harm.'

Over stiff-crusted bread and green salad, Starrett said,

'You told me you were to meet with that fellow Viereck up at the Jackson Press. I trust things went well for you, Howard. You know, you're one of the most admired writers out in the Chicago circle. In fact, Ed Baird sends his greetings – and a bit more.'

Lovecraft shot a surprised look across the table.

'Ed says he's not trying to pry you away from *Weird Tales*. Professional ethics, piracy of talent, and so on. But if you should ever decide to change your direction, move from your eldritch horror tales into something a little closer to the here-and-now, you'll be most welcome at *Real Detective Tales*.'

Lovecraft said, 'I know you feel a greater loyalty to Baird than to Henneberger, Starrett.' He chewed a sliver of tomato, swallowed, washed it down with wine and made a sour face. 'And the fact is, I rather fancy Baird over Farnie Wright myself. But I fear I could never do justice to those bang-bang whodunnits Baird runs nowadays. I think I will do best to stay with the fantastic tale.'

He turned and addressed Alex Laing. 'All of this shoptalk must be a bore to you, Mr Laing. I apologize if the topic is of no interest to a poet like yourself.'

Starrett interjected, 'I should have mentioned, Howard, that Alex is also one of those rare and fragile creatures, an editor.'

'Yeah.' Laing reached for another breadstick, snapped it with a report like a pistol firing. 'Eight to five, every day. Reading manuscripts, marking galleys, laying out pages. It's a buck.'

Lovecraft addressed Laing with more interest than he had previously shown the other. 'Do you publish books, Mr Laing?'

'Hah! Not hardly! You know Experimenter Publishing, down on Park Row? The Gernsback brothers' place.

Hugo likes to do books about the wonders of television and stuff like that. His brother Sid is more a man after my heart. He likes stuff like French humor.'

'Oh.' Lovecraft rubbed his chin. 'Perhaps you are acquainted with Dr Sloane. I sent him a manuscript some time ago and have never heard from him. Do you know the doctor?'

Laing scratched his unruly thatch of hair. 'Oh, sure, now I know who you mean. Sure, Doc Sloane, the world's oldest man! He runs that crazy *Amazing Stories* that Hugo started last year. Naw, I try and steer clear of that operation. Bunch of silly junk, all about monsters. Not my cup of gin!'

Over veal and pasta Starrett asked again if there had been any news from Lovecraft's meeting with George Sylvester Viereck. Lovecraft described their exchange at Viereck's office and at the Turkish Salon at the Waldorf.

'Some class!' Laing interjected. 'Them's the big leagues!'

'But then Viereck isn't really interested in doing a volume of your stories after all,' Starrett summarized.

'Not just now. He did hold out the prospect of such a book later on. But presently he seems to want me to play the role of journalist. Can you imagine old Grandpa Theobald with his hat on the back of his head, notepad in hand, hanging on the gilded words of some hack politico? Pah!'

There was a moment of embarrassed silence, then Starrett burst into laughter. Lovecraft turned a deep crimson. 'I am very sorry, Vincent. I had completely forgotten your own background as a newsman. I beg your pardon.'

'Don't let it bother you! But look,' he became serious, 'just what is Sylvester up to? He never struck me as anybody's starry-eyed idealist, and I've had him in view since before we got into the war. What does that fox have up his sleeve? What did he have to say about Kaiser Bill, Howard?'

Lovecraft's mouth assumed a grim set. 'You know, Wilhelm never has admitted Germany's guilt in the World War. Viereck appears to be looking toward a German revival after Hindenburg dies. He seems to be hedging his bets, but he clearly holds no confidence in any of the present parliamentary leaders. Certainly not in that Marx chap, the chancellor.'

Starrett hummed to himself. Then he said, 'I'll agree with Viereck on that score. But what then?'

Lovecraft chewed a morsel of lemon-flavored veal. 'He was not altogether clear on that point. He seems very impressed with this National Socialist, Hitler. Viereck claims that the National Socialists are not really socialists at all. It's very odd. He says that this Hitler has written a book that makes his ideas very clear. I'm to receive a copy from Viereck shortly.'

He mulled over his thoughts, then added, 'But he made some other comments – Viereck did – about a restoration of the Empire. Put the Kaiser back on his throne, that sort of talk.'

Starrett grinned broadly and nodded. 'I don't suppose he mentioned anything to you about his being near-royalty if that should happen.'

Lovecraft was astonished.

Starrett laughed softly. 'Well, Howard, you see being an old newshawk does have its points. Let me tell you a little story.' He speared a morsel of trout amandine, ate it, resumed.

'Yes, we newshawks pick up all sorts of odd information. Also, being Canadian by birth, I take a certain perverse interest in the doings of royalty. Our own Windsors and their continental cousins can put on a

marvelous show when they want to – or when they want
not to . . .

'Now, it so happens that some seventy-five years ago,
or thereabouts, before there even was a German Empire,
the King of Prussia was a good old Hohenzollern. Friedrich Wilhelm the Fourth. There was a Kronprinz
Wilhelm also. A bit of a rake and a playboy, a bit like
our present Prince of Wales.

'At the same time there was a reigning beauty of the
Berlin stage. She was a magnificent brunette named
Sophie. Sophie Viereck. A fabulous figure, as famed and
admired in the Germanic world as was Lillie Langtry in
the English. Men laid their hearts at her feet. Wherever
she traveled she was the toast of society. And of course,
she had her choice of admirers.

'One of whom was, as you have doubtless guessed by
this time, the young – in truth, by now the not-so-young
– Crown Prince.'

He interrupted his narrative at the approach of their
waiter. A small bottle of brandy appeared, certified just
off the boat. Following a moment's hesitation Lovecraft
gestured for a tiny nip.

'The informal union of Kronprinz and stage queen had
all of the glamour one might expect. It lasted for some
years, and even produced a dividend. The child was
claimed by a loyal cousin, a member of a cadet branch of
the royal house. Such was the custom at the time, such
events being far from unprecedented.

'The child was a boy. And to avoid embarrassment to
the crown, he of course retained his mother's name. As
was also the custom.

'Thus, Louis Viereck. The father of your associate,
Lovecraft.' Starrett smiled benignly. 'If you read the
man's journalism carefully, you will find that when he

went to Doorn to interview the deposed Wilhelm, the ex-Kaiser greeted him als Vetter. Cousin. I suppose that unwary readers took this as a piece of ex-imperial jocularity. But Wilhelm is hardly a jocular individual. He was simply addressing his cousin by his proper title!'

Lovecraft lowered his cup. A few drops of the brandy-laced coffee splashed onto the tablecloth.

Outside the restaurant Lovecraft's black-and-white friend waited impatiently. Lovecraft knelt and offered the cat a scrap of veal he'd filched from his plate. The cat sniffed, accepted the morsel, and carried it into an alley, tail erect as he disappeared.

'One of God's wiser acts,' Lovecraft commented, 'was the creation of the feline race. Why *Homo sapiens* rather than the *Felidae* received dominion over the earth is a mystery beyond human enravelment!'

Inside a house in Waverly Place they were greeted by a maitre d' who uncannily resembled the late Valentino and deposited at a bar manned by a jolly individual in red jacket and brass buttons. 'Hello there, Mr Laing. The usual for you?'

Laing nodded.

'And your friends, sir?'

'I'll have a martini,' Starrett said.

The bartender looked expectantly at Lovecraft.

'Oh – the same for me,' Lovecraft managed. He looked around the barroom. 'Doesn't anyone pay attention to the Volstead Act?'

Laing snorted. 'What do you think?'

Starrett placed his drink carefully on the mahogany. 'One of my town's more illustrious citizens made a statement about that recently. "If the public don't want bootleggers, all they got to do is stop buying our stuff," he said. "We'd be out of business tomorrow. It don't take no Izzy and Moe to put us out of business."'

Laing drained his glass and waved to the bartender for a refill. 'How's the martini, Lovecraft?' he asked.

'The flavor is a trifle odd.' Lovecraft watched the olive bobbing gently in his glass. 'Not precisely what one had expected.'

Starrett raised his empty glass toward the bartender. 'Reverting to an earlier topic, Howard.' He removed the olive from his glass and swallowed it without pausing to chew as the bartender tilted his silver shaker over the glass. 'Sylvester Viereck. Somehow in all our discussion, I didn't quite grasp precisely what it is that he wants of *you*, Howard. You say that you went to discuss literature and stayed to argue politics. But did he ever say what he was really after?'

Lovecraft framed his reply, found that his tongue was now slightly clumsy at forming words, and had to make a second attempt. 'Well, he wasn't exactly very clear, as a matter of fact. He said he would get me a copy of this fellow Hitler's book to read. It has not been published in English, but Viereck claims there is a translation in the works.'

He stopped and took another drink of his martini. 'And then he says . . . Viereck says . . . he wishes me to meet some friends of his and write a book about them.'

Starrett nodded.

Alex Laing said, 'Why you? Vinnie said you were a firecracker at this spook stuff. Didn't you say you'd sent a yarn to old Doc Sloane?'

Lovecraft started to nod his agreement, but he found that it made his head feel strange so he stopped. 'Yes, I – "The Colour Out of Space". Dr Sloane has not re-replied.'

'Yeah. So why's Viereck want a political book from

you? Seems to me he's got some kind of angle going, Howie. You better watch your step. I remember Sylvester Viereck from back during the war. He's one smart cookie, that one is. But I wouldn't trust him as far as I could throw Jack Dempsey!'

'A valid point.' Starrett nodded, apparently without difficulty. 'There is no question of your literary qualifications, Lovecraft. But in all candor, one must wonder why Viereck selected you for this job.' He hesitated momentarily. 'I know you won't think this is all just sour grapes.'

'No, course not.' Lovecraft forgot himself and tried to nod again but stopped very quickly. 'It actually tastes purt – pretty good.' He lifted his glass and took a sip. Some of the liquid splashed over the rim, but he managed to lower the glass safely.

'I didn't quite mean – ' Starrett leaned toward Howard Lovecraft, his broad forehead and shock of wavy hair looming astonishingly. Lovecraft reached with one hand to fend off the approaching collision. With the other he grabbed for the polished wood of the bar.

'Come to think of it – ' Starrett caught Lovecraft's arm and steadied him, ' – maybe we ought to call it a night.'

4

Brooklyn

Theodore Weiss – Theo to his family, Dash to close friends, Hardeen the Mysterious to his audiences – wheeled the tan Rickenbacker Super Sport to the kerb at Parkside Avenue and climbed from the car. He tapped his midnight-blue Borsalino to a carefully calculated angle, examined the hang of his cravat by his reflection in the front door of the building, and pressed on the buzzer with the tip of his ivory-headed stick.

Moments later he stood inside the Lovecraft apartment. He took Sonia's hands, pressed his cheek against hers, then extended one carefully manicured hand to grasp Howard Lovecraft's.

'I have not had the opportunity to extend my condolences upon the death of your brother,' the New Englander said. 'Although belatedly, may I do so.'

Theo thanked him. He knew that Sonia's husband was an odd fish, had first heard so from Ehrich before ever meeting Lovecraft or Sonia. But Ehrich had spoken of the New Englander as a brilliant mind, and as a man of scrupulous propriety in a field filled with braggarts and poseurs. Somewhere deep inside that stalactite of Yankee reserve, Ehrich had insisted, there lurked a remarkably warm person, yearning to reach the surface. Theo was less than totally convinced, but Lovecraft did seem to be an interesting character at the least. And his wife Sonia had proved to be a charming, witty person. All the more astonishing that she should be married to this prim New Englander!

Sonia retreated briefly to her kitchen, returned with a tray and a welcome pot of coffee.

They sat round a low table, sipping from their steaming cups. 'Where are you planning to take us tomorrow, Theo?' Sonia asked. Before he could answer she said, 'Howard, you've never seen Theo's new car. It's absolutely beautiful. Like a royal carriage!'

Theo laughed. 'Hardly that! It's my little orphan. You know, they stopped building the things. Fine cars, too. But they're out of business now, and I understand that Captain Rickenbacker is going to return to the aviation business instead.'

'You are an enthusiast yourself, are you not, Mr Weiss?' Lovecraft asked.

'A bit of one. Ehrich and I had quite a time in the air. You know, Houdini was the first man ever to pilot an airplane in Australia. That was quite an enterprise! It had its publicity value, of course. Houdini was always attuned to headlines, used to say it didn't matter what wonder you performed, you first had to get people to come and watch. But he was sincerely interested in aeronautics. He would have been intrigued with this fresh surge of interest that the Orteig Prize has provoked.

'Well.' He put down his empty cup. 'There will be a good many Sunday drivers out tomorrow. Shall we try to start while it's still early, then?'

Hours after Theo's departure, Sonia H. G. Lovecraft swept from the kitchen into the parlor. She checked the time by her silver Elgin wristwatch, calculating the interval until dinner must be ready. She flicked a speck of dust from the tall gilt-framed mirror and examined her appearance. For a woman in her middle forties, Sonia still managed to cut a pleasing figure.

Her hair was worn long, done up in dark graceful

swirls. Her dress was a warm russet shantung, its bias-cut hemline a fair compromise between the soaring fashions of the day and her own more conservative preference. A string of dark amber beads at the throat set off her clear olive skin and gave a look of vivacity to her slightly heavy form.

As if on cue, Howard rose from the brocade-covered easy chair that had been his favorite in their years together. He looked more wan than ever.

Sonia reached for Howard's arm; he seemed to draw away slightly, but permitted her the contact. She turned her face up and gave him a small, warm kiss on the cheek. Lovecraft stood uncertainly. 'It was most kind of you to invite me to your home,' he said.

She pressed his hand with hers. 'Please, Howard. If you would only consider this your place too. Any time you are in the city. There's no need to impose on strangers.'

Lovecraft raised his eyebrows. 'Certainly the Long family do not qualify as strangers. I have known Belknap for nearly ten years, and the senior Longs for almost as lengthy a period. We two were introduced well after that time!'

'I know, Howard. I remember it well. The amateur journalists' convention in Boston. But surely your own wife is a more intimate acquaintance than any other.

'But come, let's not quarrel, please! I have a pot of coffee on the stove, and dinner will be ready in a little while. Veal birds and wild rice, you'll love it. And tell me about everything you're doing, Howard. How is your writing going? I always look for your stories in the magazines, and I try to keep up with your career. Do you really have a book coming?'

'I'm not sure,' Lovecraft admitted. 'I promised a pub-lisher that I would meet some people he wants me to know. If I am impressed by them, perhaps a volume will grow from the experience.'

'Not your stories?'

'No.' He shook his head sadly. 'It appears that the press is more interested in the ephemeral doings of the politicians and the schemers than in my humble attempts to create any tales of enduring worth.'

'Well, come to the table, Howard dear.' Sonia took him by the hands and drew him toward the dinner table.

Over their meal they discussed Howard's work, his dealings with the magazine proprietors, and his unsuccessful attempts to find a publisher who would bring out a collection of his stories. Sonia complained that the publishing houses didn't appreciate Howard's art.

Lovecraft ate with gusto. Between forkfuls of veal he mourned, 'Poe died penniless and unknown.'

'There's no reason for you to do the same!' Sonia cried.

Lovecraft chewed the veal.

Afterward they bundled into warm clothing and walked to an ice cream parlor. Sonia told Howard that her job was going well. The millinery department at Russeks had had a successful Christmas, and they were just completing their January clearance and looking forward to the spring season.

Lovecraft grunted periodically, concentrating on his sundae.

'What I'm getting at, Howard, is that money is a little better than before. You don't have to live with your aunts in Providence. We are still legally husband and wife. I wish you would move into Parkside with me.'

Lovecraft looked up from his ice cream and syrup. He hesitated, spoon in hand. 'It would be wholly improper of me – for a gentleman to live on the earnings of a woman in trade.'

He returned to his sundae.

Sonia reddened. She clasped her hands beneath the table to steady them. 'I am not just "a woman in trade", Howard! I am your wife.'

'Nonetheless, it is out of the question.'

Sonia retreated. 'But you'll stay with me for a while, Howard? You are important to me. It's very lonely without you here.' She felt, suddenly, that she was close to tears.

'You have your friends,' Howard said. 'I notice a certain warmth between yourself and Theo Weiss. And you have your daughter.'

Sonia gripped the tortoise-shell rim of her purse with cold fingers. 'There's nothing wrong with two people being friends, Howard. And remember, I met Theo through you! He was absolutely heartbroken when his brother died, and he's been very brave in carrying on Houdini's work. There's nothing wrong with our – with his visiting me occasionally when he's not on tour.'

She stopped to catch her breath. 'As for Florence – she's living in Paris. I know I wrote to you about her. She has a job writing for the Hearst syndicate. All I have from her is an infrequent postcard.'

Lovecraft ran his spoon to the bottom of the empty sundae dish. He managed to coat the spoon with a remnant of hot fudge. 'I will stay with you at Parkside,' he said, 'on the condition that our relationship shall be wholly platonic.'

Sonia blanched. 'Howard!'

'I can make my bed very comfortably on the sofa. Unless my terms are acceptable to you, I shall be forced to decline your invitation.'

'Acceptable!' Sonia sighed bitterly. 'Acceptable doesn't mean I'm happy. But I suppose . . .'

* * *

The telephone bell was sounding as they opened the apartment door. Sonia lifted the instrument and spoke briefly. She asked the caller to wait and placed the earpiece on the marble-topped commode while she turned toward Howard.

'It's Dash – Theo,' she said quietly. She experienced a rush of anger with herself for growing red as she spoke the name. 'He's just home from his evening performance, and he suggests that we be ready by nine in the morning. You will come, Howard?'

Lovecraft stood silently for seconds that were ticked off by the aluminum-cased timepiece beside the telephone. Finally he assented.

Sonia completed her conversation, then came and sat opposite her husband. 'I know that you like Theo, really, Howard. You've said as much, that you like him much better than you did Ehrich, may his soul find rest!'

Lovecraft knotted a fist on one woolen-trousered knee. 'Yes, I must admit that Theo is at least the more polished of the two. Houdini had far too much of the aggressive *arriviste* in him, for my taste. He was a man of quick intellect, but he exhibited the crudity and pushiness of so many Jews and others. If you must know it, Sonia, it is the swirling mass of human flotsam, the Jews and swarthy-skinned Orientals, the dark-visaged Slavs and the greasy Hispanics, that virtually drove me from New York.' His jaw quivered with tension. 'If only this land could be cleansed of such mongrels and the high English stock that once populated these shores be restored to their possession!'

Her cheeks flaming, Sonia shouted, 'Howard! Do you forget who I am? You used to speak of admiring my clear mind and sympathetic nature. How could you marry me, a Jewess born in the Ukraine! Would you cleanse this land of me?'

There was a moment of stonelike silence.

Finally Lovecraft said, 'There are exceptions, Sonia. Of course there are always exceptions. The most lowly of stock can throw up a superior sport at any time. That is one advantage that the mongrel possesses over the thoroughbred! You know what the product will be when you breed thoroughbreds, but mongrels can produce anything.'

Sonia stood rigidly, her hands clenched. 'I have always loved you, Howard. In your own odd way you are a fine person. But I have never understood you, nor can I comprehend how you could ever have loved me while you entertained those vicious and despicable ideas.'

Lovecraft climbed into the front seat of the car beside Theo Weiss, Sonia into the rear. 'Since we were speaking of aviation, I thought we'd head out to Roosevelt Field and look over the activities there,' Theo said. He stepped on the starter switch. The engine began at once to purr smoothly, and he pulled the Rickenbacker away from the curb.

'Yes,' Theo said, 'the airplane is a marvel for our time. Once Ehrich had taken flying lessons he became wildly devoted to the sport. He gave me no peace until I'd agreed to learn, as well. And it is a grand experience. Have you ever flown, Lovecraft? Or you, Sonia?'

'There is an old fellow I know in Massachusetts,' Lovecraft said. 'There was an aircraft manufactory in the village of Marblehead during the Great War, run by the Burgess family of ancient settlers. They closed down the manufactory after the armistice was declared, but old Azor Burgess keeps one of the rickety machines and offers sightseeing excursions over the harbor and town.

'I did accompany him on one such flight. Had been vacationing nearby with the Longs, and young Belknap and I spent the day in Marblehead studying the Georgian structures preserved there. It was indeed an exhilarating sensation to soar through the aether on slim, flimsy wings, looking down upon green hills and white structures like sea gulls observing the ephemeral handiwork of man.'

Theo had maneuvered the Rickenbacker through the streets of Brooklyn and pointed the sedan eastward on a rural road. He glanced sideways at Lovecraft. 'Then you approve of aviation. Sonia has mentioned that you often dislike innovation. That you prefer the good old days, most often.'

'As a generality that is true,' Lovecraft conceded. 'I believe that the last Golden Age was the Georgian era, with its grace of architecture, music, painting, costume, and social conduct. It was the foolish behavior of the Hanoverian King George that set the American colonies upon the road to revolt, and thus indirectly created many of the forces of crass modernism.

'But I do not despise *all* invention. This is a splendid automobile, Mr Weiss. And as for the aëroplane, I think it is a most admirable vehicle for the cultural ennoblement of the gentry. I only fear its vulgarization into a tool of mass commerce.'

They lapsed into silence as the Rickenbacker purred through the green farmlands, now dotted with snowbanks, and the white-painted colonial villages of eastern Long Island. Weiss maneuvered the Rickenbacker off the main road and onto a winding blacktop that led to the hangars and runways of Roosevelt Field. In the chill of winter the tarmacs were largely vacant, the few parked aircraft covered with canvas tarpaulins to protect them from storms.

Weiss brought the sedan through a tricky series of barriers and parked beside a small truck inside a tin-walled hangar.

Several mechanics were working over a huge radial engine. As the Rickenbacker rolled to a halt they looked up, tossed a friendly wave to Theo, and resumed their work.

Sonia Lovecraft climbed from the rear seat of the car. 'I didn't know that everybody was your friend here, Dash.'

Weiss admitted that he liked to visit airports when he had the chance. 'Partially it's an interest that Ehrich instilled in me. But I'm enthusiastic about flying myself. And I want to investigate certain technical possibilities as well.'

He smiled as the chief mechanic left the engine crew and advanced, wiping his greasy hands on an old towel. Weiss introduced him to Sonia and to Lovecraft. They walked to a little office separated from the huge hangar by a tin partition. Inside were a few chairs, a desk, locker closet, and hot plate. The mechanic poured them hot drinks laced with alcohol from a bottle kept in the metal locker.

'Did you get the information you needed in Scotland, Mr Weiss?' the mechanic asked.

Theo said, 'I saw Baird, and he was interested in making a deal. But you know the canny Scots – hae dinna wanna gie oop hin saecrets unti' he had his money.' Weiss chuckled. 'But we'll reach a bargain, I'm sure. And he gave a very impressive demonstration.'

Weiss stopped and turned toward Howard and Sonia. 'I'm afraid that we're talking mysteries.'

'You mentioned a Baird,' Lovecraft said. 'Is this by any chance Edwin Baird, the editor?'

Weiss shook his head. 'A Scots inventor named John Baird. I suppose he might be a distant relative of your Baird. I never thought to ask, since I don't know your editor. John Baird is a wizard inventor. He's working in the fields of electricity and optics, and he's developed a new television device called the noctovisor.'

Lovecraft snorted. 'Everyone is inventing television this year. There was a report in the press about Secretary Hoover's addressing a conference in New Jersey from his office in Washington, via television. And some fellow out in California is supposed to have sent a picture over wireless.'

Weiss gestured broadly. 'I suppose it's natural for many inventors to work on the same idea. It's an obvious step ahead. With radio getting into every home, and now they're building sets for autos, with Vitaphone adding speech to motion pictures – did you see that Vitaphone film of Benito Mussolini's greetings to the American people? – it's very obvious to try and add picture where there is only sound.

'But this fellow Baird's invention is a special sort of television. He's been concerned with picking up images at night, or through dense fog. He's built a machine that uses some sort of invisible light. He calls it an infrared scanner. I saw a demonstration in Edinburgh when I toured the British Isles last month.'

Lovecraft, holding a hot cup in both hands to keep his fingers from freezing, asked what interested Theo in Baird's invention.

'I had planned an underwater escape to promote my show in Edinburgh. Things like that have to be planned to the last fraction, Howard, and I was just a bit worried about subsurface obstacles in the Firth of Forth. Baird hauled his machine out to the jetty for me and turned it on, and it worked beautifully. To the naked eye the water was utterly black, completely impenetrable. I could only have planned my escape by going down beforehand in a diving suit – Lord knows I've done that often enough! Ehrich used to say, there's no such thing as magic, no such thing as mystery. It's all in skill, in having the right equipment, and in proper preparation. He was right!

'At any rate, Mr Baird's noctovisor showed me the waters exactly as I needed to see them. Clear as a bathtub!'

Sonia asked, 'But what has that to do with airplanes, Dash?'

Weiss pointed at an engineless biplane standing neglected at one end of the hangar.

'Soon as the boys get that engine right, she goes back in the Stinson, Mr Weiss,' the mechanic volunteered.

'It seems to me,' Weiss said, 'that an airplane equipped with a Baird noctovisor could accomplish great things. Think of its usefulness in mapping channels for shipping, searching for survivors of marine disasters, charting the seabeds, even searching for sunken galleons!' At the last, he grinned broadly.

The mechanic made a rough sound. 'Put 'em on army planes! What a weapon that would make! Those zeppelin raids during the war was nothing compared to what we could do!'

Lovecraft rubbed his chin.

'Just think of it, gents,' the mechanic continued. 'And ma'am. Bombers goin' in over an enemy city in the middle of the night. They can't see you, they can't see nothin'! Searchlights – pah! If they try and send up fighter planes against us, we have *our* fighters along, all fixed out with noctos. It'd be a slaughter!'

'Well, this is all somewhat premature,' Weiss said. 'Baird still wants to dicker over prices and licenses. And besides, all he's built so far is a rather clumsy working model of the noctovisor. We've got to make it smaller and either contrive a readily portable version, or design a proper installation for aircraft. But it's a very promising machine. Very.'

5
Manhattan

Viereck sat back in the soft padding of his favorite chair, a highball at his side and a belvedere perfecto between his fingers. When he heard the door chimes sound he slid the papers from the top of his desk and sat upright waiting for his servant to announce the arrival of Otto Kiep.

A respectful knock at the door of Viereck's study; the butler's close-cropped visage. 'Dr Kiep is here, sir.'

Viereck told the butler to show the caller in. A private conference before the other guests arrived was definitely in order.

When Kiep entered the study Viereck was on his feet, moving to greet him with a warm handshake, an exchange of greetings in the German language before they switched over to English. Although Viereck's German had very little rust on it and Kiep's English left much to be desired, the latter preferred as much practice in English as he could manage.

'Quite a gathering this is to be, Viereck,' Kiep said. At his host's gesture he settled himself comfortably in a leather chair. 'You have how many groups to be here represented invited?'

'Some half-dozen, Doctor. Most of them know one another already, but there has never been a meeting of all at a single time and place. So – it seemed that a social environment would be more conducive than a formal conference. Thus, the use of my home.'

'Ach.' Kiep nodded.

Viereck lifted the lid of an ebony humidor, slid it

across glass on green felt. 'A cigar, Doctor? Or would you prefer a highball?' Kiep accepted, and Viereck reached behind him to tug at a velvet-covered cord and summon a servant. 'Not all of these elements may prove entirely simpatico with one another. So a bit of small talk, a few drinks to place them in a friendly frame of mind . . .'

Kiep, his crop-haired head and short-stocky figure dwarfed by the tall leather chair, stopped Viereck with the wave of one pudgy manicured hand. 'Simpatico?' he frowned.

'I apologize. In English, you know, they borrow words from all languages. Well, comfortable with one another. Sie lassen es sich behagen.'

'Ach so, ich verstehe schon! Gemütlich!' Kiep nodded vigorously.

Again the butler entered. Kiep ordered a drink, and the servant disappeared.

'Also,' Viereck resumed, 'we shall have a pair of journalists with us tonight. One who is already very receptive to our ideas. And another whom I intend to win to the cause. He shows some very useful attitudes – but some others that I do not so much like. But we try, eh?'

'Wieso, brauchen wir ihn?' Kiep asked. 'If einen guten Freund we already have, let him be used. Why do we another seek?'

Viereck sipped at his glass. 'Dr Kiep, have you ever met Mr George Pagnanelli?'

The shorter man shook his head uncertainly. 'Ich glaube nein. Der Name familiar ist, only.'

Viereck nodded. 'A very interesting young man. A real joiner. I think he is a member of twenty organizations, at least! Christian Front, American Defense Society, National Workers League, Yankee Freemen. I myself met him through the Steuben Society.'

'Hmph. Sehr gut, Viereck. Was fehlt ihm denn?'

'His name and his appearance are wrong, I fear. He writes and publishes a little newsletter of his own, called the *Christian Defender*. His ideas are very similar to ours. But as you know, Otto, my own writings are suspect. I am German-born, I was known to sympathize with the German cause in the war. I have spoken out for a redress of the Versailles outrages.'

'Ja, ja, ja!' Kiep nodded impatiently, his pink jowls quivering with the motion. 'Und so – ?'

'And so my words are scrutinized, my arguments are challenged because the Americans do not consider me a loyal American. I have written under other names, but that is not a fully satisfactory course. The man must emerge from behind his writings at some point, if he is to have full impact.

'And Mr Pagnanelli, you see, suffers from the same disqualifications as I. With a name like his, he is thought to be either a spokesman for Il Duce or an anarchist like those poor fish in Massachusetts.'

Kiep grunted. 'On that point, Viereck, we have done good. Carisi and Amoroso did not for nothing die. A great protest Il Duce has made. He has their bodies for burial in Italy demanded!' He gave a guttural laugh. 'So many Italians will we here win over!'

'That news is very pleasant, Otto. Mussolini can be of use to us here as well as in Europe! Good.' He paused, then went on. 'But regarding our immediate need. A pure American is required. One descended from old stock. Preferably from English stock. Pagnanelli has the wrong name, the wrong looks to him, the wrong manner of speech. But this fellow Lovecraft whom I have invited tonight – he is perfect for our needs. That is why we must win his aid. That is why he is invited here.'

A serious look on his face, Kiep said, 'I should like

more about him to know, this Lovecraft man. He is influential? His name I have never heard. He sounds odd. Like witchcraft. Die Hexerei, nicht wahr?' He laughed.

'Ja, ja, Herr Doktor. But this Lovecraft is a writer of stories and essays. Very good ones. I have read some of his work. During the World War he had some very unkind things to say about Sylvester Viereck, even. Hah!'

'But he is a frustrated and ambitious man, mein Herr. He sells his good stories to bad magazines for Pfennige. He has never seen his name on a book. *This he needs. This we offer.* If he writes a book advancing our cause, we gain the seal of respectability here.'

Kiep fidgeted in his chair, drained his glass, and placed it on Viereck's desk. 'So. Also gut. Wieviel wird er uns kosten?' Kiep reached inside his jacket and drew out his fountain pen.

'No, no, no.' Viereck waved aside the idea. 'This is a gentleman – we cannot buy him, mein Herr. Not with money. This is a fish we must catch.

'But we dangle the bait before this fish's eyes. The bait is glory. And the hook is soon in his gills. We will haul him in! The bait we dangle for him is a book of his precious stories, but first we require of him a book of political nature. He reasons so carefully, so logically. He considers the arguments of all sides.

'He opposed us during the war. Now the pure justice of our cause wins him over, and we have a spokesman and ally of the most impeccable old American credentials.'

Kiep opened his pale blue eyes wide. 'You wish for him all our intentions to open? Such confidence you feel, in this Herr Lovecraft?'

Slowly Viereck shook his head. 'No. Mr Lovecraft will be present but not for the entire evening. We will send him off after a while with the journalist Pagnanelli, to

explore their little world of words. We will tackle more
. . . substantial . . . matters after they are gone.'

In the following silence the door chimes sounded once
again.

Viereck rose. 'Now our other guests arrive.' He
checked the time by his pocket watch. 'I asked Mr
Lovecraft to come a bit earlier than the others so he
could meet them as they arrive. So I go to act the role of
gracious host.'

The butler had taken Lovecraft's hat and overcoat, and
was ushering him into the sunken living room of the
Viereck home. Viereck approached, placed his hand
briefly on Lovecraft's arm. 'I am very pleased that you
could attend our little gathering. I wish you to meet Dr
Otto Kiep, of the German Consulate.'

Kiep appeared at Viereck's elbow, made a small bow,
and extended his hand. After a moment's hesitation
Lovecraft took the pudgy hand and shook it.

Before anyone spoke the door chimes sounded once
more. A tall, youngish man in rich clothes of a subtly
exotic cut entered; on his arm, a plump woman at least
fifteen years his senior. She wore a headband with ostrich-
feather plumes, a floor-length gown, and a glittering array
of bracelets, rings, necklaces, and stomacher.

Viereck placed one hand on Dr Kiep's shoulder, the
other on Howard Lovecraft's. He said, 'Excuse me for
just one moment. Dr Kiep, you of course know the count
and countess. Mr Lovecraft must meet them.'

He strode across the room, shook hands with the count,
bent over the countess's hand, then returned with them
to Lovecraft and the German consul. 'Your Grace, may I
present Mr H. P. Lovecraft, of Providence.'

Lovecraft was uncertain how to react. He essayed a
small bow of his own, felt relief when the count extended

his hand languidly and the countess inclined her head by a few degrees. Lovecraft shook the count's extended hand.

'Anastase Andreivitch, Count Vonsiatskoy-Vonsiatsky,' the nobleman identified himself. He spoke with a heavy Russian accent. The countess smiled graciously.

'Of course Your Grace is acquainted with Dr Otto Kiep of the German Consulate,' Viereck said. 'I have asked Mr Lovecraft here so that he may become acquainted with our movement.'

The count's eyes brightened.

'Mr Lovecraft is a distinguished author,' Viereck continued. 'I hope that he will choose to write about us. We know that our cause is just, but there are those who do not understand its justice. I believe that Mr Lovecraft's words will be read and believed.'

'We're going back to Russia,' said Countess Vonsiatsky.

Lovecraft was astonished at the manner of her speech. Her voice was a warm contralto, but her inflection sounded more like an attempt at a clumsy stage-slavic than like the speech of a Russian woman using English. Lovecraft asked, 'Are you merely visiting the United States, Countess?'

A maid passed carrying a large tray of hors d'oeuvres. The countess reached for a swirl of pureed meat and dough, popped the concoction into her mouth, and continued speaking without interruption.

'I am Russian only by adoption, Mr Lovecraft. Actually I was born in Connecticut. You may know my family. Mr Viereck said that you were a New Englander yourself. We're in locomotives, you see. In fact the count has consented to let us place his name on our letterhead – it adds so to our standing.'

'Only for the time being, my dear.' The count nodded

toward his wife, inclining most of his body. A waiter
had appeared carrying a tray of long-stemmed, shallow-
bowled glasses and a tall green bottle. The count
exclaimed, 'Champagne!' He reached for a glass, his face
glowing. With his free hand he captured another glass for
the countess. The waiter moved to offer drinks to Dr
Kiep and Howard Lovecraft.

'Yes,' the countess resumed. She took a large sip of
champagne, reached between Lovecraft and Dr Kiep to
place her empty glass on the waiter's tray and draw back
with a full glass in hand. 'As soon as preparations are
completed, we will be returning to Russia, although I
think I shall wish to keep a home in Connecticut as well.
Sentiment, you know. One never loses one's fondness for
the place of one's birth.'

Lovecraft nodded. 'But would you be welcomed by the
bolshevists?'

The count turned angry. 'We shall put *them* back where
they belong. Back in the mud and the wooden huts they
understand. They have no understanding of civilization.
Look at them, now that Ulyanov is dead. He was bad
enough, that one. Lenin, he called himself. At least he
was intellectual of sorts. But these others, they will
destroy themselves!

'Djugashvili little priest, and Jew Bronstein, let them
exhaust selves fighting! They fear even to use real names.
Stalin, Trotzky, pah!

'As soon as money is raised, Mr Lovecraft,' the count
leaned forward, pointing a slim finger at Howard's dark
necktie.

'Our locomotive works are certainly helping with that,'
the countess interjected. Her husband glared at her for
an instant.

'Yes, locomotive money is helpful,' he conceded. 'Our
party will buy ships. Return to Russia. In US and Europe

are three hundred thousand Russians, Khazaks, Turk-men, Ukraines, driven out, robbed, murdered by bol-sheviki. We go back, overthrow bolsheviki, restore Tsar and justice to save suffering Russia!' A look of religious devotion suffused Vonsiatsky's countenance.

Lovecraft stood facing the count and countess with Dr Kiep at his side. Behind the couple he could see the foyer that let onto the front door of the Viereck house, opening onto fashionable West 113th Street. From time to time the butler would advance and admit guests; the salon was becoming crowded.

Viereck was visible moving from group to group, shak-ing a hand, whispering a confidence, bowing and moving on.

Holding his hands clasped before him, Lovecraft said, 'Perhaps I missed some point, Your Grace.' The sound of his voice speaking the formal terms of address was strange and pleasant in his ears. 'But I was under the impression that the entire royal family had been executed – '

'Murdered!' Vonsiatsky's eyes blazed.

' – indeed.'

'At Ekaterinburg.'

'Quite so, Your Grace. But how, then, could the Tsar be restored, if not only he but his entire family had been killed? Are there collateral Romanoffs unknown to me?'

With a half-suppressed giggle the countess replied, 'There are no surviving Romanoffs, Mr Lovecraft. But there are many other survivors of the Empire. Some with a degree of Romanoff blood, yes indeed!'

The count nodded his support.

Countess Vonsiatsky said, 'The House of Vonsiatskoy-Vonsiatsky is among the oldest and noblest of Russian houses. When Whites gather, the name of the count is spoken in tones of hushed reverence, Mr Lovecraft. Why, it makes me feel very humble to have been honored to become, by marriage, a member of the royal house.'

'Poor Nikita,' the count mooned.

Lovecraft's attention was seized by a small disturbance in the foyer. He could see Viereck separate himself suddenly from a conversation-partner, grasp Dr Kiep silently by one elbow, and draw him away from the others. The count and countess spun so that all three faced the front door.

In a moment Viereck returned in company of a small, wiry fellow with a leathery, sun-beaten complexion and an ill-fitting gray suit. He steered the man away from the salon and toward the study off to one side.

Dr Kiep appeared with a bull-necked, red-faced individual in a brown business suit and a necktie painted in glaring geometric patterns. At Kiep's other side, his face round and benevolent, strode a man wearing rimless eyeglasses and a black suit with Roman-collared shirt.

The three of them seemed to be speaking at once, the diplomat asking questions, the bull-necked man gesturing angrily, the priest patting both on their arms trying to calm them.

Countess Vonsiatsky said, 'Why, it's Mr Spanknoebel and Father Curran! How charming that they came! And wasn't that Dr Evans I saw with Sylvester a moment ago?'

She strode forward and grasped the right hands of the priest and the bull-necked man. In a moment she had brought them back to her husband and Howard Lovecraft, Otto Kiep skipping along on his short legs to stay up with the group.

The countess introduced Lovecraft and the others. The priest was Father Edward Curran, President of the International Catholic Truth Society and eastern representative of Father Charles Coughlin's Christian

Front. The bull-necked man was Heinz Spanknoebel, a chemist employed by the Ford Company in Dearborn. Spanknoebel was Chairman of the Friends of the New Germany, a Midwestern association that had succeeded the old Steuben Cultural Society.

'The count was just explaining to Mr Lovecraft,' the countess said, 'our plans for restoring the legal government of Russia once we rid her of the Jewish bolshevik clique.' She smiled at Lovecraft, holding Spanknoebel's sleeve in one hand. 'Mr Spanknoebel's good friend Mr Ford has offered his assistance. You know, those international zionist plotters will stop at nothing. Why, that terrible kike Sapiro is actually suing the *Dearborn Independent* just for printing the truth about the *Protocols of Zion*! Well, if Mr Ford could put up the cost of the Peace Ship and try to end the war like he did, then the very least he can do is to provide a liner to carry our army to Russia and throw out that Stalin and Trotzky and that awful little Premier Rykoff of theirs!'

Dr Kiep and Spanknoebel spoke briefly in quiet Germanic tones, Spanknoebel bending his head to bring it close to the pudgy Kiep's. In a moment Kiep turned and asked Father Curran in English, 'What was happening as you entered?'

Curran laughed weakly. 'A mere little happenstance, Doctor.' Lovecraft noted that Curran spoke with a slight Irish brogue. 'Dr Evans and Mr Spanknoebel and I happened to arrive outside at the same moment. In fact, Heinz and I shared a taxi from our hotel. Dr Evans arrived on foot.

'Well, you know the Imperial Wizard doesn't care too much for Catholics, nor for Irish. I'm afraid he had a harsh word or two to say as we waited for the door to open.'

Dr Kiep nodded. 'I am sure Herr Viereck will matters settle with Dr Evans.'

Lovecraft shook his head. 'Pardon me, Dr Kiep, I fear that I'm losing track of everyone. Is this a convention of medical practitioners?'

'Ah, no, Mr Lovecraft. Mein Titel aus meiner Universitätszeit ist. Dr Evans – ah, my English not so gut ist. Ein Zahnarzt. Please, the countess will – '

'Why, of course, Doctor. That little Evans is nothing but a dentist, Mr Lovecraft. And he doesn't even practice at that! He's the head of the Ku Klux Klan, you know. He calls himself Imperial Wizard, but he's just a cheap little Texan as far as I'm concerned, sitting down there in Atlanta wearing silly costumes and handing out ridiculous titles to just anybody for money!'

Lovecraft brightened. 'Why, I investigated the Ku Klux Klan some years ago. All that I could learn of it was that the organization was founded by sincere Southern patriots bent on saving a cherished tradition. Certainly their efforts to forestall the mongrelization of their race deserves nothing but our admiration.'

'Well,' the countess fluttered, 'one can hardly quarrel with such lofty goals, of course.' She reached past Howard and stopped a passing waitress long enough to remove a glass of champagne from her tray. 'But the classes to which they appeal seem to be *very* crude. The dregs, the very dregs of Southern society, Mr Lovecraft. And you know, they are recruiting in the North now, as well! We find ourselves with strange partners in our noble task.'

'It's the Klan's bigotry against Catholics that distresses me,' Father Curran said. 'The Klan speaks of keeping America a pure, moral, white Christian country, and surely one has to applaud *that* purpose! But when they start to attack Holy Mother Church and her Faithful, that we cannot tolerate!'

Viereck broke into the circle, in tow with a thin, richly dressed, gray-haired woman. 'May I interrupt, Father? I know that all of you are acquainted except – ah, this is Mr Howard Lovecraft. Mr Lovecraft, Mrs Elizabeth Dilling, chairman of the Patriotic Research Bureau.' Mrs Dilling extended her hand, and Lovecraft shook it gingerly.

'Oh, Mr Lovecraft, Mr Viereck has been telling me all about you. I'm so happy to make your acquaintance. Mr Viereck says that you're an author. So am I, in my own modest way. You know, our bureau has to get out reports and such, and I do my own little bit of the work. Mr Viereck tells me you're a short story writer. How exciting! Do you find politics interesting? I imagine you must deal with all sorts of themes in your stories, pointing out dangers to your readers and so on.'

Mrs Dilling paused for breath, and Lovecraft managed a reply. 'In fact I seldom treat political matters in my tales. I suppose I have commented, obliquely, in describing the deterioration of modern society and the greasy mongrels who clog our city streets. But my work is not primarily political in nature.'

'Well,' Mrs Dilling resumed, 'I understand that you are a native of Providence, Mr Lovecraft. A lovely, lovely city, of course. I hope that New England, at least, retains a degree of its old American identity.'

Lovecraft managed a half-sentence about the Italian and Portuguese influx before Mrs Dilling took over again.

'Yes, I can certainly see your problem. Although there are *some* nice Italians as well, you know. We shouldn't judge *all* of a race by its worst members, there are a few nice exceptions in every people. Why, do you know the Count di Revel? I see that you don't. Why, he is just the loveliest man. He's the head of the Fascist League of

North America. You know, Mr Mussolini *has* done wonders for Italy, and if he can send a splendid man like
Count di Revel, why, maybe there's something that can
be done about whipping the Italians in this country into
line as well.

'Of course,' and she lowered her voice conspiratorially,
'I still feel that we would be better off without these
people. But if we do have to put up with them at least
one of their own kind keeping them in line would be a
blessing to us all.

'Oh, where did Mr Viereck go?' She looked around
anxiously. 'Oh, there he is with that terrible little black
Mr Pagnanelli of his. I don't know what he sees in that
man. he isn't even an honest wop like Mr Capone or Mr
Colosimo in Chicago. Not that I care for those hoodlums
a bit, but at least they don't pretend to be something that
they aren't. But that Pagnanelli, I think he's some kind
of Armenian or something like that. And he goes creeping
around, always asking sly little questions, not like our
Patriotic Research Bureau at all!'

Viereck brought Pagnanelli to the circle and introduced
him. He was a short, swarthy-complexioned man wearing
cheap, ill-fitting clothes. A jacket and trousers that nearly
matched, a gray shirt with a rumpled collar and a spotted
necktie. He was greeted with coolness. After a moment's
uncomfortable silence Viereck asked if he might pull
Howard Lovecraft away from the group.

He led Lovecraft and Pagnanelli to his study and
offered them chairs. Lovecraft gazed at the Armenian,
found him less repellent than Mrs Dilling had led him to
expect. The dark young man smiled at Lovecraft.

Viereck sat behind his desk. He said, 'I have something
for each of you. I know you've heard of the NSDAP –
the National Socialist German Workers Party. This Party
is one of the growing forces in Europe. It is my belief

that within a few years it will be the dominant force, not only in Germany but on the stage of the entire world.'

Lovecraft shifted uncomfortably, noticing Pagnanelli doing the same.

'The leader of this Party,' Viereck opened the humidor on his desk and offered its contents to the others, 'happens to be a very close friend of mine.' He extracted a cigar from the humidor and shut the lid. 'Herr Hitler has set out,' (striking flame from a desk-top lighter) 'to rectify the injustices,' (pausing to draw on his corona) 'perpetrated through treachery at Versailles.

'His intention is to restore order in Germany and throughout Europe,' (sending a gray doughnut of smoke ceilingward) 'and to avert the threat of bolshevism in western Europe.'

As Viereck halted, Pagnanelli spoke in an accented voice. 'I thought, sir, that you favored an imperial restoration for Germany.'

Viereck nodded. 'One way or another, Barbarossa will awaken! Herr Hitler may make of himself another Bismarck – and for his Wilhelm, summon back the second Wilhelm, or even the younger Friedrich Wilhelm. That is to be seen.'

He paused and cleared his throat. 'But I have summoned you both to offer you a great privilege. As happens all too often – as I can testify from the experience of my own life! – the true patriot and man of vision, who refuses to bend his principles to conform to the moment's fashions, often runs afoul of his own government and spends a time imprisoned. Such was the case with Herr Hitler. But in his prison cell he composed one of the great documents of all time, a book he has named simply, *My Struggle*. In the German language, *Mein Kampf*.

'It has been my great honor to assist in the translation of this book into English, and I can present to each of you, prior to the publication of this edition, a precious copy of the translation.'

He turned in his chair, knelt at the foot of a stack of bookcases, and inserted a key in the wooden paneling. Behind the paneling was a steel safe. Viereck twirled the lock, opened the safe door, and drew out two thick envelopes. He relocked the safe and the wooden panel.

'Pagnanelli, you have already done fine work in advancing and explaining our cause. Lovecraft, we have had our differences, but I am certain that reading the words of Herr Hitler will convince you that at heart our philosophies are compatible. Please honor me by accepting these copies of the book.'

He handed an envelope to Pagnanelli; the other, to Lovecraft.

'If you are ready, a servant will fetch your hats and coats, my friends.'

The Christian

DEFENDER

GEORGE PAGNANELLI, Editor & Publisher

VOL 1 NO 5   PUBLISHED EVERY MONDAY   PRICE 2 CENTS

Hitler the German Explosive

By GEORGE SYLVESTER VIERECK

ADOLPH HITLER must be handled with care. He is a human explosive. The very mention of his name induces percussions. Some look to him as a German Mussolini, the savior of his country; others regard him as a violent agitator, thriving on religious prejudice and race contention.

Idolized by his followers, execrated by his foes, he is welcomed by Big Business as the only man in Germany who can take votes away from the Socialists. To some, however, the encouragement given to Hitler by conservative circles seems like an attempt to drive out Satan with Beelzebub.

I met Hitler at the house of a former Admiral of the German Navy. Over the tea cups we discussed problems, temporal and eternal. Through the window we saw the celebrated Meadow of Theresa where Munich foregathers annually to celebrate the October Feast. The dying sun illuminated the gigantic statue of Bavaria gazing straight at us from the meadow.

Hitler is not a native of Bavaria. His cradle was rocked in German Moravia, a region which, though one hundred per cent German, was dished out by the four foolish men at Versailles to Czecho-Slovakia. Like every son of that soil, Hitler looks upon himself as a German.

We are afforded a glimpse of the Greater Germany to be of which every German dreams, from the fact that a former Austrian subject is the leader of the German Fascisti. Hitler's shock troops are Bavarians. But his influence extends far beyond Bavaria. Though not permitted to organize in Prussia and in several other states, he has followers everywhere.

There is no one in Germany who does not recognize the importance of his emblem, the "Hakenkreuz," the ancient swastika, sometimes standing by itself and sometimes superimposed on a cross or a shield, a mystic symbol of militant Germanism.

The pugnacity of the man appears from the very choice of the name by which he designates his Party. He calls himself a "National

(Please turn over page)

6

Manhattan

Somewhere a bell tolled eleven. On the stoop of Viereck's house, Pagnanelli and Lovecraft stood, their breaths frosting the late night air. Pagnanelli turned toward the tall Lovecraft. 'Some cold night. I'm going home and make up a good hot batch of java. You like some?'

Lovecraft considered for a moment, then he nodded. He found the other a pleasant fellow despite a nondescript dress and bearing. And Pagnanelli might offer valuable advice in the field of political journalism.

They strolled toward the subway line, the sidewalk clean and dry beneath their feet. The most recent snow had been cleared away; the winter air was crisp and clear. The bright moonlight combined with the glow of streetlamps to give 113th Street the illusion of a strangely dim afternoon.

In a few minutes they were standing on the subway platform waiting for a downtown train. Pagnanelli asked Lovecraft about the latter's work. 'I try and keep up with the papers and magazines devoted to the cause. I don't think I've seen your by-line. It's an odd one, if you don't mind my saying so. I'm sure it's one I'd remember.'

Lovecraft grunted. 'I have not written for political journals, sir. Nor am I likely to do so. My work has been of a purely aesthetic nature for some years.'

'Poems and stories, eh?'

Frostily, Lovecraft gave his affirmation.

With a rattle of springs and wood and a scream of brakes, the downtown train pulled into the station. The two men climbed aboard and found seats facing each other. Their conversation dragged as the train swayed along beneath the city. Finally they surrendered to the noise and sat unspeaking until they reached Pagnanelli's stop. He motioned to Lovecraft, and they climbed off the train. At the late hour they were the only persons on the platform. Silently they crossed its width and ascended echoing metal steps to the street.

Pagnanelli's quarters were a single room four steps down from the sidewalk. He pulled an astonishing set of keys from his slightly ragged trousers and opened a series of locks on the single heavy door. 'Have to be careful,' he explained.

Inside the low-ceilinged room Lovecraft seated himself in the single tattered easy chair. Pagnanelli bustled around with a coffeepot, setting water to boil over a gas-fed hot plate. As the Armenian worked, Lovecraft's attention was drawn to the room's furnishings.

There was a small Corona typewriter set upon a rolling stand. A rickety wooden file cabinet leaned against the wall in one corner. Stacks of newspapers and magazines stood on the floor and covered an ancient desk. Bundles of a crudely printed periodical called the *Christian Defender*, tied with rough twine, were stacked in another corner. The walls were covered with parchments and certificates of membership in political groups, some of them in cheap ready-made frames, others held in place by thumbtacks.

'You been a pal of Sylvester's for long?' Pagnanelli's question broke into Lovecraft's concentration as he read the name of one group after another, all of them claiming George Pagnanelli as a loyal member.

'Eh? Why, one might say that I have known *of* Mr Viereck a good deal longer than I have *known* him. In fact we have been directly acquainted for only a short time.'

'He's a good guy.' Pagnanelli poured two servings of coffee into chipped mugs. He handed one to Lovecraft. 'Anything in it for you?'

Lovecraft asked for sugar and Pagnanelli located a cupful of it, covered with a cracked yellow saucer. He handed the cup to Lovecraft. 'Better take a little taste, I don't remember where I put the salt.'

Lovecraft sampled, then added sugar to his coffee. 'You are the editor of the *Christian Defender*?' he asked.

'My pride and joy!' The Armenian located a loose copy of the paper and handed it to Lovecraft. The New Englander placed his coffee mug gingerly on the littered floor and opened the paper.

'Hmm. Two cents per copy. Do you sell many, Pagnanelli?'

The Armenian drew up the only other chair in the room, a wooden typist's seat with several slats missing. 'Actually,' he leaned forward, 'not so many. It's something I do for the cause, you know. I'd just as soon give 'em away as sell ' em. But I got to cover costs. Printing ain't free, you know!'

Lovecraft turned the sparse sheets of the *Defender*. It was filled with notices of patriotic meetings, rallies, speeches. The tone of the paper was one of nearly panicked warnings against the dangers of communism and racial degradation.

'Good frien' o' mine named Pete Stahrenberg has a little job shop up in the Bronx. Sets my type and runs copies for me.' Pagnanelli rocked back and forth on two legs of his chair. 'Gives me a good rate, but Pete got to live too. And he got to pay for his paper, ink, type. You know, it's not cheap to put out a class product.'

Lovecraft dropped the *Christian Defender*. 'You are familiar with all the groups represented at Viereck's gathering?'

'Some better'n others.'

'I was particularly intrigued by one man there. I did not meet him, merely observed him briefly. Dr Evans.'

Pagnanelli nodded vigorously. He grunted, 'Ah-*hah*, ah-*hah*.'

'Do you know this person?' Lovecraft asked. 'I believe it was stated that he is Imperial Wizard of the Ku Klux Klan.'

'Oh, I know him, okay. Quite a guy. He came in there and took the Klan right away from the old guy, that Colonel Simpson or Singleton or whatever it was. He's a comer all right, that Doc Evans.'

'There seemed to be a certain amount of ill will between Dr Evans and Father Curran.'

'Yeah. Well, you know, the Klan don't like Catholics much.'

'Nor do I, if the truth be told. But there is no excuse for boorishness. Even if Father Curran does represent the Popish Church, one is expected to behave as a gentleman.'

'I guess Doc Evans don't agree with that, Mr Lovecraft. Mebbe it's the way he was raised, who knows?'

Lovecraft tapped his knuckles on a twine-bound bundle of *Christian Defenders*. If he was to write the book that Viereck required of him, he needed plentiful information on the background of the political groups involved in Viereck's odd coalition. And he was pretty well determined, by now, that he would write the book. Herr Hitler's manifesto – Lovecraft's copy lay atop his folded overcoat – should be a valuable source. But he needed to add to the human dimension of his writing.

'Do you know how Dr Evans was raised?' he asked Pagnanelli.

The Armenian gestured with both hands. 'Not in detail.

But I've got a little dirt on him. He started off as a small-town dentist over Texas way. Came to Atlanta to help out old Colonel Simmons running the Klan. He helped him out okay – helped him right out of the Klan, and took over for himself! Heh!'

'I imagine he would be known back in Texas, then. Don't you think so, Mr Pagnanelli? That is, if he was important in the Klan organization at home, before his summons to Georgia?'

'Yeah, I guess so. He was some kind of big noise back in Texas, in the Klan. They'd remember him out there. You planning a trip out West, Mr Lovecraft?'

Lovecraft frowned with concentration. 'Not myself, no. But I've a number of friends. Correspondents in various parts of the country. In particular, a talented young fantasy writer named Robert Howard who lives in rural Texas. I wonder if he might have known Dr Evans. Or at least have heard of him. Howard has never mentioned having Klan connections of any sort, but I should think that every small town in the state would possess a Klan presence of some kind. Howard would know – he's quite the gregarious fellow.'

'Huh!' Pagnanelli rolled some Bugler tobacco from a can on a shelf near the hot plate, lit a cigarette, and exhaled a feather of smoke. 'Certainly worth a letter to ask, anyhow. What's your pal's name again?'

'Howard,' Lovecraft said. 'Robert E. Howard.'

'Never heard of the guy.'

'I am not surprised,' Lovecraft replied. 'I fear that we fantasy writers are a rather insular school. We have our own readers and admirers, but most of us are unknown beyond those somewhat limited circles. Howard is good. You might enjoy reading him sometime.'

'Mebbe I will. I don't have much time for storybooks, though. Too busy with real stuff, if you take my meaning.'

Pagnanelli gestured to the wall covered with membership certificates. 'Tryin' to keep up with what's really going on in this country don't leave me much time for make-believe.'

'I quite understand.' Lovecraft put down his empty mug, looked at his watch, and heaved himself out of the dust-laden easy chair. 'I do believe I'll be headed back to Brooklyn.'

Pagnanelli said, 'You live there?'

'I am visiting there. A number of friends and associates of mine reside in the Borough of Churches. I enjoy my sojourns there greatly. Just the other day I was taken for a ride in a remarkable automobile. It was almost an aëroplane! 'Twas designed by the aërial ace Captain Rickenbacker.'

Pagnanelli bounced to his feet. 'A Rickenbacker Super Sport! You don't see many of those, for sure! Only one I know is Dash Weiss's.'

Lovecraft raised his eyebrows. 'I am surprised to learn that you are acquainted with Hardeen the Mysterious.'

'You've worked with Weiss, too?' Pagnanelli leaned forward.

'Our acquaintanceship is merely casual. I knew his late brother rather better than I know Theo, and it was with Houdini that I worked.' Lovecraft gathered his coat and fedora, clutched the fat envelope he'd received from Sylvester Viereck, and headed for the exit.

Pagnanelli watched intently as Lovecraft closed the door. Through a narrow grimy window he could see Lovecraft's feet as they made their way across the dirty sidewalk toward the subway kiosk.

7

Cross Plains

Robert Ervin Howard tramped stolidly up the path from the front porch of his family's house to the big tin mailbox at the edge of the dirt road. The mailman's Model T was already chugging away from the Howard home, a cloud of reddish brown dust rising in the air behind it. Robert reached into the box and extracted a small stack of envelopes. He turned and trudged back to the house, shuffling the envelopes like playing cards as he went.

Inside once more he stopped in the kitchen to accept a morsel of chili from his mother. His father, the only medico in Cross Plains, was out in his Buick Eight making rounds.

Bob closed the door of his bedroom, sat on the edge of his bed, and began to open his mail. One letter he recognized immediately by the thin, spidery handwriting on the envelope, even before he read the return address. He knew that the tiny writing inside would require patient decipherment, so he set the letter aside and opened two others first.

One came from Chicago and bore the return logo of *Weird Tales* magazine. The envelope contained a letter of acceptance for his story 'The Dream Snake'. Well and good. Too bad the magazine was so slow about payment. But at least it represented a fairly steady market, for all the crotchets of its editor.

The second letter was also from a magazine publisher; this time, *Ghost Stories*. Bob had sent them one of his John Traverel manuscripts, 'The Spirit of Tom Moly-neaux', and – hosanna! – the envelope contained a check!

Every sale was a boost to his author's ego, and the *Ghost Stories* money would help him keep up his interest in the yarn he was working on now, a boxing piece intended for *Fight Stories*.

Finally Bob slit open the letter from Howard Lovecraft and carefully unfolded the densely inscribed sheets. As usual the correspondence began with a mock-ceremonial greeting, but once Lovecraft got around to saying what he had to say . . .

Bob scanned the letter carefully. Lovecraft wanted info about a transplanted Texan named Hiram Evans, DDS. Why a dentist?

Bob read further. Apparently Evans had gone into politics of some sort. He'd joined the Klan and was now calling himself its Imperial Wizard, making his headquarters in Atlanta, Georgia. Lovecraft had met him at some kind of gathering in New York City.

Bob scratched his head. The Klan was a familiar presence in Cross Plains. He remembered the time the school board had tried to bring in that Jew English teacher . . .

He was not himself a member of the Klan, being constitutionally disinclined to involve himself with boisterous social groups. But if his friend needed information on the local Klan, he could get it.

He tugged at a desk drawer, lifted out his heavy old six-shooter, and assured himself that it was loaded. He laid it on the desk. He looked at the partial Sailor Steve Costigan manuscript and decided that *Fight Stories* could wait a little while. He picked up the gun and jammed it into his trouser pocket.

He started for the door, then turned back and grabbed his *Ghost Stories* check. Might as well kill two birds with one stone.

On his way out of the house he stopped in the kitchen

again. He tiptoed up behind his mother, threw his arms around her, and gave her a squeeze. She waited till he released her, then reached up and patted his cheek. She popped a snippet of chili beef into his mouth and told him to be home in time for dinner.

Beneath a tall old oak in the yard, Bob's dun-colored Chevrolet stood ready to go. He pulled a bandana from his pocket, swirled it across the windshield a couple of times to clear the dust, checked under the running boards and beneath the hood to make sure that his enemies hadn't laid any traps for him, and got into the car.

A few minutes later he was in town. He cashed his check at the Cross Plains bank, stopped in at the saloon for a glass of whiskey, then strolled down the town's only street to the office of the Cross Plains *Review*. He shoved open the door and whipped his revolver out of his trouser pocket, pointed it at the occupant of the front office and roared, 'Reach! Ah'm goin' to blow yew all ta hell, yew yaller-bellied snake-eatin' piece o'buzzard stew!'

The sharp-featured, leather-skinned man bent over a stack of galleys leaped into the air, whirled to face Bob, and let out his breath like a hiss of escaping steam. 'God damn you, Bob, will you ever grow up and stop playing owlhoot? You like to give me a heart attack!'

'Aw, come on, Lindsey, don't be such an old stick-in-the mud.' He twirled his revolver by its trigger guard, caught it again, and sighted on the logo of a big Oliver typewriter standing on Lindsey's desk. 'You know I was just kidding. I got to talk to you.'

'Well, God damn it, put that cannon away first and *then* you can talk to me. You know I don't like firearms. What do you think this is, some kind of Wild West show?'

Bob shoved the gun back into his pocket. 'You've got no sense of humor, Lindsey. But anyhow, I need some information.'

The newsman's eyes narrowed. 'What kind of information? Why don't you go to the library?'

Bob lowered his voice. 'I don't want to say this too loud.'

'Oh, come on. You're playing games again. Can't you see I'm working? If you want to hang around here, why don't you write some more stuff for the *Review*? I don't know why they ever stuck a good brain like yours in a body that belongs on an autumn grizzly. No wonder you come out strange. Well, what do you want?'

'Maybe I'd write for the *Review* if you paid a little better. Do you know what I'm getting from the magazines nowadays?'

'No, and don't tell me.' Lindsey walked over to Bob and slapped his biceps. 'Don't see how somebody as flabby as you are can be so strong. If you were just a little bit mean you could have been another Jim Thorpe.'

'Are you sayin' that I've got red nigger blood, Lindsey?'

'Damn it, no, I'm sayin' that you could have been a great football player up there at Payne College, Bob. Underneath all that craziness of yours you're just too nice a fellow, that's your biggest trouble.'

Bob smiled, the grin turning his face into a parody of a happy baby's. 'Well, come on, Lindsey. Can we go someplace private and have a little chat?'

'You're serious, ain't you? Okay, just hold on a minute.'

Lindsey closed up the *Review* office, put a *Back-in-15-mins* sign on the door, and took Bob Howard by the elbow.

'How do you know it'll be fifteen minutes? What if you're away for an hour?'

'I'll be back in fifteen minutes from some time, Bob. Don't you let it worry you.'

They crossed the street, got into Bob's Chevy, and

lurched away from the wooden sidewalk. Bob drove out into the post-oak country toward Brownwood. When they were a mile or so out of Cross Plains, Bob pulled the car to the side of the road and climbed out. He drew his revolver, crouched down beside the Chevy, and slowly circled the car, peering into the distance to see if anyone lay in ambush.

'I swear, Bob, you get yourself so mixed up with those wild stories you write, you don't know where make-believe stops and the real world takes on.'

Bob looked narrowly at the smaller man. 'Never mind that. I have enemies, and if I don't keep an eagle eye out they're going to bushwhack me one day. I'm just looking out for myself, Lindsey. So don't you worry about it.'

Lindsey shook his head.

'Well, will you tell me what it is you want to find out, Bob, or did you just come by to waste my afternoon and make the paper late again?'

Bob said, 'I just got a letter from a friend of mine. He needs some information about Wizard Evans.'

Lindsey looked serious for the first time. 'Hiram Evans?'

Bob nodded his head.

'Listen here, Bob, now you're a nice young fellow and most folks around here like you pretty well. But you aren't a member of the Klan. You know, it isn't such a good idea to get too inquisitive about an organization that you don't belong to.'

'I don't need the mystical stuff, Lindsey. But you're a member, and since Doc Evans is kind of a legend around here . . .'

'Klan's kind of a secret society, boy. You don't see any *kotoppotok* buttons on my blouse, do you?'

'Come on, Lindsey, everybody knows you're the county Kligrapp.'

'I never said so, son. Listen, if you want to learn about the Klan, why don't you just join up?'

Bob Howard grinned. 'Thought you didn't know nothing.'

'Son, I didn't say that. I didn't say I was in the Klan and I didn't say I wasn't. But if you want to join up, I'll try and see to it that the Kleagle hears as much and comes around your house for a friendly chat. That's how to get information about the Klan if you want it. Talk to the recruiter.'

Bob raised his six-shooter to eye level and pointed it at the newsman's chest. In a low, deadly voice he said, 'If you don't want a slug o' hot lead goin' in small and comin' out big, Lindsey, you better tell me what I want to know.'

Lindsey laughed. 'Now you're playing baby games again, Bob.'

'By the count of five.'

'Cut it out, Bob, or I'll tell your daddy and he'll take that toy away from you.'

Bob started to count.

'Now stop it!' Lindsey's voice cracked in the middle of the sentence.

Bob reached up with a massive thumb and notched back the hammer of his gun. He kept counting.

'Bob – !' Lindsey was sweating. 'Okay, I'll tell you about Hiram Evans. Good God, man, I told you, you don't know what's real and what's make-believe! You could have killed me with that thing!'

Bob didn't reply.

'Say, do you have any bullets in that gun?'

Bob pointed the six-shooter at a flat rock and squeezed off a shot. He blew the smoke away from the muzzle of his gun, then stuck it back into his pocket.

Lindsey made his way back to the Chevy on unsteady

legs. He sat down on the driver's-side running board. Bob Howard strode over and sat beside him. He kept one hand in his pocket, swiveling his wrist so the muzzle of his six-shooter traced a line up and down in the chino, pointing alternately at Lindsey's head and belly.

'God damn it, Bobby! Okay, you want to know about Hiram Evans. What can I tell you, I hardly know the man. He hasn't been in Cross Plains but a couple of times in his life. Way back when he was just a Kleagle himself, out selling memberships. And then he went up so fast, he wound up as King Kleagle for the whole state of Texas and the next thing anybody knew he was Grand Dragon of the Realm. Of Texas, that is.'

Bob nodded. 'That's like, number-one big shot for the state, right?'

'That's right, son.'

'But he isn't that anymore?'

Lindsey shook his head. 'There's no holding Hiram down. He made it to the Imperial Palace. That's Klan headquarters. National headquarters. In Atlanta. Hiram ain't been in Cross Plains since back during the World War, you was just a tyke, Bobby. I remember your daddy taking you around with him on his rounds, you and that funny dog of yours, Patch.'

'Never mind Patch! Don't speak of the dead!' Beneath the shirt sleeve the muscles of his arm tensed visibly, and the muzzle of the six-shooter pushed farther against his trousers. 'Just you tell me about Wizard Evans, Lindsey, and never mind the dead!'

'Okay, Bobby, well what about him? There wasn't nothing dramatic. You know, he just rose in the organization, that's all. From Kleagle to King Kleagle. From King Kleagle to Grand Dragon of the Realm of Texas. On up to Grand Goblin for the Southwest, and then Imperial Kligrapp.'

'Yeah, that's like national secretary, that right, Lindsey?'

There was sweat on Lindsey's face. He clenched his teeth.

Bob smiled at him and pulled the revolver halfway from his pocket.

'Son, you are crazy!'

Bob drew the revolver the rest of the way.

'Yes, he was national secretary. He didn't think old Reverend Simmons, the old Imperial Wizard, was doing right. I don't know what really happened in Atlanta, I don't want to know. All I know is, there was some kind of falling out, and Simmons got booted up the stairs to a fancy title and a pension, and Hiram got made Imperial Wizard. Then after a while Simmons left the Klan for good.

'Now, is that what you wanted to know?'

Bob scratched his thick brown hair with the blade-sight of his revolver. 'I guess it is. Except, what's in it for Doc Evans? Why's he do all that work?'

'Why, Bob, the man's an idealist. He's interested in keeping America a decent, honorable land. We're being menaced by all sorts of foes, both foreign and domestic. Foreigners, Popists, kikes, niggers, wets, adulterers. Why, the list just goes on and on.

'The Klan works tirelessly to keep America free of allegiance to causes, governments, peoples, sects, and rulers that are foreign. The Klan supports the Christian religion. The Klan esteems the United States of America and its institutions above all other governments, civil, political, and ecclesiastical, in the whole world. The Klan faithfully strives for the eternal maintenance of the supremacy of the white race.'

Lindsey stopped and took a deep breath.

'That's what it's all about, son.'

Bob Howard studied his fingernails for a moment, found a speck of dirt under one, and cleaned it out with the tip of the blade-sight. He looked expressionlessly at the newsman.

Lindsey grinned sickly. 'Well, and the Imperial Wizard does pull down a nice little salary. I don't really know exactly how much, but when Evans kicked Simmons upstairs he gave him a thousand-a-month pension.'

Bob didn't speak.

'Uh, and the Wizard does control the Searchlight Publishing Company that puts out newspapers and magazines and books for the Klan.'

He rubbed his jaw.

'And, uh, the Gate City Manufacturing Company. They make the Klan regalia and the like.

'And the Clark Realty Company.'

Bob nodded several times. He stuck his gun away. 'I guess I can answer my friend's letter now. You want a ride back to town, Lindsey? I was kind of thinking about heading over to Brownwood for a hamburger before I get home. I'll buy, Lindsey. Just got a check today from *Ghost Stories*.' Bob grinned widely.

'That'll be fine, Bob, just fine. I can always get a ride home from Brownwood easy enough.'

Bob Howard jumped to his feet and let out a loud whoop. 'Grand, Lindsey, that'll be just grand! We'll chow down a bit at the old chuck wagon, mebbe, an' mebbe we'll whet our whistles a tiny bit too, hey, ole pardner?'

He brought one open hand slamming onto the hood of his car and let out an earsplitting, 'Giddy-ap, you ole Chev-er-oh-lay!'

Lindsey, still sitting on the running board, shook his head in despair.

'Say, pardner,' Two-Gun Bob addressed him. Bob

reached for Lindsey's trembling wrist. 'Yew got an arr-glass there? Ah wouldn't want muh little ole maw tuh worry none about her favorite li'l cowpoke arrivin' late fur chow-down at thuh ole corral!'

8

Manhattan

Theodore Weiss, Hardeen the Mysterious, concentrated on working the picklock out of his thin canvas slipper. The picklock, a long flexible strip of metal, ran along the sole of his slipper so as to be indetectable when he walked onto the stage; so tiny an object, yet his career and very likely his life depended upon his having it.

Ten seconds had passed. His trained reflexes had taken over control of his breathing and simply stopped his diaphragm. His eyes were closed to aid his concentration. His assistants had poured bucket after bucket of milk over him, filling the huge can into which he had been lowered. Then they had placed the metal lid on the can and locked it in place with a set of padlocks.

Hardeen was chained in a crouching position, knees raised against his chest, ankles shackled with a set of Egyptian leg-irons. His arms were drawn around his ankles and locked with a pair of American Guiteau handcuffs. He held the picklock firmly between sensitive thumb and forefinger and went to work on the Guiteaus.

Thirty seconds had passed.

The Guiteau was turned at a slight angle. Using his free fingertips Hardeen managed to turn it back and brace it against the inside of his wrist. The picklock fit easily into the keyhole of the Guiteau. He probed, drove the tool past the first tumbler of the handcuff lock, turned it fifteen degrees, and slipped its tip past the second tumbler.

Once he'd passed the final tumbler of the Guiteau, Hardeen gave the picklock a careful twist. That was probably the most challenging part of the operation. The instrument had to be made of light, flexible material to get past the tumblers, but the final turn had to be executed with perfect precision or the picklock itself would twist in the middle and become useless.

Beside the milk can Hardeen's assistants stood guard, prepared to hold off any interference with their master's work. And ready to rush to his aid should he be in need of them.

The pit orchestra of the Academy of Music had accompanied Hardeen's entrance for the milk can escape with a medley of nautical tunes. They were still playing 'Anchors Aweigh' now, fiddles and trumpets carrying the melody, the trap drummer timing a series of rimshots to coincide with each passing quarter-minute of Hardeen's immersion.

Sixty seconds had passed.

The audience, still and silent in a nonchalant manner at the start of the escape, had begun to stir restlessly in their seats.

Hardeen had freed his hands of the Guiteau cuffs. He let the manacles fall to the bottom of the milk can. Even though extricating both hands from the Guiteaus used up five to six seconds longer than freeing one, it was time well invested when Hardeen came to the Egyptian leg-irons.

He slid his hands forward along the outer edges of his thighs, up to the bottom seam of his woolen bathing trunks. He let the picklock slip from his grasp and settle to the bottom of the milk can along with the Guiteaus. He was able now to bring his hands together and work the curved metal hook that was stitched into the seam of his trunks, through a small opening in the weave.

High above the sealed milk can a giant clockface had been erected in full view of the audience, and a large metal pointer was ticking off the seconds. The pointer passed 120 seconds and moved inexorably toward the red marker at 180 – three minutes.

The band was playing 'Asleep in the Deep'.

Inside the milk can prison, Hardeen felt a familiar small spasm as his diaphragm tried to take over autonomous operation and restart his breathing. He soothed the spasm and continued his work.

The big timer over the tank had passed 200 seconds and continued relentlessly towards 240 – four minutes.

Someone in the audience stood in his place and shouted at the stage, 'It's a fraud! He can't possibly be alive in there!'

One of Hardeen's stage crew, drilled by the magician and before him by his elder brother Houdini, stepped to the footlights and held his hands up placatingly. 'There is a committee on the stage to see that there is no fraud. There is no fraud in *any* performance by Hardeen the Mysterious!'

The trap drummer's loud report coincided with the pointer's arrival at 300 seconds – five minutes.

Within the milk can Hardeen had freed himself of his Egyptian leg-irons and raised his hands to the inside of the lid. His own subliminal clock matched the show-timer. His deft fingers crept to the upper lip of the can. Two by two he began to work on the padlocks. He knew that he could open a single lock more quickly with two hands than with one, but he could open two locks simultaneously, one with each hand, more rapidly than he could open them one after the other.

The pit orchestra had swung into a loud version of 'She Waits by the Deep Blue Sea'.

A disagreement had broken out between Hardeen's two assistants, and one had started to leave the stage. The other attempted to dissuade him, then let him go.

The first disappeared, then returned carrying a red-painted fire axe. He ran to stand beside the milk can. He shouted, holding his face near the lid of the can.

If there was any answer he couldn't hear it because of the noise of the orchestra and the general turmoil in the house. The assistant stood up and signaled to the orchestra leader. The leader cut off his musicians in the middle of 'She Waits by the Deep Blue Sea'. The second stage assistant had run to the edge of the orchestra pit and was pleading with the audience for silence so they could hear Hardeen if he was still conscious inside his prison.

The first assistant again bent and shouted at the milk can. He stood, cupping his ear against the metal lid.

Finally he rose, took one step backward, hefted the fire axe preparatory to swinging it at the first of the padlocks that held the lid in place.

Before he could swing the axe there was a metallic clatter and a thump. Then another. Another. The padlocks were falling to the wooden stage.

The timer indicated that 350 seconds had passed.

The final lock clattered to the boards. The lid of the milk can flew up, struck the stage with a loud thump, skittered a few feet, and lay in a small puddle of white.

His hair and swimming costume dripping whitely, Hardeen the Mysterious sprang from the milk can and ran to the edge of the stage, waving and bowing to the audience as the orchestra swung into a rousing, triumphal rendition of 'By the Beautiful Sea'.

After Hardeen's show, Howard and Sonia Lovecraft found their way to the performer's dressing room. Hardeen's assistants had busied themselves with cleaning and packing the equipment for their next performance. Hardeen was to depart on a modest tour for the next few weeks, and his paraphernalia was being readied for its journey.

The magician himself answered the knock at his dressing-room door. He'd showered and dried himself, thoroughly eradicating the effects of his immersion in the milk. Now he was dressed in street clothes, his stage costume laid aside to be packed along with his props.

'I was so worried, Dash!' Sonia Lovecraft exclaimed as soon as she saw him holding the door. 'Could you breathe in that can? I was certain you had drowned!'

Hardeen reached for Sonia's hand and patted it with his, laughing. 'There was never a moment of doubt or of danger, Sonia.' He drew her into the dressing room, Howard Lovecraft following closely in her wake. 'Do you know how many times I've escaped from Guiteaus and Egyptian irons under those conditions? Why, Ehrich and I used to practice that until we could do it blindfolded and handcuffed!'

'As you did,' Howard Lovecraft put in.

'Yes, yes, precisely so.' Hardeen grinned broadly.

'But you were inside there so *long*,' Sonia persisted. 'Six minutes at least, Theo! How did you do it? There was no trickery, was there?'

'Oh, no. Submersion for six minutes is no problem at all.'

'It seemed very long. People in the audience tried to hold their breath. None came close to six minutes. Why, I could hear people popping and gasping all around me. Most of them lasted less than two minutes, Dash dear. No one lasted longer than three!'

Dash swung a wooden chair wrong-way to and planted himself on it, his arms crossed atop its curved-wood back. 'That I know. We're always glad to have people try and hold their breaths. Adds to the suspense of the act.

'Of course, they're not trained. A good swimmer, now,

could do far better than that. How long do you think
Miss Ederle could hold her breath if she wished to? Five
minutes, easily. A trained vocalist could do well, also.
Caruso, poor fellow, I'd wager he could have gone seven
easily at the peak of his form. Or Rosa Ponselle! What a
voice, what breath control!'

He shook his head. 'Ehrich was a stickler for training.
He used to say, "Theo, you have the ability to become a
greater magician and escapist even than I – but I have the
drive and you have not." He may have been right, I
suppose.

'Well, anyway – what about a snack? Working always
leaves me famished.'

They left the theater and walked next door to old
Tammany Hall. Hardeen was recognized, and he introduced Howard and Sonia to a few friends. They were
seated in the ornate dark-toned dining room, and Hardeen ordered for the party. The waiter returned with a
rolling cart carrying scrambled eggs, toast, bacon, saus-
ages, sweet rolls, halved grapefruit, a silver pot of coffee
and another of tea, and a salver of hominy grits.

'You were speaking of training,' Sonia prompted
Hardeen.

'Ah. Ehrich used to train in a swimming pool. He
could hold his breath – not merely hold it, actually turn it
off – for half an hour at a time. It was partially a matter
of body conditioning and partially a matter of technique.

'The Orientals have studied such subjects for ages, and
their teachings, shorn of mystical hoodoo, are most
useful. I could never quite match Ehrich's endurance
under water, but I could come close. Certainly six minutes
is no problem at all.

'There was one thing that Ehrich had hoped to do.' He
speared a sausage, sliced half of it away, and poked it
into the yolk of a fried egg. 'Ehrich had hoped to turn off

his breathing, immobilize his body, and be frozen in a block of solid ice. Then he would be chopped out of it on stage. He never quite perfected that. I ought to have a chat with Bess and see if she wants to work on the act.'

'What was the cause of the failure?' Lovecraft asked.

'There's the irony!' Hardeen took a large bite of a sweet roll covered with strawberry preserves. 'Everything worked out fine. The cooling of Ehrich's body actually aided his endurance. There seem to be certain reflexes that act automatically at low temperatures, designs of nature to preserve us from cold. Ehrich claimed that freezing was actually easier to tolerate than immersion in warm water!

'But it took so long to freeze the ice, he would have needed to use a breathing straw for most of the time, and it would have taken a full day at least to prepare the act each time he used it!'

Hardeen swallowed half a cup of coffee, gestured to the waiter to refill his cup, reached for the platter and placed two more eggs on his plate. Lovecraft was concentrating on the sweet rolls and black coffee with vast amounts of sugar. Sonia had taken a cup of tea and was sipping carefully at it.

'Well, enough about magicians.' Hardeen spooned a mound of grits onto his plate, sampled them approvingly. 'How is your literary career progressing, Howard? Sonia tells me you're going to do a political book. Is that true?'

Lovecraft conceded that it was. 'Not purely political,' he amended. 'It will have a good deal of historical information as well, and contain projections of events yet to come.' He ruminated briefly. 'It may be classed as utopian, I suppose, although I do not usually place much credence in utopian schemes.'

Hardeen paused between forkfuls of grits. 'Have you a title for it?'

'That is yet to be ascertained. I have considered calling it *New America and the Coming World Order*. It has rather a ring, don't you agree?'

'Sounds intriguing. Then you've given up writing creepy-crawlies? I really enjoyed that one you ghosted for Ehrich. That poor fellow, tied up and abandoned in the deepest crypt of the Great Pyramid. I could hardly believe that the narrator was supposed to be my own brother!'

Lovecraft smiled. 'A bit of fancy. Farnsworth Wright and Otis Kline claim that story saved their magazine. That and a few of my more sensational ghosting jobs. Is it not odd that my own works, that appear under my own name, seem rather less popular than those of my clients?'

'No, no, no, Howard.' Sonia put her hand on Lovecraft's wrist. 'You know that you're the best author they have. But people respond to sensation, they like quick action, they like to have things made easy for them. Why, you yourself have said that the most popular stories in *Weird Tales* are those silly little mysteries of Mr Quinn's.'

'So the monthly polls indicate.'

'Don't worry, Howard darling. Your works will be recognized someday. You must never lose heart, Howard!'

Lovecraft smiled gratefully. 'There you have it, Theo. Contracts in hand, nil. Prospects, at best remote. But my loyal friends will not permit me to surrender. Sonia, Belknap Long, Robert Howard in Texas, Clark Ashton Smith in California, Vincent Starrett from Chicago. Perhaps if *New America* does well, Sylvester Viereck will take a flyer on a volume of my tales.

'Or if not Viereck, there's another prospect on the horizon.'

He paused and nibbled at a roll. Sonia prompted him to reveal the nature of his other prospect.

'Starrett has showed me a letter from Henneberger and Wright in Chicago.' He washed down the roll with coffee. 'They request his permission to use a short story of his, from a back issue of *Weird Tales,* in a collection of the most popular works from the magazine. If that book does well, I've reason to believe that they will go on to do one of my own stories.'

'It's this Viereck fellow who interests me,' Hardeen said. 'I remember his wartime capers. I really wonder, Lovecraft, what he has in mind for you. Do you really know all that you're getting into?'

'It is simply literary work, Weiss. The literary men of Georgian times did not cavil at narrow categories nor consider political topics beneath their attention. Those men are my models.'

The conversation drifted away from literature and back towards show business and Hardeen's travel plans. He announced that his tour was to be brief. Northward from New York, with performances in a number of New England theaters, then across the border to Montreal and Quebec City, and then back home.

'I've booked a more ambitious tour for later this year. But the Erlingers want me to show the colors on the northeastern wing of their circuit, and they offered good terms. I get a day or two to lay over between cities, and the northeast becomes very pleasant as we roll along into the spring.'

'How I envy you,' Lovecraft commented. 'New England, the finest and most beautiful region on this continent! But I fear that while you bask beneath green rolling hillsides and white-painted steeples, I shall be cooped up here in teeming New York, pursuing my political researches and studying the philosophy of Sylvester Viereck's friend Herr Hitler. Well, Viereck moves in intriguing circles.

'Did I mention to you – ' he turned and addressed his wife, ' – the Count and Countess Vonsiatskoy-Vonsiatsky?'

Sonia placed her teacup on its saucer and carefully wiped her mouth with a damask napkin. She folded her hands in her lap and looked calmly at her husband. 'You assuredly did not, Howard. If you had, I should instantly have given you my opinion of the count and countess.'

'You knew the count in Russia, then? The countess is herself an American, of course.'

'That I know. Vonsiatsky was a name spoken with nothing but scorn in the *shtetl*, Howard. You would understand, Theo.'

She turned toward Hardeen. 'You would understand, Theo,' she repeated. 'Even if you were born on this side, you must have heard about his kind. Petit nobility, lording it over Jew and Gentile alike, treating the poor as if they were still serfs. Ach! That one got out a half-jump ahead of a revolutionary court in '17.'

Frostily, Lovecraft said, 'He seems a most civilized gentleman, to me.'

Sonia smiled grimly. 'I'm sure that his manners are beautiful. And as the cossacks raid the villages, raping the women, murdering children, killing any man who stands to defend his family – it's always the Vonsiatskys who are too civilized to dirty their hands or bloody their swords, true enough. But they are present. They are behind that kind of thing.

'Yes, I know of your count and of his plans. Theo, you know this penniless sniveling little count and his *arriviste* wife with her locomotive dollars. Surely you have heard of them.'

Hardeen, a muffin spread with marmalade and butter already between his teeth, bit down as he nodded. He chewed and swallowed. 'Yes, I've heard of him. But I don't know his plans. I should like to!'

'I'm sure that Howard does.' Sonia nodded toward her husband.

'Indeed. The count makes no secret of his intentions. There are some three hundred thousand Russian émigrés in the United States.'

'Yes, myself included,' Sonia put in.

'And they are just awaiting the call of their nobility, to return and overthrow the bolshevists. Vonsiatsky is raising the funds necessary to hire a fleet of ships and sail with them for Europe. There they will be joined by more Russians eager to return to their homeland. Finally, the poor masses of Russia will themselves arise and smash the boorish gangsters of the Kremlin!'

'Sure,' Sonia nodded. Hardeen was listening closely, not committing himself in the argument. Sonia said, 'And when Rykoff and Stalin and Trotzky, or whoever wins control of the Party, are thrown out – what then? A new Romanoff? Will your count summon Prince Mikhail home from Switzerland? Or will he find some remote connection of blood and put himself on the throne, with his female locomotive at his side?'

Lovecraft's face grew red. 'You don't know these personages!'

'Don't make me laugh! I know them and their kind all too well!'

Hardeen raised his hand, imploring the couple to be calm. With his other hand he popped the last remnant of a muffin into his mouth. 'Rather than quarrel, why don't we wait until Howard completes his researches? Matters can then be discussed more rationally.'

No one spoke for a time. Then Lovecraft came to a resolution. 'I believe that this book of Viereck's friend in Germany is the key to the movement. There are both domestic and international elements in this webwork. We are discussing no less than a new world order.

'Of course, from a nationalistic point of view, the domestic groups are the more significant: Father Coughlin's Christian Front, and certainly the Ku Klux Klan. But there are inextricable ties to the tsarist restorationists, the international fascist organizations, and the NSDAP in Germany.

'I already possess a copy of Herr Hitler's book. I will study it and then we can hold a debate, strictly among ourselves.' He smiled thinly. 'Perhaps it would be best for me to return to Providence while I do that work. I fear for the welfare of my two old aunts anyway.

'Sonia – of course you will understand.'

She nodded sadly, said nothing.

'If we can examine your touring schedule, Weiss,' resumed Lovecraft, 'perhaps a convenient day and place can be found.'

'I'll pass through Boston on my way back from Canada.'

'Perhaps we could meet in the wholesome atmosphere of New England. Could you obtain a leave of absence as well, Sonia?'

His wife nodded.

'Well then,' Theo said, 'in Providence or in Boston. Or maybe we could meet at some shore point for a day or two. You've made some intriguing statements, Howard. For instance, regarding the connections of foreign politicians with the likes of the KKK.'

Lovecraft agreed. 'Beneath sparkling heavens we shall strive to clear New Albion's air.'

9
Marblehead

The big imported Horch automobile roared along the Post Road out of Boston, heading toward Lynn, its powerful straight-twelve engine devouring the miles without effort. The tall, beefy driver ignored speed-limit signs and the occasional police motorcycle alike. He knew that the Horch bore diplomatic license plates that carried with them immunity from local offenses.

Two men sat in the comfortable seat behind the driver. One was tall, sensuously good-looking, dressed in casually tailored but finely made clothing. The other man was shorter, proper, his jowly face rising without visible neck from his heavy-shouldered torso.

'Watch for the markers, Spanknoebel,' the taller passenger called to the driver. 'As soon as we get through Lynn, look for arrows to Salem. Marblehead is just beyond.'

Heinz Spanknoebel nodded and grunted his understanding. He was a trained chemist, a trusted lieutenant of Mr Ford. He was not accustomed to serving as chauffeur, even for such distinguished passengers as Mr Viereck and Dr Kiep. But Mr Ford had been acting strangely ever since the Aaron Sapiro matter had gone so badly. And then Viereck had asked Heinz to accompany himself and Dr Kiep on this trip, had grilled him first endlessly, along with Dr Kiep, choosing Spanknoebel out of all their associates to be taken into their confidence. It was certainly worth a momentary lowering of himself for the good of the cause.

Besides, as the Jesuits had used to say when Heinz was

a little boy just getting his schooling, *Make me as a corpse, and do with me as You will.*

He pulled around an open Bearcat full of partying sheiks and flappers, blasted once on the Horch's loud horn, and muscled the heavy car back into its lane. It was a good thing that Heinz was as huge and muscular a man as he was – it took such a driver to master the Horch, and Heinz loved the feeling of mastery as he loved no other, whether it was mastery over a woman, over another man, or over a machine. When the cause had triumphed, Heinz would be a master!

In the back seat of the automobile, Viereck and Dr Kiep were deep in conversation. Through the Consulate, Kiep had access to diplomatic pouches from Berlin, information on the developing crisis in Germany and throughout Europe. Clearly apocalyptic days were approaching. The government of Chancellor Marx had fallen; President von Hindenburg had asked Marx to form another government, but Marx was suffering difficulties. Germany was torn by factionalism that she could not long endure.

The symptoms were almost funny. 'Viereck,' Dr Kiep said, 'the reports you saw, of the reception given Chamberlin and Levine?'

'I saw them, surely. It was a salve to the insult of Lindbergh, when he followed his landing at Le Bourget with tours of all the enemies of Germany and his studied avoidance of German territory!'

'Ja. But when the others their *Columbia* at Eisleben landed, and then to Tempelhof proceeded, very nearly the government fell.'

'But why?' Behind his dark-rimmed eyeglasses, Viereck's eyes were puzzled. 'Why should that hurt the Reich? These two restored a little bit, at least, of the honor denied by Lindbergh.'

'Ja, ja. Everyone was happy. The big fight over colors was. The imperial colors to use, or the colors of the Republic, the Rathaus in Berlin to decorate. Verstehen Sie das Problem?'

Viereck removed his eyeglasses and rubbed the bridge of his nose between forefinger and thumb. 'Yes, surely, Herr Doktor. And what view did Herr Hitler express? I have not seen him lately. Since my last trip home, more than a year.'

'Natürlich, aber Herr Lüdecke better knows than I.'

'Yes, we'll see Kurt today. He always has more news from Herr Hitler than anyone else – he is the closest man to him outside of Germany. But you have no inkling – '

'Inkling?'

'Ach, wie man sagt – das Gemunkel, ja? Of his preference?'

Dr Kiep laughed harshly and patted his jacket. Viereck took the cue, reached for his own cigar case and offered a corona to Dr Kiep. 'Herr Hitler said it did not matter. A new Reich new colors will have!' Again he laughed.

Viereck held a flame for Dr Kiep, who drew on his corona until it was lighted. Then Viereck leaned forward and tapped Spanknoebel on the shoulder. 'We cut off before Salem, Heinz. Look now for pointers to Marblehead.' He leaned back into the cushions of the Horch. To Dr Kiep he said, 'Such beautiful country, this, nicht wahr? These hills, the blue sky! Nowhere else is like this New England of our Herr Lovecraft. I can understand such a man better, seeing this place. Every time I come here to inspect our progress, I learn again why he loves his homeland.'

Dr Kiep turned serious eyes to his companion. 'Sylvester, careful you must be! Too much sentiment very dangerous may become! Reich und Stamm, merken Sie sich das genau!'

Viereck nodded in silence.

Spanknoebel pulled the Horch off the Post Road and pointed its long squarish cowl toward the shore route. He slowed the powerful engine to keep the car on the narrower road that led gradually downhill, approaching the Atlantic at Marblehead.

Viereck directed him through the town, past seventeenth- and eighteenth-century buildings, and finally down Front Street, to park the heavy car at the head of Hooper's Wharf.

The three men climbed from the sedan. Spanknoebel took down their light luggage and followed Viereck and Dr Kiep. They halted before an aged hip-roofed structure surmounted by a flaking half-derelict cupola. The first storey of the building displayed a dingy storefront that gave onto the creaking timber wharf. Inside, Viereck exchanged a few words with an unshaven individual behind a rude counter, then motioned Spanknoebel to follow himself and Dr Kiep through a curtained doorway, up a flight of peeling stairs and into a square room with stained walls and flyspecked, dirt-crusted windows. The room had been furnished as a cheap office. A battered wooden desk stood near one wall. There were half a dozen chairs scattered through the room, and a row of metal lockers lining another wall.

'Put everything down, Heinz,' Viereck instructed. 'Sit down.'

Spanknoebel did as he was told. Viereck took a wooden chair opposite Spanknoebel's while Dr Kiep walked behind the desk and seated himself in a scarred swivel-chair.

Viereck looked to Dr Kiep as if awaiting approval of his actions. The consul nodded, and Viereck began to speak.

'You have done excellent work, Spanknoebel. Dr Kiep,

Herr Lüdecke, and I have watched you for several years now. We observed your work with the old Steuben Society, and your good efforts in creating from the society the Friends of the New Germany.'

Viereck rose and walked to the window facing across the harbor toward Marblehead Neck. He drew a corona for himself from his cigar case, lit the tobacco, and threw the dead match to the floor.

Spanknoebel said, 'The Steuben Society had its place, but it was too much an intellectual's circle. There was only talk there. The Freunde will be prepared to act when the time comes for action, Herr Viereck.'

'Indeed,' Viereck nodded. He paced from the window to his chair, then back again. He stood silhouetted against the afternoon sky, cigar in hand, and spoke.

'Dr Kiep and Herr Lüdecke and I have great confidence in you, Heinz. Not only have we observed your work, but also we have conducted some quiet little investigations.'

'Mrs Dilling?'

Viereck smiled. 'We are convinced that you can be trusted, and that is why we are going to show you something today. It is something that is being prepared for the future. For the time, as you put it, for action. You will see a part of our work known to very few, and you must mention it to no one. No one. You understand the importance of this?'

'Certainly!'

Viereck drew meditatively on his corona, gazing out the fly-specked window.

Dr Kiep said, 'You would your life risk, Spanknoebel, this secret to protect?'

Heinz whirled to face the consul. 'Ja! Only ask, Dr Kiep!'

The consul nodded his satisfaction.

'Very well,' Viereck said. 'We must all change our

clothing before we go any farther.' He crossed to one of the metal lockers and opened its rust-flaked door. He took out a set of nondescript garments: a denim shirt, heavy dungaree trousers, a woolen jacket and knitted cap such as dockworkers or fishermen would wear. He began meticulously to remove his soft tweeds and hang them in the locker.

'Quickly, Heinz. There are a large set in the end locker. Help yourself.'

Within minutes the three men were transformed into drably garbed seamen. Dr Kiep led the way out through the downstairs shop, to the end of Hooper's Wharf. A dinghy was waiting for them. Two burly seamen in garb similar to their own stood slouching at the edge of the wharf. As the party approached they snapped stiffly to a respectful stance. Their bearing was more that of navy-trained sailors than what one would expect of a pair of casual merchant mariners.

The party, now of five, climbed down a rickety ladder and into the dinghy. Dr Kiep spoke in German to the two sailors, and they pulled away from the wharf.

The two sailors hefted at heavy oars with a military precision, moving the clumsy dinghy into the harbor where they encountered a larger power boat. They held the dinghy alongside the power boat while Dr Kiep, Sylvester Viereck, and Heinz Spanknoebel transferred, then directed the dinghy with perfectly coordinated strokes back toward the wharf.

The engine of the power boat was already idling. As soon as the dinghy had made a few fathoms of headway, the power boat began to head for the mouth of the harbor.

Viereck and Dr Kiep were speaking with the crewmen of the power boat while Spanknoebel squatted on deck near the prow, watching the sea ahead. Marblehead

Harbor was dotted with the triangular white sails and graceful white hulls of dozens of yachts. Heavier, more businesslike vessels could be seen here and there among the yachts.

Beyond the harbor itself, more boats were visible on the ocean. The sky was a sparkling color, with only a few tiny clouds floating high above. The town climbed up hillsides on the mainland. On the other side of the harbor the low-lying Neck held the buildings of several rich men's yacht clubs and the ramshackle houses and sheds of a few die-hard locals.

Spanknoebel saw a dark-hulled steamer standing to, directly ahead of the power boat. As the boat neared the larger craft he could make out a few crewmen and some equipment on the deck of the steamer, but no meaningful activity. The power boat approached and turned, pulling around the stern of the larger craft. As it passed close to the hull of the steamer, Spanknoebel could see a few of the men on the steamer's deck. They were armed with rifles.

The power boat came about once more, the hull of the steamer now blocking off sight of land. Spanknoebel could see that lines were run from the steamer, down into the greenish water where they disappeared. Power equipment stood on the deck of the ship, and cables disappeared along with the other lines.

The crewmen of the power boat brought it to in the shadow of the steamer. A man stood on the bow of the boat and shouted a few words in German to the deck of the ship. Spanknoebel's German was limited and ungrammatical – he obtained a maximum amount of mileage from a dozen words, more as a matter of showing his colors around people involved in the cause, than of really speaking the language.

But there was no need to puzzle out the dialogue

between the steamer deckhand and the power boatman.
Davits were swung over the railing, and the power boat
was hoisted to the deck of the steamer. Spanknoebel and
other passengers climbed from the boat.

Viereck gestured Spanknoebel to follow him and Dr
Kiep. They crossed the deck, spoke again with crewmen,
and were handed three rubber-and-canvas divers' suits.
Assisted by the crewmen, they climbed into the suits.
Heinz felt a moment of panic as the heavy brass diving
helmet was lowered over his head and locked to the
metal collar of the suit, but his panic subsided to a low-
level claustrophobic discomfort as he peered through the
round window in the front of his helmet.

He heard a voice.

It was Viereck, speaking through a suit-to-suit telephone connection. 'Heinz, this will not work underwater
– we have to leave it on the deck. You will come with Dr
Kiep and myself. We have been here before, everything
is safe. You will follow us to the iron platform.' Viereck
poked Spanknoebel's arm, pointed across the deck to a
metal grating. 'When we reach the bottom, stay close.
We will leave the platform. Do not take your hand
from my shoulder. It is dark below. Dunkel hierunter,
verstehen Sie mich?'

Flattered to be addressed in the German language,
Spanknoebel replied, 'Ja, mein Herr!'

They trooped across the deck to the diving platform,
stood in their weighted costumes while winches raised the
platform over the ship's railing, then lowered it slowly
toward the water. They hit the water with a splash, then
continued to descend. Heinz gasped softly as the water
closed over him, held tightly to the metal railing of the
diving platform.

The ocean floor was in total darkness.

Viereck snapped on an underwater torch and sprayed

its light ahead of them. Each man holding a hand on the next, they crossed from the platform toward a huge shape that loomed darkly at the very limit of the torch's rays.

As they approached the object more closely, Spanknoebel could see that men in diving costume were working over it, their efforts lighted by underwater torches mounted on metal stands. They held special underwater welding gear, an oxyacetylene flame throwing its eerie glow over the sandy bottom; the curious fishes that approached gazed fearlessly at the workers, then spun and disappeared into the dark.

They entered an airlock. Spanknoebel watched carefully as Viereck and Dr Kiep disconnected the hoses and lines that ran back to the dark-hulled steamer, then waited patiently as the chamber was first pumped dry, then slowly decompressed. It was a relief to be out of the heavy, constricting diving costume.

Finally they left the chamber.

Heinz found himself in a large metal-walled room. There were flat-topped tables and chairs, maps and charts covering the bulk-heads and tabletops. The chamber resembled a cross between the field headquarters of a construction job and a high-level military headquarters.

He looked at Sylvester Viereck and said, simply, 'What is this place?'

Viereck and Dr Kiep exchanged a wry glance, then Viereck said to Heinz, '*Unterwasserprojekt Elf.*'

Spanknoebel was puzzled.

Viereck laughed at him. 'All that means is, *ocean-floor project number eleven.*'

'But – I do not understand. This is not a sunken ship or – any such thing. Is it?'

'No, no, Heinz. The project has been built from scratch, hey? It is one of a series of completely self-contained underwater seaports. Through you we will have liaison with our American allies. When the time comes, when the time comes, that is our key phrase, eh, Heinz?

'When the time comes, these projects will be of utmost importance to the cause. In America we will see uprisings, the brown, black, silver shirts, will all do their bits. The loose, immoral, undisciplined, English-dominated America of today will be transformed into a new America. An America disciplined and efficient, a part of the new world order.'

Heinz shook his head. 'Yes, this I believe. This *is* the cause for which we all work. But why do we need an underwater seaport? For trade with Europe? Why do we not use the regular ports that exist already?'

Viereck shot a question at Dr Kiep, rasping in guttural German more rapidly than Spanknoebel could follow. Dr Kiep's reply was brief. Then Viereck said:

'That will be answered in a moment. The answer does not come from Dr Kiep or from me, but from a distinguished personage whom you will meet shortly, Heinz. Before you are introduced, I remind you again, what you learn here in Marblehead you will not repeat. Neither about the office at Hooper's Wharf, nor the construction ship.' He made a curious vertical gesture with one slightly crooked finger. 'And, most emphatically, not about the *Unterwasserprojekt.*'

'I understand, Mr Viereck. Of course. If you would clarify, though – if some local resident should question me about, for example, the ship above. Or, when I return to Detroit . . .'

Viereck nodded his head vigorously. 'To the local residents, say as little as possible. If you are pressed, Heinz, we do have a – let us call it, a legitimizing device. Eh? On our ship, *Der Traum,* we're carrying out a program of commercial research. New formulas for wet-setting cement, we are developing for use in construction of heavy-duty wharfs. Very dull, you see? Very uninteresting and wholly proper.

'An international consortium is involved, including chemical firms and a research institute in Germany. But the sponsor and coordinator of the program is located in New York City. All inquiries are to be referred to them. Continental Laboratories.

'As for Detroit, not even Henry Ford knows of this work as yet. We have been distressed – I and Dr Kiep and others – with Mr Ford's behavior. He has ordered new policies for his *Dearborn Independent*, settled that unjustified libel suit over the *Protocols of Zion* . . . Even Mr Ford had better not know too much.'

Viereck rubbed his smooth cheeks with one well-manicured hand, then resumed. 'In Detroit you will coordinate the plans of the Friends of the New Germany with instructions you will receive from us. You will tell your own subordinates as little as is needful. I think your deputy Herr Kuhn is a good and trustworthy man, but even he – you will do best to simply say nothing of the existence of this place.

'Verstehen Sie?'

Heinz Spanknoebel nodded.

Viereck advanced to stand before Heinz, looked him up and down, removed a piece of lint from Spanknoebel's dark-sweatered shoulder.

'Folgen Sie mir.'

They made their way along a metal-bulkheaded companionway, then through a gray-painted port into a wood-paneled room. For an instant Spanknoebel felt the strange disorientation of having stepped into a comfortable cabin on a luxury liner. The walls were covered with polished oak wainscoting, the furniture was sumptuous, the metal deck had been overlaid with a thick carpet.

There was even a porthole rimmed with polished brass.

Through it Heinz could see some of the construction work taking place outside, the glare of the oxyacetylene torches punctuating the eerie glow of the underwater lamps.

Dr Kiep entered the room first and stood before the polished desk with an air of almost military discipline and subservience. 'Gnädiger Herr,' he said.

The man behind the desk stood up. He wore a navy blazer and turtle-neck sweater. His hair was cropped close, like Dr Kiep's. His face was almost skeletally thin. Slowly he looked up from some papers on his desk, stared into Kiep's face, then turned his head deliberately to examine Viereck, to nod, and finally to stare at Spanknoebel.

Never had Heinz seen such obdurate eyes as those of this cadaverous figure. He felt himself trembling before the stranger's glacial gaze.

The man turned his eyes back toward Dr Kiep, to Spanknoebel's huge relief. 'Who is this fellow?' the man asked.

Spanknoebel could see beads of sweat popping out on the pudgy Kiep's pink forehead. 'Darf ich Sie mit Herrn Heinz Spanknoebel bekannt machen?' the consul replied.

A chilly grin spread across the thin face. The head lowered, rose again in a slow nod. 'Sehr erfreut! Gauleiter von den Freunden, ja?'

Dr Kiep and Sylvester Viereck both affirmed the other man's suggestion.

'Herr Spanknoebel,' the icy man said, 'please forgive my accent.' Heinz did not notice any imperfection in the other's speech, but he said nothing.

'I have looked forward to meeting you,' the man went on. 'Do you know who I am?'

Spanknoebel shook his head.

'Ah.' The man looked crestfallen. 'My name is Kurt

Lüdecke. I am the personal representative of the Führer, the leader of the NSDAP.' He looked at Spanknoebel, obviously awaiting a response.

'I – I am familiar with the Party and its work. We in America work for the same cause, Herr Lüdecke. It is an honor to meet the Führer's representative.'

'Gut! Now.' Lüdecke swept Kiep, Viereck, and Spanknoebel with his cold, pale eyes. 'Did these two,' Lüdecke gestured with a thin shoulder, 'tell you the purpose of the *unterwasserprojekt?*'

Heinz nodded, 'Ja.'

'It is – ?'

Kurt Lüdecke waited.

'Mein Herr. It was explained to me – the sea-bottom project – is a port for future commerce. Between the Reich and America, mein Herr.'

'Gut.' Lüdecke nodded approvingly. 'And what will be the nature of this commerce? What will be the role of the Freunde in this commerce? Surely not that of longshoremen, Heinz?'

Spanknoebel felt himself perspiring like Dr Kiep. Only Sylvester Viereck, as casually elegant in his rough seaman's garb as ever he was in business clothes, appeared relaxed. 'Mein Herr,' Spanknoebel said. 'We have in America many followers loyal to the cause. When the day of crisis comes, they will be ready to serve.'

Lüdecke nodded again, an expression of mild impatience lingering on his features. 'Mr Spanknoebel, I am assured by Dr Kiep and by Mr Viereck that you are worthy of my confidence. I warn you that your very life is at stake should you violate that confidence.'

'I understand, mein Herr.'

'Do you see the work going on outside, Spanknoebel?' Lüdecke pointed emphatically at the round porthole. 'Those divers are doing work that is very difficult and very dangerous. This entire structure has been made in place secretly. The ship that rides above us is present only part of the time, and when we can, we will do entirely without it.

'As soon as a little more progress is made with the sea-bottom work, we will dispense altogether with the ship. Do you know the name of the ship, Heinz? It is called *Der Traum. The Dream.*' He smiled tightly.

'Our heroic divers are building submarine pens.' Again he turned to gaze through the porthole at the flaring torches and lamps. 'Soon we will be able to supply this base per Unterseeboot, entirely free of observation.'

Spanknoebel shook his head in bemusement. 'This is puzzling to me, mein Herr. Why do we need secrecy, for a trade port?'

Lüdecke smiled and nodded. 'At last, Spanknoebel, to the heart of the matter. Well now –.' He rose for the first time and walked from behind his desk. Spanknoebel could see that he wore neatly pressed woolen trousers and perfectly shined shoes. 'When we come to power in Europe, we hope to see our comrades do the same here in America. The Freunde, and their allies here of the Count di Revel's Fascist League, and their other helpers.

'But you in turn may require some assistance, eh?' He stood confidently gazing out through the porthole, his feet spread, his arms crossed oddly behind his back, each hand cupping the bent elbow of the other. He spoke directly toward the porthole, his face luridly illuminated by the flaring oxyacetylene torches, using the polished glass of the porthole as a sounding board for his cold, precise voice.

'It is required that you use your imagination, Heinz. I know you are a chemist, accustomed to rigid formulas and precise rules. You mix a base with an acid, the result

will be a salt and water, eh? Always and everywhere. But
now you must use your imagination.

'I want you to see riots in the streets of America.
Violence and disorder. A rabble marching on Washing-
ton. The army called to keep order. The president help-
less – and who will be president when comes the day?
This silly nobody Coolidge? The foolish rummy Smith?
No matter. America cannot respond to a real challenge.

'The call for help. Silver shirts, Klansmen, in the
midst of the turmoil, helping the civil authorities, you
understand, Heinz. But still disorder spreads. Food is
short. Currency loses its worth. And then, Spanknoebel,
then – '

He turned to face the room again, gesturing broadly
with one elegant slim hand. 'Then imagine, Heinz, an
army of trained, disciplined Aryan soldiers, rising from
the sea. Marching into the harbors of America, like
invaders from – ' he paused to smile at the image, ' – like
an army of invaders from the lost continent of Atlantis.

'Each man armed with carefully waterproofed weapons,
Spanknoebel. Each man supplied with diving gear, and
enough oxygen to reach the shore. Each man wholly a
dedicated soldier of the cause. And as they invade the
seacoast towns of America, their brothers in the cause
rise to take power in the cities of the American heartland.
In Detroit. In Chicago. In a hundred cities!'

Lüdecke clenched a fist, held it before his eyes as if
seeing it for the first time.

'Your role is to prepare your followers to play their
part in this. They must be ready to welcome the troops
who will come from the sea. You must understand all
that this entails, and set to work at once. Are you
prepared to do this?'

Spanknoebel's reply was a whispered 'Ja.' He felt a
hard, searing core flare in his broad chest. It was as if a

piece of white-hot iron were glowing within him, sending its heat and its strength to every extremity of his body, pounding with every pulsation of his heart. He could see the figures rising from the surf, could see his own followers, splendid in their uniforms, waiting on the shore to greet their comrades in arms, to crush their opponents, to obliterate from America the weakness and the softness of her mongrel cities.

'Ja,' he repeated, 'ja, mein Herr! We will be prepared! Give us our instructions! Give us our timetable! We will be ready when the time has come!'

Lüdecke smiled approvingly at Heinz Spanknoebel, then at George Sylvester Viereck, then at Dr Otto Kiep.

'I am pleased,' Lüdecke said softly. 'I am well pleased, and so, I am certain, will be mein Führer.'

10
Chicago

940 Buena Park Terrace
Chicago
29 April 1927

Dear Howard,

I hope you won't be too surprised by the postmark on this
letter. The Beechhurst house was fine, and I was well into my
book for Doran when I received an urgent summons from Walt
Howey, my old chief on the Windy City Inter-Ocean. Walter is
in dire need of an experienced hound, as our crack police-beat
man Billy Black is wildly overworked and there seems no one
else in the house who can handle the job.

Specifically, the Inter-Ocean is trying to match its betters in
covering the bootleggers, racketeers, and vice lords of
Chicagoland. And Walter has asked me to check up on the
early career of our current chieftain-of-all-chieftains, Mr Al
Brown nee Alphonso Caponi aka Al Capone-with-a-silent-e,
popular dealer in fine used furniture.

Anyway, starting in New York I spent a few days checking
out the Big Fellow's minor league record on the Lower East
Side. He was a fair utility player for the Five Points Gang there
and did some remarkable pinch-hitting duty on a few road trips
out Brooklyn way. But nothing to suggest the Ruthian stature
he's achieved since he got the call from Big Jim here in Chi.

Thus the trail led back here and as you can see from the
Buena Park address, I've managed to recapture my old digs.
But to my point . . .

You mentioned having an interest in various rightish political
groups when last we chatted in New York, especially those
associations having some foreign connections. This does raise a
question of how the local criminal element, with its heavily
Sicilian bias, might relate to various political entities on both
sides of the water. I should mention that Al Brown is not

himself a member of the Unione Siciliana (although he has maneuvered his man Tony Lombardo into its presidency). Nor is Brown presently nor ever will be a mafioso. The Unione and the mafia are strictly Sicilian outfits, and Al is a mainland Italian. And for these tradition-bound orders, that settles that!

Of course Capone simply owns the local political structure. I don't know that Al has any national ambitions, although he has his perfectly open investments in Florida to think about. Our Mayor Thompson is playing a chummy game with a fellow named Huey Long down in Louisiana, some sort of rabble-rousing po'–country-boy politician, and in my book any alliance between a fast-rising demagogue like Long and a weakling who plays cat's paw for the likes of Al Brown is very bad news.

Locally there is an oddly mixed feeling among Italian and Sicilian residents, when it comes to the fascisti. A lot of mafiosi have flooded in here of late. Mussolini is trying to suppress the mafia in Italy, and is even pushing against their stronghold in Sicily, and seems to be succeeding with his efforts. The organization hardly has a toehold on the Italian mainland any longer. (That's a joke, Howard.) And a lot of soldiers and dons are packing up and moving to America the land of opportunity.

They lose no love on Il Duce, but they do still love their dear beautiful Italia. (Did you know that the mafia was originally a patriotic society? Founded A.D. 1282 as guerrillas during the French occupation. The name's an abbreviation for Morte alla Francia Italia anela, 'Death to the French is Italy's Cry'. Or at least I'm told that's the meaning, not having been in Italy in A.D. 1282.)

There's at least one openly fascist organization here, bossed by a Dr Ugo Galli. Ties in with the national outfit headed by Count Ignazio Thaon di Revel. Don't you wish you could concoct monickers like those for your characters?

Paradoxically, Howard, the American-born Italians seem to have a warm regard for the old country but not for its current bossman. And the newer-comers were chased out by Il Duce, so much of the local 'Italian' populace is very, very American! My 'friend' Mr Brown-Caponi-Capone belongs to the former class – American-born, says that he got his famous scars in a machine-gun unit during the Great War. A machine-gun unit fighting in the famous Five Corners campaign? But no matter.

En fin, Howard, is there a tie-in between these local mobsters and your political playmates? I'll have to answer with an unequivocal <u>maybe</u>. And my apologies.

Strangely enough, the Big Fellow is not himself that unpleasant or unapproachable a person. (Not that I'd like to have him angry with me. He isn't above sending a visitor to see you whom you'd rather not receive.)

Billy Black and I took a little tour of the South Side the other evening, and stopped in at the Midnight Frolics to have a drink or two and listen to some old musician friends of mine. A nice little band called the Wolverines run by a piano-player, Dick Voynow. They used to have an astonishing cornetist name of Bix Beiderbecke. Dickie told me Bix has gone to New York to work for Jean Goldkette. Voynow replaced him with a youngster, Jimmy McPartland. I know that the charm of jazz music escapes you, Howard, but you really ought to give it a try. You could do worse than to hunt up the Goldkette orchestra; maybe we'll find them together if I get back East again.

Anyway, there were Billy Black and I sitting over a couple of highballs, exchanging data on the New York and Chicago scenes, and talking about Al Brown in particular, when in troop a phalanx of bodyguards, outriders, camp followers, and sutlers; and in the center of them all the Big Fellow himself, replete with pin-striped suit, silken shirt, diamond jewelry, and broad-brimmed sombrero.

He recognized Billy, called us both over to the royal pavilion, and told the waiter to take away the rotgut Billy and I had been swilling and bring us some private stock. (It had been rotgut, too!)

Al introduced us to some of his party, including one Bathhouse John Coughlin, a Republican alderman. More about him later, Howard. Al yells at Basil DuPre, one of Voynow's sidemen, to ask what tune they were playing, and Basil yells back, 'A Good Man Is Hard to Find'. Al thought that was so funny he bought a round for the entire house and gave every musician a hundred-dollar tip!

After about an hour he turns to Billy Black and myself and says, 'You boys need a story or you'll be in dutch with your editor, won't you? Well, come along and we'll do something for you.'

Howard, out we march to Al's personal limo. We drive over to his headquarters in the Metropole Hotel, elevate up to his private suite, and Al announces, 'Anything you boys want to know, just ask me!'

Well, Howard, I won't duplicate the write-up that Billy and I did for the Inter-Ocean: see clipping enclosed. But at one point, Al got onto the subject of politics and declaimed on the Red Menace at length. That didn't make the Inter-Ocean story, but you'd probably be interested. By my notes, Al said:

'Bolshevism is knocking at our gates. We can't afford to let it in. We have to organize ourselves against it and put our shoulders together and hold fast. We must keep America whole and safe and unspoiled. We must keep the worker away from Red literature and Red ruses; we must see that his mind remains healthy.'

Isn't that precious?

As for the man's claim about 'just providing a service' (see clipping), the fact is, Howard, that it's hard to quarrel with him. Nobody has to drink his hooch, nobody has to patronize his whorehouses, nobody has to play the ponies. Of course, some of the other things these racketeers are engaged in, are a different matter. The protection racket hasn't hit the East Coast very hard as yet. But it's a beauty, and the victims do have to kick in or they're in dire peril. And Capone and the others are moving in on some of the legitimate labor bodies, too!

But Al is a bootlegger above all else, and he doesn't make anybody drink beer who doesn't want to. So much for the good Senator Sheppard and the holy Congressman Volstead.

Anyway, we finished up our interview, enjoyed Al's hospitality (a trifle nervously), and then received free transportation to our respective homes. I must admit to a moment of terror when Al said, 'How would you like to go for a little ride?' I must have looked pretty funny – at least if I looked anything like Billy Black at that moment.

Al doubled over laughing at us. But he meant just a ride, not a ride. Newsmen are pretty sacrosanct, at least so far, and Al did nothing to molest us.

Now, Lovecraft, I said I'd have more words about Alderman Coughlin. He's called Bathhouse because of a little incident hereabouts a few years ago. He's a medium-distant relation of

Charlie Coughlin, your friend Father Curran's priest-buddy. By the time Bathhouse and I finished comparing notes, we discovered that Charlie and I, if not Bathhouse himself, were boyhood acquaintances! We're all three of us native Torontonians (aye, sinister foreigners, Howard, beware our tinted hides and oddly formed eyes), all more or less of an age (I was hatched in '86, Howard, which causes me an occasional moment of puzzlement at your own grandfatherly pretensions), and even roamed the same neighborhood around Oxford Street.

Half my family is Irish, as is all of Father Coughlin's, iv carse. But my own Irishers are of that curious breed, Erse Protestants. So I missed out on the benefits of Charlie's ecclesiastical education. What if I hadn't! Can you imagine <u>me</u> in a Roman collar? Ho ho!

At any rate, Charlie has his own parish now, although one would hardly call Royal Oak, Michigan, a center of world influence. I visited the town, spoke with some of his parishioners (he seems a popular enough priest), and called upon Charles Himself, conveying the greetings of his umptieth-cousin Bathhouse and trying to locate the links in our common Toronto past.

(Charles C. by the way, claims to be unaware of some of the more unsavory goings-on in the First Ward of Chicago, which Cousin Bathhouse owns in partnership with a colorful character known as Michael 'Hinky-Dink' Kenna. Charlie tut-tuts a good deal when it comes to his disreputable reputation.)

To come to the point, Charlie's politics are more than slightly vague and contradictory. He seems to be a capitalist, socialist, fascist, and anarchist; a liberal, reactionary, bigot, and advocate of toleration; and an internationalist isolationist. But let me not make too light of the man, Howard. <u>I am afraid of him</u>! He is utterly magnetic. In ecclesiastical terms, <u>he is a charismatic</u>.

And he <u>lusts</u> for power! One can feel it!

At the moment he is a relatively obscure parish priest, but he is reaching out. Last October he initiated a weekly radio broadcast out of WJR in Detroit. Mainly he devotes himself to tepid homilies and children's games, but who knows where he is going to finish?

As for his relationship with your friend Edward Curran and their fledgling Christian Front . . . all I have to say is, Beware,

Howard! I know, of course, that you do not consider yourself a Christian. Well, all things being what they are in this chaotic century of ours, I'm not even sure what a Christian is. But by my own Christian forebears, I don't think this man is a Christian. Not if the word has any meaning left in it at all!

At any rate, when Father Charles gets onto politics, the phrase that keeps popping through his circuitous pronunciamentos is 'Social Justice'. I suppose we'd do well to keep an ear out for that phrase, and any time we hear it, at least we know its source. The Shrine of the Little Flower, Royal Oak, Michigan.

Howard, beware!

Well, enough of this doom-crying on my part. All is for the pretty-good in this most mediocre of all possible worlds.

Another incident while I was up at the Weird Tales office this week. Who should stroll in as I sat conferring with Wright and Henneberger but Farnie's predecessor and Clark's onetime compatriot, Edwin Baird. They have yet to make their break final and complete, and was I ever embarrassed as they proceeded to get into a violent quarrel!

It started over some minor matter like free back issues of Weird Tales, but soon everyone was raking up coals dating from March 1923 onward.

I kept edging toward the door – I despair of family quarrels! – but all of them kept pulling me back. All of the names of people at the magazine kept popping up – Otis Kline, Tony Rud, Prince Otto Binder, Donnie Keyhoe, Harry Houdini. All of the artists – Joe Doolin, and Brosnatch, old man Epperly, and so on.

And, of course, H. P. Lovecraft.

Wright finally admitted that he had, on occasion, rejected a story of yours and then taken it after all, on resubmission. To which Ed Baird replied that if Farnie had to look twice to see a talent like HPL's he'd better have his optics examined, and that if you were ever dissatisfied with Weird Tales you would be welcome any time in the offices of Ed's current pridanjoy, Real Detective Tales.

And so it went, around and around and around.

Howard, I've done a number of yarns for Baird's deteckatiff books. Perhaps you've seen my Jimmie Lavender stories, with apologies to the fine onetime moundsman of the Windy City Cubs. Lord knows I've used Jimmie enough times, and he always seems to be good for a quick sale and a decent check, which is more than can be said for many a more ambitious creation.

Okay, okay, I'll mind my own business!

That's really all I have to report just now, Auld Theobaldus. So I will close off and try to get some shut-eye – if I can sleep through the tommy-gun battles that rage day and night in this bastion of municipal tranquillity.

> Yours for bigger and better Czechs,
> (also Slovaks, Serbians, et cetera)
> (That's a joke, Howard!)

VINCENT STARRETT

Vincent signed the letter, donned a heavy cardigan against the still uncertain evening, and strolled to the corner mail-drop. On his way out of the apartment building on Buena Park Terrace he noticed a large new automobile parked across the street. Two men sat in it, hats tugged low, gazing at his building.

As Vincent stood at the mail-drop the engine of the car roared into life and the sedan made a rapid U-turn, pulling to the curb behind him. A window rolled down, and the passenger ordered Vincent to freeze. He did so. In that single moment he noticed both that the passenger held a Thompson submachine gun, and that the car was a new Buick. He marveled at the workings of his mind.

The passenger reached out of the car. 'Let me see that letter before you mail it.'

Vincent handed over the envelope. The man took it, scanned the address, passed it to his companion sitting in the driver's seat. In seconds he received it back and handed it again to Vincent.

'Okay, go ahead and mail it.'

Vincent dropped the letter into the mail receptacle. The car roared away. Vincent walked slowly back to number 940, climbed the wooden stairs to his apartment, opened a bottle of almost decent whiskey, and poured out half a tumbler. He went to the sink and added a dribble of cool water.

Then he sat at the kitchen table and drank down the contents of the tumbler. It would take a few minutes for the alcohol to reach his brain, and he used the time to change from street clothes to pyjamas, brush his teeth, and climb into bed with pencil and pad. It was a funny way to get drunk, but he could feel the liquor doing its work.

He gazed at the spiral-bound sheets through wavering eyesight, jotted a few notes, and began working on a sonnet. He could rhyme Capone easily enough, without even calling upon the disclaimed older version with the i on the end. Capone, stone, moan, crone, phone, loan. Who else would find his way into the poem? Big Al's archrival, Bugs Moran. Buggsy would have to get his lines, and he was a tougher nut to rhyme. Moran. Catamaran? No good. Rataplan? That was better.

But nobody would recognize *rataplan* except drummers. *Man, fan, tan, can.* It was coming easier. But he *liked* that word *rataplan*. Maybe he could get in a play on words, compare a rattling machine gun to a rataplanning drummer. Who drummed for the Wolverines these days? He tried to remember from the Midnight Frolics but instead kept seeing Al Brown's face with its ruined cheek.

He could do no more. No more. Oh – that was it! Vic

More. No, the drummer's name was *Vic Moore*, same as the Ziegfeld banana.

The pad slipped from Vincent's hand onto the woolen blanket, the pencil tumbled to the bare floor with a brief rattle. Vincent started to reach for them, but the room spun around and a first warning of impending nausea rose from the pit of his stomach and helped him decide to let it ride for now. Let it slide, let it ride.

11
Boston

Some crude humorist pointed and hollered, 'Hey, lookit, it's Mutt 'n' Jeff in the flesh!'

Pete Stahrenberg, as hot-tempered as he was huge and brawny and tough, was out of his seat and launched halfway across the Boston Elevated car before he felt George Pagnanelli grasping him by the arm, pulling him back to his seat. 'Don't start a fight,' Pagnanelli urged. 'You'll get in trouble with the cops, and we don't want that.'

Stahrenberg stood hesitating as the subway car's doors rolled shut again, leaving his antagonist laughing on the platform as the train rolled toward Boston Common. There the final and most dedicated assemblage was planned, in vain hope of saving the convicted Braintree killers and their bizarre fellow-inmate Celestino Madeiros from imminent execution.

'Besides,' Pagnanelli went on, 'we do look a little like Mutt and Jeff. You must be a foot taller than I am, and weigh two or three times as much.'

Pete stood over George for a moment before resuming his seat. 'Yeah, I guess so,' he conceded.

'Come on, Pete, sit down.'

'I don't know, though. I think you're too easygoing. You let these lousy punks get away with that kind of crack, they think they can get away with anything.'

George made a placating gesture. 'He was just some kind of joker.'

'How do you know that? Maybe he was some stinking Red, or a dirty kike or something. Everybody's in this

burg today, every kind of scum from all over the East
Coast. I don't mind a bit if there's a good scuffle, hey,
George? I'd kind of like to crack a few Jew skulls before
I go home. They're all a bunch of Reds comin' here to
cry over them two lousy greasers, they ought to send 'em
all back to the other side.'

He was silent for a moment, listening to the rattle of
the subway, then looked at Pagnanelli's olive visage and
prominent nose. Stahrenberg clapped the smaller man
resoundingly on the shoulder. 'But you're okay, George.
I know you're a guinea, but you're all right in my book
anyhow!' He laughed heartily.

They climbed off the subway at Boylston Street and
walked toward the Common, each man carrying a bundle
of *Christian Defenders*. They stopped across the street
from the Common. 'Will ya look at that,' Pete Stahrenberg exclaimed.

Pagnanelli gaped.

The Common was completely filled with milling crowds
of men and women. The afternoon air was warm and
muggy, the sun relentless. Banners waved over parts of
the Common, denouncing Governor Fuller and Judge
Thayer, calling upon Chief Justice Taft to stop the
execution, demanding a new trial for the condemned
men.

In several corners of the Common rough platforms had
been set up and orators were haranguing the crowd,
whipping them to greater heights of indignation, urging
them to make ever stronger demands of the authorities.
But others in the throng seemed to regard the rally as an
occasion for a sunny picnic. Baskets of food were opened,
sandwiches were passed, along with ill-concealed bottles
of wine and beer.

'Well, I'll be damned,' Stahrenberg spat.

Pagnanelli grinned. 'Looks like Coney on the Fourth.'

'Yeah. Rotten bolshies. They oughta fried them two the day they caught 'em! Come on, let's go see if we can do any good over there.'

He caught up Pagnanelli by one elbow and all but carried him across Boylston Street and onto the Common itself. They set down their bundles of *Christian Defenders*, opened the twine bindings, and began to hawk the newspapers. A few of the people crowding the Common turned to see who these newcomers were, and what they were hawking.

'Get your *Christian Defender*,' Pagnanelli yelled. 'For God and America – read the patriotic truth.'

Stahrenberg's pitch was more vigorous. He called headlines from the current issue of the *Defender*. 'No Mercy for Red Murderers! Jew York Red Rally Fails!'

Angry sympathizers of the two anarchists began growling and circling around Stahrenberg and Pagnanelli. 'Are you sure this was such a good idea?' George asked his printer.

'Come on, come on, don't funk it, George!' Stahrenberg stuck out his big jaw belligerently. 'Come on, you Red punks,' he challenged, 'buy a real American paper, don't be scared of the truth!' He brandished a *Christian Defender* in one beefy fist, raised the other beside it, and shook it at the crowd.

A man in a rumpled gray suit and octagonal eyeglasses stepped from the crowd and came up to Stahrenberg. 'You want a paper?' Pete asked the man. 'You a real American, buddy?'

There were furrows between the man's eyes. 'I'd like to discuss this with you,' the man said. 'Have you really investigated the facts in this – '

Pete cut him off with a roar. 'You commie punk! Go on back ta Roosha!' He shoved his open hand into the man's face, knocking his glasses off, sending the man sprawling against the backs of a group of people facing the other way. There was a small uproar.

George pulled Pete away from the crowd before anyone could react. 'Take it easy,' he urged. 'Pete, we're not among friends, hey? Don't start a fight!'

Stahrenberg muttered angrily about Reds and wops and kikes, but permitted himself to be dragged to a quieter section of the Common.

Across Beacon Street Pagnanelli could see a row of uniformed troopers mounted on horses, surveying the crowd. Several State Police cruisers were drawn up also, at the ends of the line of mounted police.

Not far from the mounted police and motor cruisers, Pagnanelli and Stahrenberg saw a finely ordered formation of young men in identical dark uniforms. A grin crossed Stahrenberg's face. 'Ha! Blackshirts! They'll show 'em how to demonstrate! Not with a mob half-full of women and kids! Trained men! That's the way to do it!'

At the end of the Common nearest the Blackshirts and police the demonstrators were fewer and quieter. A group had gathered opposite the Blackshirts and were shouting taunts at them, waving placards; the Blackshirts held their ranks and their silence. They appeared to carry no arms.

There were plenty of other vendors hawking their newspapers. Most of them were radical papers, crudely produced sheets that echoed the demands of the crowd for a new trial for the Braintree killers now in Dedham Prison. But others were patriotic sheets that Pagnanelli and Stahrenberg both recognized as the work of colleagues – *The Blackshirt*, *Lightning*, *The American Patriot*, *The Christian Mobilizer*.

Vendors of the two groups glared their hostility at each other as they cried their wares to the crowd. Pagnanelli brushed against one ruffian, a hulking fellow with a week's growth of beard and a filthy cloth cap pulled over his ears, waving copies of *The Militant* and shouting incoherent slogans.

Some of the demonstrators facing the Blackshirt formation had apparently grown tired of shouting and being ignored by the uniformed men. They borrowed ripe vegetables from picnickers and lined up facing the Blackshirt unit. The mounted police and their horses seemed to stir restlessly.

Someone in the line of demonstrators shouted another taunt at the Blackshirts and hurled a tomato through the air. It landed short of the Blackshirts but splattered the trousers of the nearest members of the unit. As though the first tomato had been a signal, the radicals facing the Blackshirts began hurling food.

The Commander of the unit lifted a glittering whistle to his lips and blew a single piercing note. The Blackshirts, without breaking ranks, charged ahead and began swinging fists. From somewhere, they produced truncheons and laid into their tormentors.

The mounted police started a precision movement, wheeling across Beacon Street, the end of their equestrian squadron sweeping the nearest mob of protesters before them. A plainclothes officer had climbed atop one of the parked motor cruisers and was shouting commands through a megaphone, ordering the demonstrators to disperse at once.

For a while the struggle seemed to be all in favor of the Blackshirts. While the motley-garbed demonstrators within the Common by far outnumbered them, they were an undisciplined, almost helpless mob, while the Blackshirts were ordered, trained, armed, and working under the firm control of their leaders.

The mounted police were pressing farther on the demonstrators, tacitly ignoring the Blackshirts.

But then a series of shouted signals worked through the Common and a crew of burly shirt-sleeved radicals filtered from the crowd and began assembling near the scene of action. Tough men, not the ineffective intellectual type who had challenged Pete Stahrenberg at the opposite end of the Common. Men carrying wooden clubs, rocks, and bottles.

At least two score of them assembled and squared off opposite the Blackshirts. Then both factions charged. George Pagnanelli saw Pete Stahrenberg throw down his bundle of *Christian Defenders* and reach for his hip pocket. His face showed a savage light of joyous anticipation.

Stahrenberg slipped a spring-loaded folding knife from his pocket, whipped it open; its stiletto blade caught the afternoon sunlight for an instant and flung a dazzling blast of light at Pagnanelli's eye. He blinked and saw Stahrenberg lunging at a shirt-sleeved demonstrator. The demonstrator was armed with a long-necked empty green bottle. As Stahrenberg drove for the demonstrator's belly with his knife, the man swung the green bottle in an arc aimed at Stahrenberg's skull.

Pagnanelli was jounced sideways by something huge and mahogany-colored. He spun toward the grass, vaguely aware as he fell that he'd been struck by the flank of a police horse as its rider headed into the fray of Blackshirts and radicals. George lost sight of Pete Stahrenberg and his bottle-wielding foe. The entire end of the Common near the battle was surging toward Charles Street as demonstrators struggled to aid their comrades.

George struggled back to his feet, found himself face to face with a broad-chested radical. The radical grabbed George by the front of his clothing and lifted him into the air, brandishing a stick in his free hand. He shook George violently, but before he could swing the stick George saw a Blackshirt raise his truncheon and smash it against the side of the demonstrator's head.

Once again Pagnanelli was hurled violently to the ground, this time by the force of the tumbling demonstrator. The heavy man tumbled on top of George as well, knocking the breath from him. He lay quietly, unable to move under the weight of his assailant until he had recovered his wind. All around him he could see the feet of hundreds of scuffling demonstrators, Blackshirts, police horses.

With a moan George managed to suck air back into his lungs and shove the demonstrator off his chest. The man rolled onto his back, groaning, then struggled upright and began to stumble away. Pagnanelli felt a strange relief when he saw that the man was still alive, not out of concern for the radical but because he was himself freed of an entanglement with another human being's violent death.

George struggled back to his own feet and staggered in a direction opposite that taken by the recovered demonstrator. He could hear the shouting of the police official atop the parked cruiser but could not make out the substance of the message. On the Common the sounds of battle were pierced now and then by terrified shrieks of women and children caught up in the fighting.

The mounted police squadron had completed a sweep of demonstrators, who were now being packed into Black Marias in Beacon Street. The mounted troopers reformed their line and began a second sweep, moving now in the opposite direction, rounding up a second group of demonstrators. Somehow as the horses and their riders swept through the crowd, any Blackshirts they encountered managed to slip between the flanks of the sweating mounts leaving only radical demonstrators to be gathered up by the troopers.

A light wind had arisen, and George suddenly detected the odor of burning newsprint upon it. He peered through the weaving masses of bodies and saw that someone had started a bonfire with the stacks of newspapers and pamphlets being hawked. He looked around desperately for his bundle of *Christian Defenders*, but they were nowhere to be seen.

. A third time the mounted troopers began their sweep. On this occasion George saw that he was near the middle of the group of demonstrators and Blackshirts caught in the concave line of horses and men. He struggled to make his way to the edge of the mob so he could escape the roundup, but the press of bodies was too thick. He was stymied.

He looked up and saw a sweating, foaming horse; the trooper on its back seemed to tower as high into the sky as a church steeple.

George tried to yell at the officer, to tell him that he should not be arrested, but the trooper was shouting something back to him, something about foreign revolutionaries and cleaning up Boston for good. The trooper raised a truncheon apparently identical to those used by the Blackshirts. George threw one arm up to protect his face from the descending club. He felt a heavy wallop on his forearm, and a split-second later his head was jarred. At the same moment, a thousand lights flashed on and off in his brain and a sound like a tree snapping before a tornado filled his ears.

He tumbled toward the ground but had no recollection of reaching it.

Pagnanelli awoke in a soft bed with clean sheets, the astringent smell of medication in his nostrils. He looked around thinking that he was in a hospital room but saw instead the furnishings of a luxuriant hotel apartment. The face of a stranger leaned over him and nodded once, then withdrew. George heard words spoken a few feet from his bed, then saw a second face peering into his own.

It was that of the unshaven radical who had been hawking copies of *The Militant* at Boston Common. The man had removed his filthy cloth cap but was otherwise identical in appearance to George's earlier view of him in the Common. 'Are you all right, Arthur?'

The word *Arthur* struck Pagnanelli with as much force as the mounted trooper's heavy truncheon. He looked down to see himself lying in the fresh-smelling bed. He saw that his right arm – which he had thrown instinctively between his head and the descending club – had been cleaned and splinted. He could move the arm slightly, but his first effort brought such pain lancing from it that he ceased at once. Instead he raised his left hand to his head and found that it, too, was heavily bandaged. When he moved he felt a dizzy nausea. He moaned and shut his eyes. The unshaven man did not speak again, and Pagnanelli lay undisturbed in the bed.

He was only semiconscious. The dirty face wavered in front of his mind's eye, a maddeningly familiar face. He knew that he recognized the man. He'd looked only slightly familiar in the Common, with his cap pulled down over his ears, concealing most of the upper half of his face, and his growth of whiskers obscuring his cheeks and chin and mouth. With the cap gone he was even more familiar to George's mind. But who was he?

Who was he?

And why had he been able to call him Arthur?

Pagnanelli slipped quietly over the brink into oblivion and slept for long hours.

When he awakened again his dizziness had diminished and his nausea had disappeared. With his uninjured arm he pushed himself upright in the bed and looked around. The door of the bedroom was open, and through it he could see into the sitting room of the suite. It was beautifully furnished with tables and couches in gilt and silken period style.

Pagnanelli called out once.

There was a stirring in the sitting room, and Theodore Weiss, Hardeen the Mysterious, strode through the doorway. He was clean-shaven and immaculately groomed. For undress he wore a silken dressing gown of glossy black with Chinese magical symbols and astrological signs stitched as decoration. About his throat was knotted a shimmering silken cravat. Knife-edged trousers extended beneath the robe, to the tops of Hardeen's gleaming patent leather shoes.

'You were – ?' Pagnanelli managed only the two words of enquiry.

'Yes, I was the vendor,' Hardeen answered. 'How are you feeling, George? You look a lot better than you did. The doctor has his own suite here in the Copley, we can have him back in two minutes if you need him. But he said you'd be all right.'

Pagnanelli raised his splint-covered arm.

'Nasty sprain there, but not quite a break,' Hardeen said. 'And a good thing you got that arm up. You caught a nice wallop on the cranium as it was, but the headaches shouldn't last more than a few days and the swelling should be gone in a week. You're starting to show a nice shiner, too!'

'I feel like I ran into Dempsey,' Pagnanelli admitted. 'It was a cop that bopped me, wasn't it?'

Hardeen shrugged. 'State trooper, Blackshirt, bolshie – what's the difference? How's your appetite? This is a dangerous business, George. Are you sure you don't want to get out? You're playing so many games one on top of another, trouble is almost inevitable.'

'I can't get out. If you'd seen what it was like when I was a kid in Armenia, Theo. You're lucky, you were born on this side. But over there . . . Nothing but armies sweeping through. If it wasn't the Bulgarians slaughtering the men and raping the women, then it was the Greeks. If it wasn't the Greeks, it was the Italians. Or the Russians. Or the Turks. I think those bashibozouks were the worst. They weren't satisfied with murder and rape, they liked to torture, too!

'So, we made it here to America, but even America isn't safe. Those foreign terrorists want to come here, too, and turn America into another Europe. Reds, Black-shirts, fascists, National Socialists, tsarists . . . They're all the same in my book, Theo.'

Weiss said, 'You sound pretty strong. I'll get us food, eh?'

Pagnanelli smiled gratefully. Weiss lifted an ornate European-style telephone painted in ivory and gilt, and ordered for them.

When Weiss hung up the earpiece, Pagnanelli said, 'You had me fooled at the demonstration. Then when I woke up in this bed and you called me Arthur, I was at a loss.'

'I shouldn't have done that,' Weiss conceded.

'The doctor heard?'

'He's trustworthy. But we should maintain the roles anyway. George Pagnanelli at all times. Never mind, Arthur Derounian.'

'Yes, please.' George paused. 'But I didn't know you were going to be at the Common. I had to be there. To keep up my credential, you know. When Viereck suggested that Pete Stahrenberg and I attend – '

'I didn't notice Viereck there.' Weiss pulled up a gilt-encrusted chair and sat beside Pagnanelli's bed. 'You don't happen to know where Sylvester is these days, do you?'

Pagnanelli tried to shake his head, decided better of it and whispered, 'No.'

'We try to keep close tabs on him,' Weiss said. 'But he's a slippery one, Mr Viereck, Mr James Burr Hamilton, Mr George F. Corners, Mr Donald Furtherman Wicketts, Dr Claudius Murchison. And God knows what other names that viper uses! Not only does he slip in and out of New York like a shadow, he seems to have ways of slipping in and out of the country as well.' He shook his head despairingly.

There was a discreet knock from the door, and Hardeen exited to admit the room-service attendants. He directed them to Pagnanelli's bed and followed the rolling carts as the staff propelled them. Pagnanelli found himself in the midst of a surreal landscape of gleaming silver, white linen, and glittering crystal. Weiss scribbled his signature on the service card, and the waiters departed.

Pagnanelli discovered that even with one hand immobilized he was able to tackle the meal with relish. It was minutes before he looked up from the food. He swallowed a morsel and said, 'I don't even know what time it is. How long was I out?'

Weiss walked to the corner and pulled back a drapery. The bright Massachusetts sunlight beamed into the room. 'It's noon. You took that clout yesterday, and were out of action overnight. You were lucky not to wind up in a prison ward. Your friend Herr Stahrenberg, by the way,' he chuckled, 'spent the night in the pokey, sharing a common cell with a score of anarchists and Reds. I hope he enjoyed the experience! I had quite a job getting you away from the Common!'

Pagnanelli said, 'Thanks, I didn't say that before, did I? Thanks.'

'We don't get many people with your kind of courage,' Hardeen said. 'When we get one, we try to take care of him. Think of yourself as an asset!' He laughed. Pagnanelli shook his head. He winced, but managed to say, 'I'm sure it's more than that.

'But, Theo – What do you think is really going on here? I mean, I know all about Sacco and Vanzetti and how every extremist group in the country is using their case to generate passion.'

Weiss nodded.

'But – what's really going on? I've infiltrated every weird fascist hate-group I can find. I know that they're dangerous. But – I have the feeling that this is all building up to something *now*. Or at least, soon. And I can't get a line on *what*. Revolution? War? Anarchy? I just can't find the master key to it all.'

'Yes,' Hardeen said, 'that's the grand puzzle, isn't it? I'm sure that Viereck is somewhere at the centre of a grand spider's web. And every one of these groups is a strand of his evil nest. The Ku Klux Klan, the Blackshirts, the strange political priests running in and out. The fascists, the tsarists.

'The information you've gathered for us, George, is invaluable in trying to fathom what they're all doing.' Hardeen paced back and forth, a golden dinner roll in his hand, waving it like a conductor before an orchestra.

'But what is Viereck's scheme? Who is *his* master?'

Pagnanelli sipped at a tumbler of water. 'Dr Kiep?'

Hardeen stopped pacing and turned to face Pagnanelli's bed. 'You're right, without question. Dr Kiep is involved intimately with this. We know that Viereck was getting German Embassy money at least as early as 1915.'

'I was a terrified boy hiding in my parents' cellar from

the bashibozouks in 1915. I was little Arthur Derounian then.' Pagnanelli's voice dropped with the final name. 'That's why I was so distraught when you called me Arthur. I didn't realize who *you* were, Hardeen – and no one but you is supposed to know my true identity. Not even Washington. Not as long as I have any surviving relatives.'

Hardeen nodded. 'I really didn't mean to startle you that way.' He stood with his hands clasped behind him, gathering his thoughts.

'Well, you know Viereck's history anyway,' he said finally.

Pagnanelli grunted assent.

'And his long connection with the Hun,' Hardeen continued. 'Have you seen the things he's been publishing?' he asked suddenly. 'Of course you have. Never a word of repentance or reform. Germany betrayed by the whole rest of the world, persecuted and despoiled. You know that he claims some sort of left-handed connection with the Hohenzollerns, which is itself a dangerous fact. And far worse is his association with the National Socialists. It's a dangerous game, Pagnanelli!'

'Don't I know it,' the diminutive Pagnanelli fingered his bruises. 'What do you think is in the cards, Hardeen? What does Washington think?'

Hardeen shook his head. 'If the German republic survives, there's a fair chance of a stable order for Europe. Germany is the lynchpin. Fascist Italy is dangerous enough, but we think that situation can be held under control. Red Russia – well, she may bluster of course, and she has a terrible inclination to meddle in the affairs of others. You know, the bolsheviki have rattled sabers with England, Poland, and China all in the past few months.'

The two men exchanged wan grins.

'But they seem so inclined to go for each other's throats, as Trotzky and Stalin are doing just now, that I think they're of little concern to the rest of the world. At least for now.

'But Germany . . . Germany . . .' He paced the room as if eager to run off and engage an enemy in single struggle. 'Once von Hindenburg goes, things look very dark, Pagnanelli. Germany's own Reds are eager for their turn at power; the National Socialists, for theirs. If either so much as quivers, the other will surely use it as a justification to leap.

'And Viereck. Viereck!' He stuck the dinner roll in his dressing-gown pocket to free his hands, and struck one fist against the opposite palm. He stood stock-still with a determined set to his jaw. 'We are going to unravel that scoundrel's game, George!'

12
Marblehead

The Lovecrafts' visit with Howard's aunts in Providence was a qualified success. Mrs Clark had resumed her old hobby of painting landscapes, and Howard and Sonia dutifully admired her latest canvasses. Mrs Gamwell's work as a city librarian was also going well, and the family finances were in a reasonably sound state of health.

No mention was made of Howard's even considering a permanent move back to Brooklyn – or of Sonia's returning to Providence except as a temporary guest – and so neither Lillian nor Annie objected when the couple moved on to Boston.

There they found Hardeen the Mysterious awaiting them in the sitting room of his suite at the Copley. Two large rolling tables littered with empty dishes and soiled utensils stood ready for pickup by the housekeeping staff outside Hardeen's suite. Within, Theo greeted the Lovecrafts. He told them that his tour had been a success. His assistants had already departed for home with his stage equipment, and he was free to join them for a holiday at the shore.

In short order the tan-and-gray Rickenbacker was rolling down the old highway through Saugus, Lynn, Salem, and on into Marblehead.

As the summer landscape fell away toward the glittering ocean, Sonia half quoted Howard's description of witch-haunted Arkham and ancient Innsmouth with its rotting wharves and decrepit gambrel-roofed houses. Theo swung the Rickenbacker along Washington Street and into Orne, then pulled up at the Spite House. They entered the old structure and claimed the rooms they had reserved.

From the porch of the Spite House they looked over old buildings, over Fountain Park and Gas House Beach, to the low crags of Orne and Gerry Islands, Marblehead Harbor and the Atlantic beyond.

They took a light luncheon, strolled around the old burial ground while Lovecraft lectured on local history, then decided to hire a shallop and sail around Marblehead Harbor. Standing beside Sonia, with Howard Lovecraft at her other side, Hardeen laughed. 'You know, I've seen a hundred harbors from bridges and wharves. But once I'm in my shackles and straitjacket and they throw me into the drink, there's no time for sightseeing. It's strictly business, then!

'So I look forward to the opportunity to sail around in the sunlight and just enjoy myself! I hope you won't consider it a waste of time.'

Sonia took Theo by one arm and Howard by the other. 'On the contrary! I know that Howard loves everything about these old towns. The ancient buildings, the hillsides and parks.

'Howard,' she pressed her face against his shoulder for a second, 'for all that you say about your belonging to Providence, I believe that some even greater reservoir of joy and vitality lies for you in these villages.'

Howard grunted, 'Perhaps.'

'You can't fool me,' Sonia went on. 'And anyway, I can see far more beauty here. I know that a little sail will do wonders for us all. Theo must be stale after all his work, and I'm so pleased to be out of the city for a while! Come along and don't be a spoilsport, Howard!'

They hired a shallop out of the little harbor above Fort Sewall. Howard Lovecraft briefly claimed ignorance of the harbor, then admitted to some slight knowledge and gave directions to the crusty seaman who owned the boat.

They sailed north of the Marblehead Light where great yachts basked in the summer brightness and hardworking fishercraft beat toward schools of silver wealth. They passed southward of Cat Island without incident, but near Satan Rock they saw a dark-hulled steamer standing at sea anchor, a couple of motorized trawlers moving around her hull. Lines and ladders hung over the sides of the steamer and disappeared into the ocean.

The shallop drew near one of the trawlers, and a deckhand hailed them. The New England sailor shouted back. The hand on the trawler shouted again, in a thick foreign accent. The New Englander yelled once more, that they were out for a pleasure sail and headed for Satan Rock. The trawler hand ordered them off.

In the shallop the grizzled New Englander cursed beneath his breath and guided the little boat ahead on its original course. 'That's them damned krauts and their damned science,' he grumbled. 'They got no business in our waters, no matter what they say they're doin'!'

The hand aboard the trawler shouted again, then raised something that glinted in the sunlight. As Hardeen yelled, 'He's got a rifle,' a puff of smoke appeared from the weapon, followed by a crack as the bullet splintered the gunwale of the shallop.

On the deck of the trawler an officer appeared suddenly, ran to the deckhand and struck his rifle aside. He produced a pair of field glasses and peered through them at the shallop. Its four occupants stared back. The officer shouted, 'Are you there all right?'

'Damned right we are, you Hun!' the sailor called back. 'And the harbor master's goin' to get an earful of this! What in hell do you think you're doin', anyhow?' Without waiting for an answer he started to bring his boat about, but the officer shouted, asking him to stand to and parley.

Hardeen laid his hand on the sailor's oilskinned arm. 'I'd rather stay here and find out what this means than turn tail and run crying to the harbor master.'

The old sailor remained motionless.

The officer left the deck of the trawler. A dinghy had been lowered, and the officer had himself rowed toward the shallop by a pair of hefty sailors who moved with an almost military precision.

Speaking in heavily accented English the officer apologized to the New Englander. 'We here are conducting delicate soundings and other scientific experiments. In our immediate vicinity, traffic can cause bad interference with our work. So the crewman on guard we set. We do not wish our work to have disturbed, hah? And also to you some danger exists.'

Hardeen raised his voice. 'Scientific research? What kind of scientific research is this, shooting a rifle at a harmless sailboat? It looks more like piracy to me!'

The officer pulled off his cap and wiped his forehead with his sleeve. 'Yes, you are in the right. My man on deck,' he inclined his head toward the trawler, 'he should not at you have shot. I will see to his discipline! Also, we will pay indemnity. What is the value of the damage, please?'

The old sailor spat over the gunwale of his boat. He named a figure for the damage to his shallop, and the foreigner settled in cartwheels. Then he clambered back into his dinghy and returned to the trawler.

The old sailor turned toward Hardeen. 'Well, you learn anythin' from that? Damned foreigners, think they own the hull ocean! Well, you still want to see some more islands?'

They decided instead to turn back to the harbor, and Hardeen paid off the sailor for the use of his shallop.

They returned to the Spite House for fresh clothing, then strolled along the waterfront as evening began to settle in. Sonia brought up the afternoon's incident. 'What kind of work did that officer say they were doing? Taking some kind of soundings?'

'He didn't really say,' Hardeen answered. 'Scientific work, he said, but that's no real explanation. I wonder if the harbor master's office is still open.' He looked at his watch, then added, 'I think I'd like to make a little enquiry. Shall we meet later – say, for dinner?'

Howard and Sonia agreed, and Theo set out alone. The Lovecrafts wandered back to the old burying ground on Orne Street and strolled among the half-fallen grave markers. Howard stood before a board carved with the date 1638. 'Nearly three centuries ago,' he said, 'this clay, this dust, was a woman. And as long from today, we shall be as she is now, Sonia.'

Sonia took his arm and shuddered despite the warm air. 'Those Germans nearly took care of that for us this afternoon.' Behind them the ocean was dark and rippled with a mild easterly breeze. The sky was filling with stars. 'Sometimes you talk like a character out of one of your own stories,' Sonia complained. 'Do you think it matters at all to . . . to . . . the dead? Will it make any difference to us, once we are gone?'

Lovecraft stood, stroking his long jaw. 'Much as it appeals, I cannot believe in any survival of the individual consciousness beyond the dissolution of the body. But there may be other forms of immortality available to us who seek them out.

'Great sculptors, architects, whose buildings long survive their preceptors, philosophers whose thoughts influence the lives of the common herd or better yet are treasured by a few enlightened minds of any generation. Even the authors of tales that find their way between the boards of books, and onto the shelves of librarians and fine bookmen. These fortunate few live on, not eternally, of course, for in the end we shall all go down into the unending night. But for a while, at least, for a matter of years or decades, and in rare cases even for some centuries, it is possible to hold the ultimate darkness at bay.'

'Is that why you want so much to have a book of your own?' Sonia asked. 'Your stories are certainly popular with your readers, but I can tell that you aren't satisfied, Howard, with having them in the pages of the magazines.'

Lovecraft confessed that Sonia might be right.

Theo returned to the Spite House and found Howard and Sonia Lovecraft awaiting him, ready to proceed to dinner. They obtained an old-fashioned New England meal, Dash and Sonia carefully avoiding sea fare that might provoke the violent reaction of Lovecraft's boyhood aversion to fish in any form.

Afterward they sat at their table near the old fireplace, consuming pie and ice cream and pots full of heavy coffee. Sonia asked what Theo had learned from the harbor master.

'Essentially,' Weiss told her, 'nothing. That steamer has been at anchor for a number of weeks. Its name, incidentally, is *Der Traum.*' He smiled wryly. 'Howard, that's German for *The Dream*. They haven't bothered anybody, except to keep everyone away from their work. They claim that they're making studies for a construction firm in New York, testing underwater building techniques.'

'Isn't someone supposed to be in charge of that?' Sonia asked.

Theo nodded. 'Normally it's under control of the Coast Guard. But there's nothing to prevent private surveys of the ocean floor. I asked the harbor master about that, specifically. You know, I sometimes do routine surveys of river or lake bottoms myself.'

He made a little gesture with his hands, holding them palms-up. 'It's a fuzzy realm, legally speaking.'

'It seemed to me that we experienced nothing less than an encounter with a pirate craft,' Lovecraft put in angrily.

'It was surely not a group of dedicated scientific investigators.'

Theo Weiss smiled lazily. 'I thought you were snuggling up to that bunch, Howard.'

Lovecraft's visage grew stern, but he held back.

Weiss pressed him. 'Weren't you undertaking some work for Sylvester Viereck? Or did I have a false impression about that?'

Lovecraft reached for the tray in the center of their time-smoothed table and lifted another slice of apple pie to his own plate. 'I have discussed some work with Viereck,' he conceded. He removed the end of his slice of pie carefully with his fork and transferred it to his mouth. After swallowing he said, 'In fact, I have already drafted the preface to my book for the Jackson Press. I have perused the preliminary translation of Mr Viereck's patron's book, *My Struggle*, and have found in it uncounted nuggets! Perhaps you would care to wait here while I return to my room and fetch my manuscript.'

Weiss nodded.

'I don't think I want to spend the evening turning over the fine points of that person's manifesto,' Sonia put in. 'If you'll both excuse me, I think I'll just go to bed. I could use the extra sleep anyway – it's been quite a day for me!'

Lovecraft saw her to their room, then returned to the nearly empty dining parlor of the Spite House and sat opposite Theo. 'I'm afraid that my penmanship leaves something to be desired,' he said. 'I shall be pleased to read you selected portions.'

Weiss assented. He poured himself a fresh cup of coffee from the pot their landlord kept filled and waiting on a trivet. Then he reached beneath the table, brought out a flask, and added a few drops of golden fluid to his cup. He turned a questioning glance toward his companion, then did likewise to Lovecraft's cup.

'I must state at the outset,' Lovecraft began formally, 'that reading Herr Hitler's book created in me a most remarkable feeling of spiritual kinship.'

Weiss stared at Lovecraft inquiringly.

'You see, Herr Hitler was born just a year before I was,' Lovecraft explained. 'In an old Austrian village, Braunau. It was apparently a charming and old-fashioned place, where the passage of time had erased few of the characteristic evidences of past ages.

'This was very much my own experience in my native city of Providence. And when Herr Hitler, as a young man, traveled to the great metropolis of Vienna, he reveals a retrospective impression not unlike my feelings which I recall experiencing when I myself first visited our own great metropolis, New York. But here.'

Lovecraft fumbled inside his jacket and drew out a slim sheaf of pages covered with his usual spidery script. 'Let me quote to you from Herr Hitler's book, Theo. "The purpose of my trip was to study the picture gallery in the Court Museum, but I had eyes for scarcely anything but the Museum itself. From morning until late at night, I ran from one object of interest to another, but it was always the buildings which held my primary interest. For hours I could stand in front of the Opera, for hours I could gaze at Parliament; the whole Ring Boulevard seemed to me like an enchantment out of *The Thousand and One Nights*."

'You see?' Lovecraft looked up from his transcription. 'Can you appreciate the sense of kinship which this creates?'

Hardeen sipped at his cup and urged Lovecraft to go on.

'"I believe that those who knew me in those days," the text continues, "took me for an eccentric. Amid all this, as was only natural, I served my love of architecture with ardent zeal. Along with music, it seemed to me the queen of the arts. Under such circumstances my concern with it was not *work* but the greatest pleasure. I could read and draw until late into the night, and never grow tired."

'You see, Theo? A soul of true sensitivity is speaking here. This young man, this pilgrim from little, old-fashioned Braunau. How like myself, I keep exclaiming! His love for the fine and graceful old architecture, his nocturnal instincts, his dedication to literature and the arts, his keen understanding that the *work* of the true artist is not work at all, but the most unspoiled of pleasures – all of these are sentiments which arouse in me a sympathetic response. A feeling of psychic union!'

'That's all very nice, Lovecraft.' Hardeen drew the abandoned pie tin across the tabletop and stared at its meager contents. With a spoon from his saucer he picked at a bit of crust that adhered to the tin. 'If the book were entitled *Bohemian Memoirs* or something of the sort. It's the same as your feelings about New York, you say.'

'When first I encountered the denizens of Greenwich Village,' Lovecraft confessed, 'I was utterly captivated. Here, I believed, I had found a world of true intellectuals and sensitive artistry. Here I could immerse myself in the company of poets and fantasists as sincerely dedicated to the muse as was I.'

'But you were disappointed,' Hardeen prompted Lovecraft. 'You came to be disillusioned?'

'"Only our decadent metropolitan bohemians can feel at home in this maze of reasoning and cull an 'inner experience' from this dung-heap of literary dadaism, supported by the proverbial modesty of a section of our people who always detect profound wisdom in what is most incomprehensible to them personally."'

'Hey?'

'That's more of Herr Hitler.' Lovecraft waved his pages of transcript. 'You see, Theo? The man speaks my own mind! Here is a conservative of the truest and highest kind. A personage who clings to the finer things of the past not because they are old per-se – but because he is capable of detecting the fraudulence and pernicious quality of so-called modernism!'

Theo shook his head. 'I'm not really interested in hearing Herr Hitler's theories of literary criticism.'

Lovecraft shot him an angry look.

'I'm sure you are qualified to judge the man's theories about writing,' Theo said. 'I've heard your praises sung by Sonia and by Ehrich for a long time, Lovecraft. And I don't question your own literary attainments.'

Lovecraft was mollified.

'I'm more concerned with the fellow's political program than I am with his literary judgements,' Hardeen resumed. 'I'm frankly very concerned that you're getting mixed up with a crew of people who are quite out of your depth, and there may be dire results.'

'Your concern for my welfare is most appreciated,' Lovecraft replied coldly. 'I believe, however, that a person of some thirty-seven years age, and of respectable intelligence and education, might be regarded as capable of managing his own personal relationships.'

Hardeen clucked his tongue. 'Listen, that's not what I'm saying at all. I don't know you as well as my brother did, Lovecraft, and certainly not as Sonia does. But it's obvious that you're an idealist. An artist. An intellectual.' He saw Lovecraft swell at the characterization. 'You're not particularly interested in crass things like business and politics, except on some theoretical level.' Lovecraft shrank back a bit.

'And you're dealing with people,' Weiss pointed with his pie fork, 'who are very ruthless, very determined, very energetic. They may not be too clever in the sense that you and men you admire are, but they are certainly sly and deceptive in getting to their goals.'

Lovecraft dropped his eyes to his folded sheets of

notepaper and shuffled the pages. He began to quote again. '"Once, as I was strolling through the Inner City," that's the inner city of Vienna, of course, "I suddenly encountered an apparition in black caftan and black hair locks. Is this a Jew? was my first thought. For, to be sure, they had not looked like that in Linz. I observed the man furtively and cautiously, but the longer I stared at this foreign face, scrutinizing feature for feature, the more my first question assumed a new form: Is this a German?

'"I was repelled by the conglomeration of races which the capital showed me, repelled by this whole mixture of Czechs, Poles, Hungarians, Ruthenians, Serbs, and Croats, and everywhere, the eternal mushroom of humanity – Jews and more Jews. To me the giant city seemed the embodiment of racial desecration."

'Why, Greenwich Village, Williamsburg – the man might be describing any of a hundred sections of New York, Weiss. He writes of Vienna, but he might as well write of Brooklyn! Ah, the endless nights even in 259 Parkside, listening to the unceasing reedy piping of the Syrian in the apartment next to Sonia's and my own! There must have been a whole tribe of Orientals in there, taking their turns at the pipes, for they seemed never to cease! And the faces in the streets, and the odors in the subways! We have lost our America to these mongrel herds, just as the Germans and the Austrians have lost their nations to the thronging multitudes of Slavs!'

Hardeen put down his fork. For a moment he seemed to be absorbed in thought, chewing his full lip and saying nothing. He shook his head. 'Howard, you leave me at a loss.'

They faced each other silently. A few feet away the pine fire crackled in an old brick fireplace. Some moisture must have remained in the logs: there was a steady hiss of heated sap beneath the crackle, and a loud, sharp sound when a log would split now and then along its grain.

'No,' Hardeen said. 'Not at a loss. Just at a point of momentary despair. So your Hitler has his theories of human racial types.'

'They are not his alone,' Lovecraft interrupted. 'He bases his arguments not upon his own experiences solely, but upon the solid works of such men as Houston Stewart Chamberlain. Have you read his *Foundations of the Nineteenth Century*, Weiss? An astonishing work! Massive, closely reasoned, irrefutable!'

'Irrefutable nonsense!' Hardeen shot back. 'Yes, I know Chamberlain's work. I staggered through as much of it as I could, in the German original.'

'And I suppose you know Herr Hitler's book, also?'

'Also, in the original.'

'You are better read than I had suspected.'

'There's a lot that you don't suspect!' Hardeen snapped. Then, more gently, 'I don't mean to quarrel with you, Lovecraft. If for no more reason than my affection for Sonia. But don't you see, you play with these ideas as if they were *purely* ideas. You must make yourself understand that they are not just concepts, that people and nations are involved.'

'I have met individuals. Count Vonsiatsky, for example.'

'Yes, your count. But you have never traveled in Russia. Ehrich and I were there, you know, back in the old days. In 1903.'

'Houdini's escape from the prison transport is legendary,' Lovecraft acknowledged.

'Not my point. You can't imagine what it was like to visit Russia in those days. The whole country was like a single, huge prison. There were more privileged and less privileged inmates. And there were keepers – but even they were prisoners, in their own way.

'And as for your Herr Hitler's attitude toward Jews, Lovecraft, the plight of Russian Jews was not pretty. Ehrich and I were wined and dined by the aristocracy, but we saw the treatment of our brothers. They could not, for instance, live in the city of Moscow. I suppose Herr Hitler would like that notion. It might have made Vienna a pleasanter place for him. No one in caftan and side curls. Everyone like him.'

Lovecraft squirmed uncomfortably in his seat. 'You dress in proper and civilized manner, Weiss. There is no reason why those Viennese Jews could not do likewise. Conform themselves to the respectable norm of their society. Why must they defy the people who were their hosts by deliberately wearing such outlandish and offensive garb?'

Hardeen brought his fist down upon the table. 'You've put your finger on it exactly, now! You see – the Jews were not the guests in Vienna! Hitler was! He was from where – Braunau, Linz. He was the bumpkin visiting the metropolis, unable to cope with the variety of types and the diversity of styles which he encountered! And rather than recognizing a shortcoming in himself, he laid all the blame on those around him! And rather than correct his own short-comings, he would banish those whose presence made him conscious of his own failings!'

Lovecraft was thunderstruck. The silence between the two men was filled with the hiss and the pops of the pine fire. The room was deserted now except for Lovecraft and Weiss.

With a creak the door opened from the kitchen. The dour innkeeper appeared, removed the coffeepot from the trivet on their table, and returned in moments with another pot, steaming and fragrant. 'I'll be retirin' now,' he told them. 'You gents want ta sit up a-talkin', you can put another log on the fire in a while.' He turned and disappeared once again.

While Weiss refilled his own and Lovecraft's cup with black coffee and brandy from his pewter flask, Lovecraft pondered. Finally, his hands to his brows and his eyes fixed on the black steaming fluid in his cup, he said, 'You mean to say, Weiss, that *I* am the . . . the *alien*? I am of old English stock. There have been Lovecrafts in New England for a century and a half. And these . . . Syrian mongrels who inflict their presence on the real Americans who try to live in New York . . .'

He had been jarred by the other, but now he felt his confidence coming back. He became almost jocular. 'Surely, Hardeen, you don't mean to say that these Orientals are true Americans, are truer than you or I – '

'*I* was born in Wisconsin, Howard. But my parents were from Hungary. Sonia is from the Ukraine.'

'Tempered by her girlhood in England.'

'But you see, Lovecraft, you are making an argument for cultural influence. No doubt that persons deprived of nurture, of education, of cultural influence, can be raised to a higher level of achievement, if we just make these things available to them. But you don't accuse a starving man of guilt or inferiority because he's deprived of food. You try to offer him a chance to better himself!'

Lovecraft rubbed his chin. He was himself the scion of a wealthy heritage. Whipple Phillips, his maternal grandfather, had turned a fortune in the East India trade of the nineteenth century. His own father, Winfield Lovecraft, had done well in trade, also. But Howard had always been of an unworldly bent, devoted to art rather than commerce, and the family fortune had declined under his guidance. Declined, nearly to extinction.

Hardeen did not wait for Lovecraft to reply. He pressed on. 'I just wish you would think this thing through. Not just as concepts and theories. There are concepts and theories aplenty in this world, and they're harmless as long as that's all they are. But when governments and armies start treating human beings as if they were concepts and theories, civilization is threatened!'

Lovecraft sipped at his cup, pursed his lips, held his breath, swallowed. For some reason he thought of the little journalist he had met at Viereck's. 'George Pagnanelli speaks thus of the way his people are treated.'

Hardeen said, 'Eh?'

Lovecraft looked up. 'Oh, I was just thinking of a man to whom I was introduced at Viereck's. Chap named Pagnanelli.'

'Oh,' Hardeen grunted. 'Part of *that* bunch.'

Hardeen heaved himself out of his chair. 'Enough for one night, Lovecraft. We'll have more to say about this. Now I think I shall head for my own room and a good night's rest in my own bed.'

'A good idea.' Lovecraft sat gazing into the fireplace. 'I shall remain for a while, and see what fancies the writhing flames may help me to conjure. Then I too,' he looked up, 'shall hie myself off for the restorative of slumber in *my* own room and *my* own bed, but a yard from Sonia's.'

'More the fool you,' Hardeen muttered.

13
Marblehead Neck

'You two must have enjoyed a wonderful conversation!' Sonia Lovecraft, dressed in a breezy summer frock of shantung print, patted Howard and Theo's hands as they sat at table awaiting the arrival of their meal. 'Here we are eating breakfast in the afternoon!'

'It was a most fruitful and stimulating exchange,' Howard Lovecraft said. He looked into the fireplace, now swept clear of any sign of last night's logs. 'I learned from Weiss that Albert Michelson, the discoverer of the speed of light, was himself a Hebrew.'

'That wasn't exactly the point I was trying to make,' Theo said. 'My real objection to this National Socialist program is its – oh, its disregard for any human value, any human desire. Any – *anything* except the schemes of the Führer. Everything builds up and up to one man's will, and that's all that matters. Herr Hitler may actually be a dedicated idealist. I imagine that he is, in his own peculiar way. But he would squeeze and crush all of the people to fit his particular notion of the ideal society.'

'That is no worse than the bolshevists are doing,' Lovecraft countered.

'I make no brief for them, either.'

'I thought you and Ehrich so despised the ancien régime. You spoke of – '

He was interrupted by the arrival of their meal: dropped eggs, sweet rolls, coffee, fried dough, jellies, buckwheats, juices, and muffins.

'You were so critical of tsarist Russia, I should think you would be a great admirer of the new government.'

Hardeen shook his head. 'No. One tyranny, another

tyranny. But, don't you see, there is a situation very similar to that of your Herr Hitler. I'm sure that Lenin was an idealist, that this fellow Stalin and his associate Rykoff are idealists. They have their dream of the perfect society, and it means nothing to them to make themselves despots of the most terrible sort. All in the service of their ideals, don't you see?'

Sonia patted them both. 'I see last night wasn't enough. Can't we have a holiday today?'

Hardeen settled back in his seat and plucked a sweet roll in half. He held one piece before himself. 'Of course. What shall we do this afternoon? I wish I could get a better look at that marine research project we saw yesterday. My curiosity is piqued, to say the least!'

Sonia shook her head. 'I hope you don't intend to go out there again, Dash.'

He smiled. 'I don't like being shot at. If there were some other way . . .'

'You might wish to look at it from the air,' Lovecraft suggested.

Weiss returned an inquiring glance.

'There was an aircraft manufactory here in Marblehead,' Lovecraft reminded him. 'Back during the World War. Long since dismantled, of course, but old Azor Burgess – it was the Burgess Aircraft Corporation that operated the factory – takes visitors on sightseeing flights now and then.'

Hardeen's eyes lit up. 'Do you know this Burgess?'

'Only slightly. Old Azor Burgess, the family eccentric. The Burgesses were among the early settlers of Marblehead, a wealthy mercantile family. When it appeared that the United States might be drawn into the World War, they set up a line to produce aëroplanes for the government.

'On the occasion when I was vacationing nearby with the Longs, young Belknap and I paid our fee and were taken into the air for a sightseeing excursion over the town and harbor. A most exhilarating experience!'

Hardeen asked Lovecraft to direct him, and the three piled into his Rickenbacker. Lovecraft guided them through the town, across the narrow causeway to the Neck, and to Azor Burgess's ramshackle house halfway out Harbor Avenue to the lighthouse. Hardeen parked the car, and they made their way to the porch where Burgess sat rocking and smoking a pipe.

'Mr Burgess!' Lovecraft called.

The old man turned a grizzled face to them and nodded. 'I remember you, Mr Lovecraft. What can I do for you?'

Lovecraft introduced Sonia and Hardeen. Burgess acknowledged the introductions with a nod for each. Lovecraft asked if the old amphibious aëroplane was still in working order.

'Don't get many skylarkers anymore,' Burgess said. 'Guess with everything so modern and efficient, Lindy and them other fellas flying across the ocean all the time, nobody wants to risk their hide in an old creakin' biplane.'

There was a moment of silence.

'But I've still got 'er under the canvas, there.' He pointed with his pipestem. 'Still a customer every now and then. Enough to make it worthwhile to keep her in flyin' condition. You lookin' to take another spin today, Mr Lovecraft?'

'Actually I was hoping to go up, Mr Burgess.' Hardeen took a step forward as he spoke.

'I'll take anyone who want t'go,' Burgess said. 'Anybody willin' t'pay the fare, I'll take 'em anywhere they want. The old bird's like an old woman, you know. She creaks and she moans, and she's a little bit slowed down and she handles a little on the stiff side. But she's a reliable old girl, and she gets her job done!'

Hardeen reached for his wallet and extracted a bill.

Burgess hoisted himself from his rocking chair. 'Any of

the three of you,' he repeated. 'T'others can wait here till we get back.'

'I'd hoped that Mr Lovecraft and I could go up together, Mr Burgess. We wish to do some observation work. Mr Lovecraft knows the local waters better than I.'

'But who'll fly her? Can't take but two at a time. I've got t'fly the old girl.'

'I'm sure I can handle the controls,' Hardeen reassured. 'I've been an aviator for over fifteen years now. Learned on an old Voisin biplane, not much more than a motorized box-kite! I know the Burgess aircraft. This is an "H" model, with the Renault aircooled?'

Old Azor stood in his tracks. 'You do know your aircraft, mister. But are you sure you can handle this girl? She's fixed out with a planing float, y'know. Got it off an old Sopwith Bat Boat, God knows why anybody wanted t'haul one of them things back here, but some fella had one for a while after the war. Let 'er go for salvage, finally. I almost put in her engine, but ninety horses, my Lord, would've torn this old girl right into shreds. But that planing float, why, my old girl can get up and down on the water smooth as cream. Only she handles a little foot-heavy in the air, if you know my meaning.'

Hardeen nodded seriously. 'I understand.' He moved across the scrubby grass toward the wooden pier where the biplane was moored beneath its gray tarpaulin. 'And it's a pleasure to swap prop-wash with a brother aeronaut!' He grinned broadly.

Suddenly old Azor's dour face split into a similar grin. 'Well, if you can vouch for her, I guess I can trust you not t'fly off like Lindy and never come back.

'Besides,' he cackled, 'she'll only hold enough fuel for a couple of hours flight. You'd be lucky to reach Bangor, no less Paree!'

They pulled the canvas from the biplane. Lovecraft

and Weiss climbed into the observer's and pilot's seats of the aeroplane while Sonia stood watching on the pier. 'Thought about puttin' in an automatic starter,' Azor said, 'but it's a lot of money if I'm going to have to retire the old girl any time.'

He climbed down a ladder from the end of the pier and edged along a little platform attached to the heavy piling that supported the pier. He exchanged another word with Hardeen, reached up and grasped the aircraft's propellor, and swung it.

Minutes later Burgess was back on the pier with Sonia. They watched Hardeen maneuver the biplane across the rippling water of the harbor and point her nose northeast toward the Marblehead Light. The old Renault engine ran smoothly but with a steady, loud sound. They could hear the engine roar as Hardeen pushed the airplane forward, reached top taxi speed, and kicked her into the air.

The Burgess 'H' rose with a sort of lumbering grace, weighted down by her Sopwith float. Hardeen circled once over the Neck, and Sonia, her eyes shaded by her broad-brimmed summer hat, waved a handkerchief at the airplane. Then the Burgess leveled off and moved toward the northeast once again.

In the pilot's seat Hardeen tested the controls, muttering to himself that Azor Burgess had been right in his description of the aircraft's handling. He yelled a few words at Howard Lovecraft, struggling to make himself heard over the roar of the Renault engine and the rush of the slipstream. This flight might have a significant purpose, Hardeen thought, but while his mind was occupied with serious concerns, his feelings were bursting their bonds. The excitement and exhilaration of flight were magnificent, and the sensation of hanging suspended between azur sky and gleaming sea was unmatched in the world.

In response to Hardeen's question, Howard Lovecraft was shouting and pointing over the side of the aircraft. Hardeen saw that Lovecraft had jammed his fedora down on to his head to keep it from sailing away in the slipstream. Below them he could make out the islands of Salem Sound. Hardeen reached into a pocket and extracted a tiny folding map. He located Cat Island on the map and on the shimmering blue below the airplane, then flew over the island and banked through a turn above the channel that separated Cat Island from treacherous little Satan Rock.

There were a number of shapes in the channel. He dipped the biplane's nose, leveled her off into a slow spiral, finding her too eager to dip over and dive, and reluctant to pick her nose up again. The Sopwith float, of course. Maybe it would have been a better idea if Azor had put in the Daimler engine after all, despite the additional weight and torque problem, to get the extra twenty horsepower it would have offered. But there was nothing to be done about that now.

Hardeen could see the looming bulk of the steamer, two or three motor trawlers, and a number of dinghies in the channel, with the figures of men moving around on the decks of the larger craft. More intriguing was –

He couldn't make out the bottom here, the water was too deep for that. But there seemed to be something large and dark submerged beneath the ships. He pointed down and shouted a query at Lovecraft. The response was one of puzzlement. Hardeen reached into his coat and extracted a small, flat metal case. This he unfolded and reassembled, transforming it into a pair of compact but powerful binoculars.

He held the biplane's stick steady with one hand, leaned over the edge of her fuselage, and peered down through the binoculars while the airplane stayed in her slow, steady bank-turn. The men on board the steamer were pointing up at the Burgess now, and a deck officer was conferring with a man in dark costume.

They seemed to be shouting something at the airplane, but their words failed to carry. In a minute several of the sailors disappeared belowdecks, reemerged carrying weapons, and pointed them at the biplane.

Without delaying longer, Hardeen wrestled the nose of the Burgess upward and kicked her out of her turn. He headed the aircraft toward the town of Marblehead, circled, directed her nose back toward the harbor and the Neck. In a short time they were taxiing along the beachfront by the Corinthian Yacht Club, and just short of Azor Burgess's pier, Hardeen cut the engine.

The airplane floated a few yards farther toward the pier, then came to a halt. Burgess paced stiffly out to the edge of the pier and threw a line to the airplane. Sonia Lovecraft was beside him, beaming and waving to the men.

Soon they sat in Burgess's parlor, a pot of tea brewing for the four of them.

'You really did a fine job of pilotin',' the old man said. 'Had my eye on you all the time you was up, Mr Weiss. Thought you might be just blowin' hot air when you said you could pilot an aircraft. Then I saw you really could do that, but I kind of suspected the old Bat Boat float would throw you!'

'I'll have to admit, she's a difficult aircraft,' Hardeen conceded. 'You pull back on that stick and wait for her to pull her nose up, and she comes up so *slowly*. I'll admit, I was afraid of stalling a couple of times.'

'Heh! Don't worry about that! The old girl doesn't stall easy, whatever else she does. Now,' he stood up and walked to the iron stove, 'who takes lemon and who don't?'

After the tea was poured, Sonia asked, 'Did you see what you wanted to, Theo? Howard?'

'Our friends of yesterday's altercation seem to be as busy and as hostile to observation as ever,' Howard answered. 'One would think that yesterday's run-in would suffice, but their behavior pattern is unaltered.' He sniffed his cup of tea suspiciously, added sugar and sipped happily. 'Foreign interlopers! They ought to be blasted out of the sea and sent home to their dens!'

'Mr Burgess,' Sonia turned to the old man, 'have you had any dealings with those people working out beyond the harbor?'

'Don't get into town very often, Mrs Lovecraft,' Burgess grunted. 'Don't keep up too much with comin's and goin's. But I know who you mean. Them scientist fellas, they stay on their ship most of the time. Come into town onct in a blue moon, pick up a few marine supplies an' charts. Haven't met 'em myself. Don't much like what I hear of 'em. Hear they're kind of rough and unfriendly.'

'Well,' Hardeen said, 'I'm afraid that the flight was pretty disappointing from that angle. I had a fine time – did you, Lovecraft? It was hard to tell, up in the slipstream.'

Lovecraft considered, sipping his sweetened tea. 'A most pleasant excursion, yes. This was, you understand, only my second venture into the blue empyrean on wings of fabric and wood. The first was a greater thrill, but perhaps too unsettling. This aërial adventure could be appreciated with the greater calm of custom.'

Sonia smiled and ventured a statement. 'Maybe I'll give it a try sometime. There's no reason for the air to be an exclusively masculine realm. But I think I'll settle for the role of spectator for now.'

They crossed the causeway again, Hardeen guiding the Rickenbacker along the narrow sharp-sided road. Back in town they decided on a late supper, a good rest, and a return home in the morning. They left the Spite House and dined heartily on plain New England fare, then strolled slowly through the historic streets. Finally they retired, Hardeen to his room; the Lovecrafts, to their own.

Even after Sonia had climbed into bed, Howard sat in a padded chair, hunched over paper and pen, jotting brief letters to his correspondents across the country. Sonia watched him, chin in hand, quietly waiting until he stopped writing.

'Howard,' she said softly, 'did you and Theo – ' She paused expectantly, hoping that he would take the half-question and respond to it, but he returned her look and also waited. She felt herself flush. 'Well, you seemed to be very involved last night, Howard dear. When I went up to bed. And today, you and Theo – well, I just wondered. About your conversation.' She felt as if she had botched her question hopelessly. What *was* she trying to ask, anyway?

'It appears that Mr Weiss is really more conversant with my affairs than I had anticipated, Sonia.'

'How so?'

Lovecraft shook his head. 'I don't know his sources of information regarding the Viereck circle, but he seems to be knowledgeable regarding its members and their activities. He is also surprisingly well-read for a cheap conjurer and escape artist!'

'Howard! A cheap conjurer? I thought you admired Dash. You said you thought he was very cultured and intelligent.'

Lovecraft released a long hissing breath. 'He has read – or at least claims to have read – both Chamberlain and *My Struggle* in their original forms. I did not question him closely on the Chamberlain, but his conversation indicates a good knowledge of Herr Hitler's book.'

'And? Did the two of you reach a meeting of the minds?'

Lovecraft hesitated before answering. Finally he said,

'Mr Weiss is a convincing spokesman for the Hebrew race, my dear. He defends them eloquently against Herr Hitler's attacks. But somehow, there seems to be a . . .' He stopped and leaned back, gazing at the ceiling of their old room. 'You used the term, "meeting of the minds". I think that Mr Weiss and Herr Hitler don't quite have a meeting of the minds. Hitler speaks of races and peoples as groups, while Weiss speaks of individuals among them. Not exactly the same. What Hitler proposes is a sort of grand housecleaning for Europe, bringing about a single, noble, advanced race of the highest intellectual and moral type.'

Sonia snorted. 'You're slipping right back into his spell, Howard. I have seen the kind of world that man would make. Theo has not lived in it as I did when I was a girl, but his parents knew it well and he at least has visited it.'

'And I deal only in concepts, is that it? That was Weiss's line, which I now hear echoing in my very sleeping chamber. Ah,' he shook his head despairingly. 'I think I shall stroll around the village for a while.' He rose and headed for his fedora.

Sonia sat up straighter in bed. 'Would you like some company, Howard? It looks like a beautiful night.'

Lovecraft went to the window and peered out. 'Even in summer, the ocean cools the air after dark. I think it would be best for me to take my stroll in solitude. I shall return in a few hours, thank you.'

He donned topcoat and fedora against the evening chill, drew shut the door behind him, and set off through the town, gazing raptly at the ancient buildings as they dozed in the summer moonlight. For an enchanted interval it was as if he had stepped back through some fissure in the substance of time, to stroll at his leisure through the era of periwigs and small-clothes, clipper ships and coaches,

when New England was young and swore fealty still to
the antient crown.

He wandered down Ferry Lane and stood with his
back to the lapping waters. He gazed uphill at the town,
then decided to stroll along Hooper's Wharf and look at
the shipping tied up in the harbor. Most of the commerce
of Marblehead had disappeared with vanished centuries,
replaced by a mixture of pleasure craft and commercial
fishers, but occasionally some cargo was still consigned to
the old harbor.

Upon Hooper's Wharf Lovecraft halted in a moment
of enchantment. One of the buildings, drab though it
must be by daylight, had been somehow transformed by
the moon into a vision of an earlier age. Its stern hip
roof was relieved by the incongruous but oddly pleasing
presence of a Georgian cupola. An upper room in the
building was illuminated, the only such on the entire
wharf. As Lovecraft stood studying the structure a face
appeared in the lighted pane, then quickly disappeared.

In the storefront beneath the window electric beams
flashed and a door swung open. Two men in seamen's
garb emerged and strode purposefully toward Lovecraft,
walking in rapid lockstep.

As the seamen advanced without a word, Lovecraft
decided that he wanted nothing of their company and
started to walk hurriedly back along the wharf. He could
hear footsteps behind him. He increased his pace, but the
footsteps pounded louder and faster than his own. His
breathing became labored.

He felt a hand grasp his shoulder and stop him in his
tracks. He whirled to confront his assailant, white with
rage at this affront to his person.

He clenched his fists, swung wildly at the uncouth face
that peered at him from beneath a black knitted cap. His
blow missed by a foot or more.

The man released his grip on Lovecraft's shoulder,

swung a fist at his belly. Howard doubled over in pain and psychic shock. One part of his mind was caught up in the reality of the instant. Another calmly surveyed the scene, dismayed that he'd been struck in anger by another person. That had not happened to him in more than thirty years, since he had been a small child and become involved in petty fisticuffs with others from the neighborhood.

He managed to rise halfway and cocked his arm despite the heavy folds of his topcoat and suit jacket. He tried a straightforward blow at his opponent, felt the thrill of achievement as it landed high on the man's torso – but then saw the second man's fist lash out against the side of his head. He tumbled to the rough roadway, got his hands beneath him and started to push himself off the ground when a shocking impact pounded into his ribs.

He was knocked sideways, saw heavy boots, felt a massive toe jolt into his shoulder. He rolled into a ball, instinctively covering his face and the soft parts of his belly and groin. He felt blow after blow and was unable to do more in defense of himself than roll helplessly, hoping that the boots would land on his back or limbs rather than his head.

When the kicking stopped he lay half-conscious, vaguely aware of two gruff voices engaged in dialogue above his body. Strong hands grasped him by the arms and hauled him upright. He felt himself trembling. He was led back toward Hooper's Wharf, his legs half functioning, half dragging beneath him.

A growled command and he was shoved through a doorway, up a staircase, and thrown into a rough wooden chair. Strong hands patted his pockets, extracted his wallet and papers, took them away.

Lovecraft managed to raise his head and peer about him. The room was dingy. Gray metal lockers lined one wall, and the two seamen who had beaten him stood nearby. Directly opposite him was a battered desk. A small, dapper man sat behind it, contemplating him from pale blue eyes set within an almost delicate face.

One of the seamen laid Lovecraft's wallet and belongings on the desk in front of the man. Howard saw him pick up the crumpled papers – he recognized them as his transcriptions from the translated copy of *My Struggle* – and examine them with interest. The man opened the wallet, studied its contents, then lowered the materials and gazed calmly across his desk.

'You are Mr Lovecraft?' The man's enunciation was precise, with only the suggestion of an accent.

Lovecraft sat staring ahead of him.

'You must tell me,' the man said. 'You *are* Lovecraft, are you not?'

Howard stared. One of the seamen approached and stood over him menacingly. He grasped Lovecraft's clothing with one hand, brandished a fist before his face. The man at the desk barked a brief command to the seaman, who dropped Lovecraft's coat front but remained ominously in place.

'You must cooperate,' the man behind the desk said.

Lovecraft raised his hands slowly to his face and rubbed his temples. An incoherent moan escaped his lips. There was a moment of silence. Then he said, 'Who are you? What is this about?'

There was no reply.

'I am a lawful citizen,' Lovecraft attempted again. He had regained most of his breath. His body felt more numbed than pained by the pummeling and kicking he had received. He was attempting to grasp the situation and assert his rights. 'These thugs beat me and dragged me here.' He indicated the two seamen. 'I demand that you summon the authorities at once and have them arrested.'

The dapper man said, 'I do not think you understand

the reason you are here. But first you must identify yourself.'

'Yes, yes. I am Howard Lovecraft.'

'This is very unfortunate,' the man said. 'We knew that we were under observation. My two men believed that you were an enemy.'

Howard groaned again. 'Enemy? Enemy of whom? Are they *your* men? Then I demand an explanation.'

The man shoved Lovecraft's wallet aside, picked up his note pages, and examined them for several minutes before laying them down again. 'Yes,' he said, 'you are the man doing that work for us.' He looked at Lovecraft sharply. 'Who is your employer? For whom have you done your work with *Mein Kampf*?'

'Sylvester Viereck.'

The dapper man nodded. 'Of course. We shall have to correct what has been done.' He barked a command, and one of the seamen disappeared from the room. 'Mr Lovecraft, you must understand – '

'Who are you?' Lovecraft interrupted.

The dapper man sat unspeaking for a moment, as if startled at being broken in upon. Then he said, 'My name is Kurt Lüdecke. Perhaps you have heard it before?'

Lovecraft thought he had not.

Lüdecke sighed. 'I am the representative of a scientific research organization based in Europe. We have been conducting a series of observations offshore, not far from here.'

The seaman reappeared with a bottle and glasses, placed them on Lüdecke's desk. Lüdecke poured a tumbler for Lovecraft and a smaller glass for himself. He nodded at the seaman, who carried the tumbler to Lovecraft and held it for him. Lovecraft wrinkled his nose in distaste. 'If you please,' Lüdecke encouraged. 'It will help you to recover from your unfortunate accident.'

Lovecraft took a tiny sip of the burning, smoky-flavored

liquid. For a moment it threatened to come back up, but the sensation passed and he felt a warmth begin to spread through his body. He leaned forward and took the glass from the seaman and forced himself to swallow a larger dose.

'Our work,' Lüdecke resumed, 'is intended for commercial ends. We are concerned with the future of world trade, particularly that between the continent of Europe and North America. As you can understand, Mr Lovecraft, our rivals will try to find out our secrets, and this we wish to avoid. Thus, we keep a very quiet appearance here and wherever we work. This modest facility,' he gestured around the room, 'is our office. And when I saw you on the wharf, studying our building, I asked my assistants to summon you for a discussion.

'You should not have run away, Mr Lovecraft.'

'I have every right to stand upon a public wharf, Mr Lüdecke!' Lovecraft, strengthened by the schnapps, grew heated. 'And I also had the right to leave if I chose!'

'You are correct,' Lüdecke soothed. 'It was all a most unfortunate error.'

'And I demand that these ruffians be turned over to the authorities for punishment!'

'If you insist, that can be done. But I beg you to reconsider. They acted on my instructions.'

'Then you too should be prosecuted!'

'You would have difficulty obtaining proof. If we three decline to incriminate ourselves under your country's laws, what evidence is there? No, Mr Lovecraft, you would only embarrass yourself. You would appear very foolish.'

'This is outrageous!'

'No, please.' Lüdecke was conciliatory. 'I did not mean to threaten you, Mr Lovecraft. I wish to apologize. And if you will accept an indemnity, I would be able to provide compensation for your discomfort.' He reached into a drawer of his desk and extracted a checkbook.

Lovecraft half rose in anger. 'I have been affronted and physically assaulted, sir! Do not compound the offense by trying to purchase my forgiveness! This is not a matter of commerce, but of honor!'

'I appeal to you,' Lüdecke said. But he looked past Lovecraft at the two burly sailors. Lovecraft did not fail to notice them moving closer to his chair. 'May I offer one further proposal. Wait until the morning. Then place a trunk telephone call to Mr Viereck in New York.'

'And what has Sylvester Viereck to do with this?' Lovecraft pointed his finger at Lüdecke. 'You represent a European research firm; he, a New York publishing enterprise. Why do you wish me to telephone him?'

'Only because he is an acquaintance of both of us. I have met Mr Viereck when he visited the Continent in the past. You yourself told me that he is your employer.'

'Not my employer,' Lovecraft disagreed. 'I have been exploring some projected enterprises with Viereck, but I am by no means an employee of his.'

'As you will. I offer you my sincere apologies for this event. Tomorrow, you will find that Mr Viereck will vouch for my good faith.'

14
Providence

George Pagnanelli watched the buildings flash by the window of the New Haven train as it entered Providence. Lush, rolling countryside had already given way to neat suburban houses and shops; now the train approached the downtown section of the city where older, taller industrial structures shouldered against hotels and department stores for space.

Pagnanelli's was a complex mission. He closed his eyes and rubbed them with the tips of his fingers, sorting things out for the hundredth time. Viereck was his sponsor. Getting into the good graces of the publisher had been one of the major coups of Pagnanelli's checkered career. Through Viereck he had gained access to a more elevated and more influential stratum than he could have hoped to reach via his paper *The Christian Defender*. Yet he could never have reached that level on his own, even if he'd made the *Defender* a more respectable and intellectual sheet. He just didn't have the money or the connections – but Sylvester was able to serve as his mentor and to put him in the company of everyone from Father Curran and the Count di Revel, to blue-bloods like Mrs Dilling and blue-noses like the haughty New Englander Howard Lovecraft.

Theo Weiss was right – George had picked a difficult role to play. But it was worth playing, it was worth it if he could ferret out the truth about the men who were working to destroy the freedom that Arthur Derounian had come to America to find, and that as George Pagnanelli he was willing to risk everything to protect.

The train ground to a halt. Pagnanelli stood up and

reached as high as he could to retrieve his canvas bag from the luggage rack overhead. He climbed down from the coach onto the gray cement platform and made his way through the station. Outside, he walked carefully to Gaspee Street, as had been arranged. He stood on the corner of Gaspee and West Exchange, his canvas bag between his feet, conspicuously reading a copy of *The Christian Defender*.

In a few minutes a closed Pierce automobile pulled to the curb and a man opened the rear door. 'You sell *Defenders*?' he called to George.

'Two cents a copy. Or you can subscribe.'

'Only if you'll deliver. I know of a subscriber here in town.'

He waved George into the car. As soon as Pagnanelli sat down the man said, 'Hold still. I'm going to blindfold you.'

George let the man tie a cloth over his eyes. For just one instant he felt a tremor of fear. If everything was really as planned, he was placing himself in the hands of men who used murder as cold-bloodedly for their purposes as others used logic or the offer of money or the appeal of loyalty. But then – there was no reason for them to kill Pagnanelli, and if there had been, there would surely have been no need to lure him into this elaborate trap.

He leaned back against the soft cushions and managed somewhat to relax. The Pierce was comfortable enough. Never before had he ridden in such a luxurious car, and the soft, plush covering of the cushions was a revelation. The car rode smoothly on its shock absorbers, too. Pagnanelli could tell that it was crossing a bridge by the distinctive sound and vibration of the tyres; then the car swung through a series of turns and proceeded uphill.

When the Pierce halted, he felt the man who had exchanged passwords with him grasp him firmly by the elbow. 'Here we are,' the man said, his first words since they had left Gaspee Street. Pagnanelli heard the driver open his door and slam it solidly again after climbing out of the car, then open the door of the rear compartment. 'Out – carefully,' Pagnanelli's guide said.

George picked up his canvas bag and climbed from the car, still blindfolded. His guide kept a grip on his elbow and ushered him for a short walk. The hard surface beneath his feet suggested a concrete pathway, probably from street to house.

He heard a chime sound and a door open, then felt himself propelled up a short flight of stairs, forward a few steps . . . the feel beneath his feet was softer now, probably a carpet. The door behind him slammed shut with a solid sound of wood against wood. Now he was guided forward again and turned about. The canvas bag was taken from him, and the blindfold removed from his eyes.

He was standing in a comfortable living room. There were cloth-covered overstuffed easy chairs and a large dark-colored sofa. The table before the sofa was topped by a huge lace cloth; a hand-tinted photograph of a young woman stood on the table. She wore clothing of recent style and obvious quality, and was smiling slightly for the camera.

A short, stocky man stood on the other side of the table, facing Pagnanelli. His features and coloring cried out his Mediterranean origins; his hair was growing thin on top and gray at the sides, but showed signs of having been thick, black, and curly in his youth. His olive complexion, rounded features, and dark liquid eyes resembled those of the young woman in the photograph. He wore a conservative blue suit, a sparkling white shirt and quiet tie.

'Signor Pagnanelli,' the man said, 'capisce italiano?'

George shook his head. 'Poco o niente, signore, scusate!' George managed to stumble. 'I've been on this side since I was a small child, and my parents insisted on speaking English at home.'

The man said, 'Bene, that's good. Well, I am Giuseppe Morelli. Welcome to my home.' He stuck out his hand, and George took it gingerly. Despite his obvious age, Morelli commanded a grip like Jack Dempsey's. Pagnanelli's eyes flashed from his host to the photo on the table. He brought his attention back to Morelli in an instant, but the older man missed nothing. 'She don't like me to call myself Giuseppe. Joseph, she says, my name is Joseph, or Joe. I'm an American, Mr Pagnanelli, but nobody's such an American like my girl. She doesn't even want to be Stella, she says her name is Estelle, that's real American, Stella is too Italian for her.'

He released George's hand and gestured for him to be seated. Morelli lowered himself into an easy chair. Behind Morelli was the door through which George had entered the house. It held a small rectangle of stained glass covered with a decorative grid of black wrought iron. The stained glass depicted a pastoral scene that glowed in the afternoon sunlight. The wall of the room that must face onto the street, George deduced, would contain several large windows. But heavy drapes were drawn from ceiling to floor.

'Mr Pagnanelli,' Morelli said, 'I invited you here because some very good friends in Illinois asked me to. You got very good connections. You know, I'm just a businessman trying to raise my girl like a good American citizen. We got a little community here,' he gestured with both hands, raising his shoulders in a half-shrug as he did so, 'and I do my duty, every good citizen's duty, to help out, to try and keep this town clean. I got my papers, you know. I been a citizen for eight years. I was a doughboy in the war!'

Pagnanelli cleared his throat. Viereck had briefed him on Morelli's business and on the identity of his friends in Illinois. 'Yes, sir,' George said.

'So what can I do for you?' Morelli asked.

This was the moment, Pagnanelli thought. All of the work he had done with Viereck, and all of the work he'd gone through using Viereck for connections, led to this. From Viereck to Count di Revel and the Italian *alleanza*, a twisted skein leading through the American *fascisti* of both the plainclothed and Blackshirted varieties to the Five Points Gang in New York and thence to Chicago. All of this had brought him here.

And at the same time there were his instructions from Theodore Weiss, involving this same Morelli!

Pagnanelli took a deep breath, clutched one hand with the other to steady himself, and flicked his eyes toward the picture of Morelli's daughter. 'Mr Morelli,' he said, 'we are both of us immigrants. And we are both of us Americans . . .'

That was on Federal Hill.

On College Hill, Howard Lovecraft sat in the kitchen of his aunts' house facing Lillian Clark across the oilcloth-covered table. Annie Gamwell bustled between pantry and stove, preparing black coffee and sweet rolls for her nephew. Howard had just finished describing the odd architecture of the Spite House in Marblehead when the telephone bell sounded.

The shrill signal drew Lillian away from the kitchen table and into the parlor. Howard and Annie sat in silence while Lillian's voice wafted back to them. Whatever the nature of the call, Lillian's flusterment was obvious. She spoke in half sentences, querulous syllables, inconclusive strings of words.

Finally she returned to the kitchen and stood irresolutely in the doorway. 'That was the police, Howard. They have a message for you.'

Lovecraft shoved his chair away from the table. 'I'll come to the 'phone.'

'No,' Lillian shook her head. 'There's no need for that, Howard. It was about that terrible drowning last winter. The man who called was the lieutenant who talked to you last winter. He said he was sure you would remember him.'

Lovecraft nodded.

'He said that he needs to speak with you again, dear, there's been a new development in the case.'

Lovecraft smiled wanly. He thought for an instant of his friend Starrett grinding out those silly Jimmie Lavender stories for Ed Baird's detective magazine and beseeching him, Lovecraft, to do the same. If only Vincent knew!

'I suppose I shall climb aboard a streetcar and make my way to headquarters,' Lovecraft announced. He rose from his seat and started for the parlor, but Lillian still stood in the doorway.

'There's no need for that, dear. The lieutenant said he would send a car for you. I must say that the police have been very thoughtful. He said he didn't want the neighbors to stare or embarrass us by asking odd questions, so instead of sending a squad of police he is sending a detective and a driver in plain clothing, and sending a nice Pierce automobile instead of a police cruiser.'

15

California

Clark Ashton Smith berated himself. He owed Lovecraft a letter. He'd promised to undertake some research for his New England friend, to check into the activities of certain political groups in San Francisco. Lovecraft had written and asked Smith for assistance. The Easterner was becoming deeply involved with these people, and he sought information regarding how far their web was flung and precisely what its true nature might be.

Clark had responded with a promise to investigate and report back, and then never had. But he would. He vowed to himself that he would.

For a moment, however, he had a more immediate task. He owed his meager living to the *Auburn Journal*, and he owed the *Journal* a column.

He raised his glance from the dingy cabin halfway up the slope. Higher up, the snow lay as it did the year around. And higher still the mountains were silhouetted against the thick clusters of stars that seemed so often to call to him, to offer a welcome and a solace if he could only gain the peak and climb still a little more, just a little more, through some mystical portal to other worlds.

He'd go to San Francisco and do that checking for Lovecraft. The trip would represent a momentary reprieve from this world of chicken houses and enfeebled parents and church raffles, and back to George Sterling's world of tall buildings and glittering lights. Only for a little while. But it would get him there.

He turned back to his desk and sat down. The page in his old Corona was still blank. No miracle had occurred.

He put his face into his hands and rubbed his cheeks,

making the blood flow, feeling the bristles of his natty moustache beneath his palms. A lock of dark, lank hair fell across his forehead. He'd arrange to have a day man cover for him at the *Journal* the next couple of nights. He would have to get somebody to take care of the god-damned chickens and his goddamned incontinent parents, too. Then he'd head for San Francisco.

Maybe he could get double-duty out of his trip. If there was anything really interesting in these political odd ones that Lovecraft wanted information on, he might also get a column for the *Journal* out of his research. Maybe a couple. Or even a series of articles. That would make it easier to get time off for the trip. Perhaps even some expense money.

But for now, he had to fill his allotted column-inches. And he was still feeling a little melancholy because it was the anniversary of his friend Sterling's suicide.

He dropped his hands to the keyboard of the heavy upright, snapped his head back so the hair cleared his eyes, and started to type. ' "A Wine of Wizardry" was the first work of George Sterling's that I ever experienced the pleasure of consuming,' he pecked out on the old typewriter. 'The poem, spreading its necromantic music, its splendors as of sunset on jewels and cathedral windows, across the pages of the old *Cosmopolitan* magazine, glowed like a titanic fire-opal cast somehow accidentally into a potato-bin.'

He stopped typing and read the paragraph. It was pretty good. Okay. At least that problem was taking care of itself – Sterling hadn't exactly been a local character to the readers of the *Auburn Journal*, but he'd been close enough that Smith could justify using him for the column. And Smith's own friendship with Sterling strengthened the link.

He kept on typing.

* * *

The next day he had the stationmaster flag down the Southern Pacific flyer as it passed through Auburn on its way from Truckee to Roseville. Clark traveled light; a change of clothes and a set of toilet articles crammed into a little overnight bag, a notebook and pencils, and for reading matter on the dull ride down through the Sierrras and into Oakland, the newest issue of *Weird Tales*. He read Lovecraft's story, a pleasing yarn about a painter named Richard Pickman, as the train clacked along.

He had a good solid meal in the dining car, climbed down the iron steps in the Oakland terminal, and took a ferry across the bay to San Francisco.

At the Embarcadero he set out on foot, jostling through crowds of tourists and commuters, shoppers and long-shoremen and off-duty merchant sailors.

He made his way through the shabby waterfront district and wound up on Clay Street, a narrow old thoroughfare near North Beach. Clay was bordered by crumbling brick structures, some of them prequake. Even the newer ones (and those at most twenty years old!) looked tired and dispirited. He checked into the Thor Hotel and unpacked carefully in a dingy room on the top floor of the walk-up.

Smith scanned a few notes that he'd transcribed from Lovecraft's letter, names of some of the people Lovecraft was interested in and the organizations they belonged to. Certainly the Blackshirts and the Ku Klux Klan were familiar enough. Not that much of interest ever went on in Auburn – but both had popped up in San Francisco.

He had heard more of the Freundc des Neuen Deutsch-lands that Lovecraft also inquired about. Those were the fellows Howard seemed most to have had dealings with, although of course things would be different in San Francisco. With the city's heavy concentration of Italians the fascisti had made considerable progress. And for that matter the Russian settlers in the avenues between Geary and Clement might have some links to the Vonsiatsky group as well.

Clark Smith sighed, left the Thor Hotel, and started up Clay toward Chinatown. He stopped at the first commercial telephone station that he passed and placed a call with Central. In moments he was speaking with Martin Larrabee, his onetime chief at the *Auburn Journal* but in recent years a staffer for the *San Francisco Call*.

Smith identified himself and got a warm welcome from Martin. 'Is this business stuff or is it personal?' Larrabee asked. 'I'll be off shift in a couple of hours. Why don't we meet at John's for a glass of Irish?'

'I'm mixing business and pleasure,' Smith replied. He was in town to get away from the chicken coops and general dullness of Auburn, he told Larrabee – but also hoping to uncover a story or two while he was at it.

'Want to come over to the *Call*, then? If there's business to transact . . .'

Smith looked at his watch. 'No, I feel like a little hike around the city. Five-thirty at John's?'

Larrabee agreed and rang off.

Entering John's, Smith wondered if the password for the barroom had been changed since his last visit to San Francisco. It hadn't, and he felt a thrill go through his chest when the bartender remembered him. 'Too bad about Mr Sterling, eh, Mr Smith?'

Clark nodded and agreed.

'Well,' the bartender sighed, 'you'll have the usual?'

Clark nodded, and the bartender reached behind him for a green-labeled bottle. He poured a glass of Irish for Clark and set a tumbler of water beside it.

'You going to have dinner, Mr Smith? Or just a drink? I spotted some nice fresh crabs out in the kitchen.'

'Oh – I'm not sure. Depends on Martin Larrabee.'

The bartender moved along the mahogany, waiting on

other customers. Clark studied the rows of bottles standing before the huge back-mirror. Then he studied his own image: he was still a good-looking man, even though he was pushing thirty-five. Aristocratic features, large dark eyes that women seemed to fancy, and the thin face and body that made them all want to take care of him. He exchanged a bitter glance with his reflection, then spotted Larrabee in the mirror, advancing behind him.

Larrabee raised a hand and cordially greeted the bartender; as Smith turned on his barstool Larrabee's grin widened. Smith slid from his stool, and they exchanged handclasps. 'A good day, Martin?'

'Got a hot story to push the crazy politicians off the front page for once!' Larrabee grinned. He leaned his heavy dark-suited frame against the mahogany. To Smith's raised eyebrows he elaborated. 'The city isn't like Auburn, Clark. We're a lot more interested in the rest of the world. You ever look at the *Call*?'

Smith nodded.

'Yeah,' Larrabee mused, 'it took a big change from working on the *Journal*. Lot of Washington news in the *Call*. Lot of foreign stuff, even. Joe Stalin and old Trotzky – you know he's really named Bronstein, that scrawny little kike – the two of 'em are really fighting it out. And a bunch of Chinks want to have a war with each other. Around here, that stuff makes Page One.' Larrabee gestured with both hands, miraculously balancing the glass of Irish whiskey so it didn't lose a drop as he waved it through the air.

'But anyhow, Clark, you said you had some business. I could stand here and booze with you all night, but maybe you've got ants in your pants to get to work. What's doing with you?'

Smith gestured deprecatingly. 'I've a friend named Howard Lovecraft, a New Englander, very skilled craftsman with words.'

'Never heard of him,' Larrabee said.

'He's doing a book on politics,' Smith continued. 'Not the usual Republican and Democrat stuff. He's interested in some rather startling groups. The Ku Klux Klan. Friends of the New Germany. Social Justice, Blackshirts, Russian fascist restorationists, German Imperialists . . .'

Larrabee whistled, put his glass on the bar, signaled for a refill for himself and one for his friend. 'Does he know what he's getting into, your friend Lovelace?'

'Lovecraft.'

'Hey?'

'Lovecraft. Craft, not lace.'

'Oh. Anyway, Clark, I paid enough dues running the damned *Journal*, I know what reaches as far as Auburn and what doesn't. Probably, you have no concept of what these groups are all about. The Klan, the Freunde, the Blackshirts. I don't suppose you walked through North Beach today, did you?'

Smith shook his head.

'The Duce's boys are all over the place,' Larrabee said. 'Mussolini doesn't figure those people belong to us, they belong to *him*. They're still Eye-Talians, and he wants 'em on his side if there's any trouble. The local wops don't all like that idea, but there's a Blackshirt gang that leans on anybody who squawks about it. It's not pretty, Clark, not like the gold-country, believe me!'

Smith chewed thoughtfully on an oyster chip. He washed the salty flavor away with a large sip of whiskey. 'Do you have any connections up there, Martin?'

'In North Beach?' Larrabee shook his head. 'Don't speak the language. But I know a couple of people in the Freunde. You know how to keep a straight face on, Clark. We can head up to Freunde headquarters, look over their literature, talk to a couple of people. If you'd like.'

Smith glanced at his watch. 'Maybe we could get a little food afterwards.'

Larrabee agreed.

They left John's and headed up Stockton. The sun had set, and the San Francisco evening was chilly and wet. Smith stopped under a dripping lamppost and patted his pockets, found a cigarette and a box of matches, and lit up. He pulled his collar around his face and turned down the brim of his hat. He breathed a sigh of pleasure that he'd substituted the soft felt hat for his usual beret when he headed toward the city.

They strolled up Stockton as far as Clay Street, then turned down Clay through Chinatown. They halted facing the Thor Hotel.

'You're kidding,' Smith exclaimed.

'What?'

'The Thor. I'm staying on the top storey.'

Larrabee grinned. 'You have a knack, Clark. The western office of the Freunde is in the cellar. Just hold on a couple of minutes.' He drew Smith back into the shadows of a darkened storefront.

Two men dressed in drab merchant-sailors' garb came tramping in lockstep from the Embarcadero. Larrabee nudged Smith in the ribs and pointed.

The sailors were talking in low tones. Smith could hear their voices, thick with gutturals. They stopped in front of the Thor, knocked on an inconspicuous panel a few feet from the shabby main entrance, and were admitted.

'Is that a secret outfit?' Smith whispered to Larrabee.

'Nah. Not exactly. They serve beer and schnapps, though, so they have to keep quiet.' He pressed Smith's elbow, and they crossed the street.

Down a flight of unlighted stairs they found a small low-ceilinged cellar. At the rear of the dank room a stained curtain hung behind a battered lectern. At the other end of the room was a diminutive bar. An unshaven man stood behind it, leaning forward in earnest conversation with another who sat perched on a wooden barstool. The center of the room contained half a dozen tables and thirty or forty cheap curved-wood chairs, all of them empty.

Larrabee steered Smith across the room. Passing the grimy bar, Larrabee grunted, 'Hello, Siggie. Anyone inside?' He nodded toward a doorway marked *Private*.

The bartender looked up from his conversation. 'Hallo, Martin. Ja. A bigshot in town. Nimm dich in acht!'

Larrabee pulled Smith to a halt before the door.

'What's that?' Clark asked softly. 'I didn't know you spoke German.'

'A few words. Siggie just said to be careful.' He knocked on the door. There was a moment of silence, then a chair scraped and a voice spoke one word that was muffled by the closed door; it might have been *come in* or *kommen*.

Larrabee opened the door and stepped inside, drawing Smith along behind him.

Looking around Larrabee's beefy shoulder, Smith saw a hulking figure seated behind a desk. The man looked up at them, recognition visible in his eyes when he spotted Larrabee.

'Well, Martin, hello. This is a surprise.' The man stood up behind his desk. He was as tall as Larrabee and as heavily built. He wore a business suit that made a poor fit on him.

Larrabee shook his hand, then introduced Clark. 'This is my friend from Auburn, Heinz. Clark Ashton Smith. We used to work together on the paper up there. Clark, meet Heinz Spanknoebel from Detroit. He's the head of this outfit.'

Smith shook hands, felt relieved to get his back uncrushed.

'You bring him around as a recruit?' Spanknoebel asked Larrabee.

'No. Just interested. Thought I'd bring him in so he could get some straight info, that's all.'

'You plan to write about us?' Spanknoebel asked Smith.

Clark considered his answer for a fraction of a second. 'I doubt it. Auburn's a pretty insular community. Most of the people up there wouldn't be very interested in what's going on in San Francisco.'

The man behind the desk grunted. 'Okay. Then what do you want?'

'Oh. I just . . . had heard a little about your group. Wondered, ah, what sort of association it was.' He felt a nervous tug at the corners of the mouth.

Spanknoebel shifted his gaze from Smith to Larrabee. 'You guarantee this man? We can't have every stranger wandering in here, Martin. If I didn't know you myself, I'd be plenty worried about – ' He inclined his head toward Smith.

'Take it easy, Heinz. I told you we used to work together. He's a reliable man. Don't worry.'

'We can't trust just anybody. Who might wander into this place, especially in a town like Frisco, eh? The place is full of Chinks and niggers and kikes and every other kind of scum. Even the wops are stirring around, but fortunately the Blackshirts seem to have that under control. But we're not too happy.'

Larrabee patted his pockets, then reached onto the desktop to take up a package of cigarettes and light one for himself. 'It's a cosmopolitan town. Every place isn't going to be like Detroit, Heinz.'

'Well, come on.' Spanknoebel advanced from behind the desk and laid a heavy hand on Smith's shoulder, another on Larrabee's. He half shoved, half escorted them out of the private office, stopped and locked it behind him, then accompanied them to a grimy round table. The three sat down.

Spanknoebel gestured to Siggie for a bottle of schnapps and three shot glasses. 'Bringen Sie auch einige Flugschriften mit!' He turned toward Clark. 'I don't know what ideas you got, Mr Smith, but this is a social club, eh? Friends of the New Germany, you know, there are a lot of German-Americans, everybody got some feelings for the old country. That's all. See our slogan over there?' He pointed.

'You know any German, Mr Smith? I don't know much myself,' Spanknoebel admitted. 'I was born on this side, grew up speaking English. I studied a little German, but I still got some problems with it. Look. *Wir Amerikaner deutschen Blutes ehren die Heimat.* You savvy that? All it means is that Americans with German blood cherish the fatherland. You see?'

The slogan was carefully lettered on a sign that hung on the wall above the lectern and curtain.

'Nothing sinister in that, is there? What do you think?' Spanknoebel asked.

Clark shook his head. 'I suppose not.'

The bartender put the bottle and glasses on the table. He pulled a stack of pamphlets from under his arm and laid them before Spanknoebel. 'Die Flugschriften, mein Herr.'

Spanknoebel nodded and waved the bartender back to his post. 'Take a look, Mr Smith.' He spread the pamphlets in front of Clark. They were rather crudely printed, half in German and half in English. Smith read a few headlines. They praised Hitler and the NSDAP, condemned Bolshevism and Jews, called for revision of the Versailles treaties.

'May I keep these?' Smith waited for a suggestion of a nod, placed the pamphlets in the notebook that he carried, and shoved them back into his pocket.

'Purely a social club?' Smith asked. 'It seems pretty quiet to me. Couple of men at the bar, is that all?'

'It's a quiet night,' Spanknoebel replied. 'I'm not in town often myself. Live in Detroit, get out here or the East Coast once in a while. Most of the boys who come in here are sailors. They come in on freighters, there's nothing to do in this town. Not much to do in this town, and, you know, blood calls to blood. So we provide a little home atmosphere for them. Look, here come a couple of the boys now.'

He stopped speaking as a small group of men in sailors' garb tramped down the stairs from Clay Street and into the room. One of them called a greeting to Spanknoebel, then they bellied up to the bar and ordered.

'Tell you what,' Spanknoebel resumed. 'You sure you can vouch for Smitty here, Martin?'

Larrabee reassured him.

'Okay, then, here's what we'll do. Smitty, you have the litterchure I gave you. You want to see what our boys do on a dull night in Frisco, I'll ask 'em if they'll take you along with 'em for a while. A little outing. You're responsible for Smitty, though, Larrabee, you see? He makes any false moves, you'll answer to the Freunde.'

Smith looked back and forth at the others. What was Larrabee doing in this place? And what was Smith doing here with him? Visiting a social club? A dingy cellar speakeasy? That would be commonplace enough. But this big out-of-town character was no mere bootlegger. And whatever was going on between Spanknoebel and Larrabee, the *Call* man was dragging Clark into it – like it or not – right up to his ears!

Spanknoebel called to the men at the bar, and a few of them came over to the table where they stood awaiting instructions. 'Grab some chairs,' Spanknoebel ordered.

'Now, I want you boys to meet a couple of friends of

mine. You've probably seen Larrabee around. Oh – you boys all know English, hah?'

The sailors nodded and mumbled assent.

'Okay. You got a car? Fine. You know what you're going to do. Martin is a good friend of mine, and Smitty, he says, is an all-right guy. So you boys take 'em along with you. Don't get into any trouble and don't let Martin or Smitty get into any trouble. I'll see you back here later. Have a good time for yourselves, you deserve it.'

They climbed the stairs, Smith and Larrabee and the sailors. One of the sailors had the keys to a large Chandler sedan that stood nearby on Sansome. Smith and Larrabee clambered into the back seat with one of the sailors, while the other three entered the front. There was a brief conversation among the sailors, entirely in German.

Speaking softly, Smith asked Larrabee if he knew where they were headed. Larrabee admitted he didn't know.

'I didn't realize you were on such good terms with that Spanknocbel fellow,' Smith muttered. 'I didn't know you were so chummy with the German club at all.'

'Old friends,' Larrabee said. 'Lot of Germans in my own family. Blood calls to blood, like Heinz says. Just keep low, keep your eyes open, Clark. I doubt that you'll be able to do anything with this for the *Journal*. I keep it strictly out of the *Call*, too. But you'll learn something about what needs to be done in this country, Smith. And in the world, for that matter!'

The driver maneuvered the Chandler around the Embarcadero and the Marina, out to the Richmond district. He parked in a dark avenue near Funston and California Street, and the six men climbed out of the sedan.

Smith watched as the sailors made their way to the rear of the automobile. Their leader opened the trunk and passed around lengths of two-by-fours. He pulled a sack open and the men reached in, drew their hands back with rocks in them.

Larrabee lit a cigarette and passed one to Smith.

The leader of the sailors issued a few commands in low tones, and the four dark-clothed men started walking. Smith and Larrabee hung back, keeping in easy sight of the others.

They rounded the corner, and Smith saw that there was a synagogue in the next block. There were lights behind its windows. One of the sailors walked to the door and pounded on it with a heavy rock until the door opened and a face peered out.

Smith could barely see the figure within. It appeared to be that of a man on the far side of middle age. He wore a business suit with some sort of fringed shawl and a black felt hat.

The sailor spoke to him in German.

The man seemed to wince at what the sailor had said. He responded tersely, also in German.

The sailor began to shout and the man shoved the door as if to slam it in the intruder's face, but the sailor thrust his heavy shoulder in the way and forced the door open. The other sailors followed him as he pushed into the building.

Clark Smith started forward, but Larrabee held him back. 'Stay out, Clark! You don't want any part of this. You stay out here and just watch!'

Larrabee walked up the cement pathway to the front door of the synagogue and stood with Smith, watching.

Clark could see into the vestibule of the synagogue. The sailors had seized the elderly man and knocked him to the floor. Two of them were kicking him while the others had disappeared into an inner sanctuary of some sort. Clark could hear thumps and voices, the two deep voices of the sailors and a number of higher ones, screaming or pleading or shrieking. Clark started to pull away from Larrabee to run through the vestibule to the back room, but Larrabee held him firmly and growled. 'Don't try it, Smith! There's no way you can stop this! Just keep still!'

A young girl – Clark guessed her age as twelve or thirteen – came running into the vestibule. She stopped, staring in horror at the old man on the floor and the two sailors standing over him. She started to scream, and one of the sailors turned and slapped her heavily across the face. She was knocked backward and struck the wall with a thump.

Another child appeared in the doorway, but before she could emerge into the vestibule Clark saw her seized by a dark-clad arm and pulled back.

He slipped away from Larrabee's grasp and ran into the synagogue. On the floor the old man had stopped writhing and the two sailors standing over him were exchanging comments in German. Clark darted through the inner doorway into the back room.

He saw the second pair of sailors terrorizing a group of young girls. At the moment they were holding one dark-haired child between them. Her clothing was torn, and one of the sailors was fondling her roughly while she struggled and tried vainly to turn away from him. The other sailor laughed. When he saw Clark enter the room he asked him something in German.

Clark shouted, 'Stop it, you animals! What are you doing?'

One of the sailors released his grip on the girl and faced Clark, again muttered something in German.

'Stop it! You're hoodlums, criminals! Get out of here!' He grabbed the second sailor and tried to pull him away from the girl. He could hear the first sailor shouting, out of a corner of one eye saw him move to pick up the two-by-four he'd tossed aside.

The sailor raised the club. Clark let go of the other

man's arm and turned to face the one with the club. He was halfway around and saw the heavy wooden bludgeon descending toward him. In a strange way he thought that he heard its impact along his hairline and saw a flaring display of lights, but he felt no pain as he started to fall.

16
Providence

At first delighted at the opulence of the Pierce automobile, Howard Lovecraft settled into the cushioned rear seat with a sigh and a kind thought for the Providence Police Department. The shiny black coachwork, the gleaming metal trim, the carpeted floor and plush appointments, the softly purring engine of the Pierce, all marked it as a suitable descendent of Grandfather Phillips's handsome carriage. Theo Weiss's Rickenbacker with its sleek lines and sensational performance might be the twentieth-century analogue of a low-slung phaeton, but the Pierce was a more appropriate vehicle for the gentleman of middle years and comfortable means.

The driver, although fitted neither in police uniform nor in chauffeur's livery, was well-groomed and respectful. He appeared, strangely, more of a Mediterranean than a Celtic type.

Two plainclothes officers climbed into the passenger compartment of the Pierce and sat on either side of Lovecraft. The officer to his right said, 'We have to blindfold you, Mr Lovecraft. I hope you won't mind.'

Lovecraft was jolted from his reverie of Grandfather Phillips and the coach and the house on Angell Street. 'Blindfold? What?' He could hardly believe his ears.

'Yes, sir. Orders.'

'But why? Everybody knows where Elbow Street is. Don't tell me that the police have moved their headquarters to some secret hideaway.'

The officer didn't smile. 'We have an appointment. Don't worry, Mr Lovecraft. You're safe, and we'll return you to your home afterward.' As the plainclothesman leaned toward him, blindfold in hand, Lovecraft took note of a slight odor about the man, a mixture of wine and garlic – and of the man's massive dimensions.

Lovecraft fumed but submitted. But as soon as the blindfold was adjusted over his eyes and the automobile pulled smoothly away from the curb at Barnes Street and headed down the slope of College Hill, a transformation overtook him. He was no longer Howard Phillips Lovecraft, the gentleman of Providence-Plantations, but C. Auguste Dupin, the scourge of the Paris demimonde and scornful superior of the official police.

Like Poe's detective he substituted his ears and the sensibilities of his hands and feet for his eyes. Every turn, every pitch up or down a slope, he recorded mentally. He knew when the Pierce crossed over the Providence River, when it passed through the downtown section of the city near the railroad depot . . .

They were certainly not going to Elbow Street!

And then, rising again, headed in what must be a westerly direction, almost certainly up the verge of Federal Hill! Fortunately the three men in the car with Lovecraft did not insist on jabbering as they rode, so he was able to concentrate on the sounds and sensations of the journey. He nodded to himself as the automobile drew once more to a halt, feeling almost smug at his certainty of the neighborhood if not the precise street to which he had been brought.

He felt a shifting of pressures as the man to his right made a movement. He heard the door being opened and felt chill air enter the car. Then he was taken by the elbow and guided from the Pierce and along a short path. He could feel the hard but roughly textured sidewalk give way to an equally unyielding but smoother texture; this, he inferred, was likely a path of flagstones laid onto common earth, leading from sidewalk to the front door of a private home.

He was halted by a pressure on his elbow, heard the
muffled sound of a doorbell ringing inside a building,
then was guided up onto a low stoop of some sort, across
a raised threshold and into a thickly carpeted room. C.
Auguste Dupin was at his most formidable tonight!

His blindfold was removed, and he found himself
standing in the center of a comfortably furnished parlor
filled with well-made but somewhat worn fittings. A short,
swarthy-complexioned man with a thick, dark moustache
was facing him.

Veireck reached the other's desk in a single quick
'You have the advantage of me, sir,' Lovecraft-Dupin
replied, 'as I seldom have occasion to visit residences on
  Lüdecke raised one blond eyebrow toward Viereck.
sir?'

Even through the man's olive skin, Lovecraft could see
him pale with anger. He clutched the back of the sofa for
an instant, made a negating gesture with his free hand.
Lovecraft assumed this was a signal to the 'detectives'
from the automobile, who must thus be still behind him
in the room.

you wish. All have the same story. About the *S-4*.' He
He snapped a gesture toward a far corner of the room.
'And here is your friend Mr Pagnanelli.'

Now Lovecraft spun halfway to the right and saw
his acquaintance from Viereck's social gathering, the
immigrant publisher.

when the *S-4* tried to surface and the *Paulding* was just – '
Lovecraft, got answers that were obviously negative and
obviously delivered with an uneasiness bordering on fear.
Then Morelli spoke once more to Lovecraft. 'How do
you know me? My men say you was blindfolded and they
told you nothing. Was you warned by the cops?'

Lovecraft-Dupin shook his head, relishing the moment.
'A telephonic communication instructed my aunts that a
car was on its way. I assure you that your henchmen have

obeyed their instructions, Signor Morelli. Your identity and the location of this house I determined by a simple process of ratiocination.'

'Sit down.' Despite the Italian's diminutive stature and foreign accent, Lovecraft obeyed. George Pagnanelli crossed the room and drew up an easy chair. Morelli seated himself on the sofa opposite Lovecraft.

'Now, Lovecraft,' Morelli said, 'Mr Pagnanelli here tells me that you are a good American and an intelligent man.'

Lovecraft felt himself swelling at the words. Morelli was clearly a complex individual – able in cold blood to commit murder, yet perceptive of higher qualities in another. Starrett's Caponi must be not unlike this fellow.

'He also tells me that you got yourself involved with some very bad men,' Morelli continued. 'This Sylvester Viereck, he sold out America one time and he would do it again. These Klan men who hate Catholics and immigrants. Wasn't their parents immigrants? Are they Indians? These Irish priests. And the Blackshirts!' A sneer curled his lip at the last.

'Signor Mussolini is working to restore Italy's discipline and her honor. Would you not let him do it?' Lovecraft challenged.

'He wants to rule all Italians,' Morelli said. 'He don't care that people came to America to be Americans. He thinks, all Italians is his army. He's a bad man, Mr Lovecraft!'

Lovecraft nodded, acknowledging the Italian's statement. He addressed himself to Pagnanelli. 'What is going on here? I believed that you were an ally of Mr Viereck's plan. I find your presence in Signor Morelli's household surprising.'

'Howard,' Pagnanelli said. 'Is that okay, I'll call you Howard? I hope we can trust you. If we can't, you could blow us all right out of the water, and all we could do to stop you would be . . . well, not very nice.' He nodded toward Morelli and toward the silent men standing behind Lovecraft's chair.

Lovecraft's head was whirling. 'I don't follow. Whose side are you on?' He raised his hands to his temples. 'For that matter, who are the *we* to whom you refer?' He looked from Pagnanelli to Morelli.

'The *we* is this country. A government agency that is working to counter a big threat that's coming both from inside our borders and from Europe. We need Mr Morelli's help. And we need yours.'

Pagnanelli continued with a question. 'Howard, what do you think you've been involved in for the past year? What do you think that Viereck and Curran and Dr Evans and that slippery Russian Vonsiatsky are up to? And what do you think their foreign friends, Count di Revel and Dr Kiep and Herr Lüdecke are working for? Do you think they're a bunch of lunatics who like to dress up in bizarre costumes and play at revolution? Those men are serious. They represent different factions and they don't get on all the time – that's our biggest advantage against them.

'But if they have their way, there will be a dictatorship in this country. Or another great war. Maybe both. You would not think their world was a utopia.'

'And you – Pagnanelli, Signor Morelli – what are *you* up to?' Lovecraft asked.

Before Pagnanelli could speak, Morelli stopped him. 'You understand, Mr Lovecraft, the more you learn the more harm you could do. If you choose to harm.'

Lovecraft's head rang. C. Auguste Dupin sped away, a wisp of imagination, back to his long-dead creator. It was difficult for Howard Lovecraft to realize that he wasn't engaged in some fantastic game of make-believe, a child's fantasy of spies and counterspies or an authors' session in which plots were tried out by one writer while others listened and picked holes in their logic, suggesting twists of event or of character.

'Could I have – '

'A glass of wine?' Morelli asked.

'A cup of coffee.'

The Italian made a sign to one of the silent men near the doorway. The tall man crossed the room and disappeared through an open arch.

Pagnanelli leaned forward in his easy chair. He gave Lovecraft a look that seemed uncannily to say, *I know what you're thinking. This is no game. This is no mental exercise.*

A small procession entered the room through the archway where Morelli's henchman had disappeared. First came a tall young woman carrying a tray. Her hair was a glossy black, shingled in the latest style. Her clothing also was the latest, a soft blouse cut loosely of pastel shantung and a flapper skirt. Her features resembled Morelli's, modified to a feminine softness of mouth and chin. Her skin was a Mediterranean olive and her eyes were huge and black and liquid. Behind her came the dark-suited henchman, who returned silently to his post near the doorway. Last of all a small gray-and-black striped cat pranced, its ears pricked and face filled with curiosity, its tail held high.

The young woman placed the tray on a low table before the sofa. It held a silver coffeepot from whose spout steam rose slowly, and cups and cream and sugar.

Howard Lovecraft rose silently to his feet.

With a minimum of conversation the young woman poured coffee for Lovecraft, Pagnanelli, and Morelli, then retired. The little cat followed her.

'My daughter,' Morelli said proudly. 'She's a real American girl. She says she don't even speak no Italian, hah! I know she does, but she's so American she don't want to admit it. What was you saying, Mr Lovecraft?'

Lovecraft sank slowly into his seat. 'I beg your pardon, sir.' All the heat of a moment ago had fled. Miss Morelli was a cultured woman, he realized. And lovely. He let his eyes rove the parlor around him. No, this was not the oily yellow verminous subhumanity that had so repelled him in his New York years. These people might yet manage to absorb the culture and refinement of their betters. How much of civilization was in the genes, how much might be absorbed through proper education and the influence of a superior congeries of precept and example?

George Pagnanelli sipped at a cup of coffee, then put it down on the table with a rattle. 'Howard, we know that you were lured into this thing by Viereck. That's the funny part. I've been trying to get close to him for three years now by joining every hate group I could find, publishing my own rag, swilling with all of these freaks and monsters like Dilling and that phony countess from the locomotive factory, and all it's got me is a glass of beer at Stahrenberg's hole once a month when I go to pay him.' He blew out his breath as if expelling an unpleasant miasma from his mouth.

'But Viereck dances around you,' Pagnanelli pointed a dark finger at Lovecraft, 'like you were the Prince of Wales!'

'Blood,' Lovecraft said softly.

'Eh?'

'My real work,' Lovecraft said. 'My real work is the creation of tales designed to play upon the oldest and strongest emotion of mankind, which is fear. Horror stories, if you will. I have even achieved a certain modest success in this endeavor. You will recall, Pagnanelli, a passing reference to my works which I made when you kindly invited me to your home in New York.'

The Armenian nodded.

'Sylvester Viereck has worked in the same realm,'

Lovecraft said. 'He produced a rather good novel called *The House of the Vampire* in which the revenant sucked not his victims' blood, but their talents, for the furtherance of his own unholy career. And if all that you say is true, he is attempting to do the same thing to me!

'He wants me to write a book promoting his movement. A sort of American *Mein Kampf*.'

'You've read that?' Pagnanelli demanded. 'You've gone through that manuscript he gave you? I have, and it's a corker!'

Lovecraft nodded confirmation. 'I must admit that I was somewhat carried away by Herr Hitler's obvious passion, at first. By his passion and by certain similarities between his own experiences and beliefs, and mine. But as my friend Hardeen and my own wife have pointed out, the application of Hitler's system might lead to mass murder.'

'I'm glad you realize that. His kind of hate-mongering and hysteria can drum up a mob at any time. I've seen what that kind of blood-lusting, pillaging mind can do.'

'The noble savagery of the blond Nordic berserker – ' Lovecraft began.

'Is a myth,' Pagnanelli broke in. 'No, it isn't even a myth. It's a deliberate lie. It's an excuse for gory-handed killers to smash and torture and rape and rob. I've seen it. The Greeks and the Turks and the Russians have all done it to my people for centuries. And when they've finished – '

'When they've finished,' Lovecraft supplied, 'perhaps at a terrible cost, one must concede, yes, but they may then build an utopian regime of refinement and elevation.'

'Never! Mr Morelli, you've seen where that leads.'

The Italian's face showed its pain. 'You think Mussolini is a good man, Mr Lovecraft?'

'He is striving to restore the glories of Rome.'

'He's a killer!'

'But if only people would help him to build, not obstruct his efforts!'

'No, Mr Lovecraft. I will tell you something.' The compact, dark-suited Morelli leaned across the coffee table. 'You think you understand. But you don't understand. Killers like Mussolini don't kill because people fight them. They kill because they love to kill. They love to see blood, they love to see corpses, they love to destroy human beings. They love to kill because it makes them feel powerful. Every killer is weak and scared, and when he kills he gets a moment of relief from that. When he kills, he is like God! You know that Satan lures our souls to Hell because every time a man falls he can forget for one second that God threw him out of Heaven! That's what a killer is. He knows himself and he hates what he is, but when he takes a life he can forget for a minute what he is. That's Signor Mussolini and Herr Hitler, and your patron Viereck is luring your soul to fall like theirs.'

Lovecraft held his long chin in one hand. He did not look directly at the Italian. But he forced himself to speak. 'What is your business, Signor Morelli? Is it peaceful and law-abiding? Does the name Constantine Madeiros mean nothing to you, sir?'

There was a stir from behind Lovecraft. Morelli looked sharply toward the door of the house, and there was silence.

Morelli spoke in a voice so low that Lovecraft could barely make out his words. 'Mr Lovecraft,' Morelli almost whispered. 'Yes, I killed Constantino. I. Not with my hands.' He held them before his face, studied them as if to see if they were clean or were dripping red. 'Not with these hands. But I killed him.

'And I have killed others.' He threw a look over his shoulder, toward the kitchen. 'She doesn't know it, so you keep your voice quiet, Mr Lovecraft.' He put one hand to his cheek, then lowered it again. 'She knows,' he whispered bitterly, 'but she don't let on that she does. You think she hates me, my American girl?'

Lovecraft did not speak.

'I kill. And every time I kill, my soul finds Hell. Yes, I feel for a minute like God, but like an evil God, like Satan. And I know he got me. I know I'll burn for all eternity in Hell with Satan. But maybe God will let me off a little. Maybe he'll let me off a little bit.

'Mr Lovecraft, you got to give us your help. I kill a man and a man. I know I'm going to roast forever. I know that. But this Hitler, this Viereck, they don't want to kill no man. They want to kill the world. They want to kill the soul of the world, Mr Lovecraft.'

Morelli covered his face with his hands.

Lovecraft was not certain, but he thought he heard a small sound in the archway that led to the kitchen. When he looked, there was no one there. He sped a glance toward George Pagnanelli but received no aid from him. 'Signor Morelli,' Lovecraft said. He felt an impulse to reach forward and place his hand on the Italian's, but instead folded his hands upon his lap. 'Signor Morelli,' he repeated.

17
Manhattan

In the quiet hours before dawn broke over the neat homes of Brooklyn Heights and a weak autumnal sun would set the towers of Manhattan agleam in the clean, quiet air, Theo Weiss's sleek Rickenbacker purred smoothly across the Gothic architecture of the Brooklyn Bridge and descended into the dank canyons of the Lower East Side. Weiss, handling the polished mahogany wheel, managed his customary elegance of dress even at this early hour. Sonia Lovecraft, beside him, wore a heavy fall dress and woolen coat. A thick forest-green car rug was spread over her lap, and she held a clumsy vacuum-jug of coffee to keep it from tipping.

Early tugs hooted on the river; fish and produce vendors made their way through the dark streets, bringing fresh goods to market. Late revellers might still be making their ways home by taxi or subway, but they kept to the posh neighborhoods farther uptown.

As the Rickenbacker Sport picked its way toward Coenties Slip by the light of its own streamlined headlamps, Sonia plucked nervously at the dense, dark fringe of the lap rug. She turned to face Hardeen and raised one hand uncertainly toward his shoulder as she spoke to him.

'I understand why you want to make this test, Theo. I really do. But I don't see why it has to be this early in the morning. It's so chilly out, and the river must be even worse. There was a photo in the *Graphic* of regular icebergs coming down the Hudson. The paper says a few more days of this and the river will freeze all the way to Hoboken.'

Hardeen tipped his head sideways to brush his cheek against Sonia's hand. 'I'll be in full diving gear. It isn't as if this were an all-out escape stunt. We'll just be testing Baird's machine. Please don't worry.'

'I thought you liked me to worry about you.' Sonia's voice was warm despite the frigid morning air.

Theo laughed. 'I do. I do. But you see, this will be perfectly safe, Sonia. My crew will be standing by, I know this part of the river anyhow. There's nothing to worry about.'

'But it must be pitch-black down there!'

'Of course! But not just because of the hour. It's pitch-black down there at any time. The brightest noon doesn't penetrate all that way down, and even if it did, the riverbed is so muddy that a diver would stir up a black cloud of his own. What point would there be in using the noctovisor if the water were clear and lighted?'

'But, Dash – '

He turned for a moment to look into her face, then shifted his attention back to the narrow street.

'Dash, why go down there at four in the morning if it would be just as dark – I mean, just as good for your test – in the middle of the day? Then at least your helpers could see better what they're doing up on the pier. And it might be a little warmer.'

Hardeen shook his head. 'You know, Ehrich used to be such a bug on publicity. Circusing, he used to call it.'

He pulled the sleek car to the edge of the pavement and switched off its purring engine and its headlights. Then he dropped his hands from the polished steering wheel and turned toward Sonia. He took her hands into his own and rubbed them to restore some warmth.

She said, 'But this is the very opposite of circusing, Dash. Sneaking down here at four o'clock in the morning when there isn't a soul about. Slipping into the East River like some eel sliding out to sea.'

'There *will* be a few souls about. My crew, of course.'
He peered through the windshield and out onto the pier.
'Look,' he pointed.

Sonia saw a group of figures moving murkily around.
She said, 'Is everyone here?'

Hardeen nodded. 'Let's get started.' He released her
hands, then took her by the shoulders and drew her
toward him. She held back for the barest moment, then
responded. She felt his cheek, smooth-shaven even for
this early-morning test, against her own. She felt his lips
against the side of her neck. Then he released her and
they climbed from the sedan and walked onto the pier.

A point of fiery orange-red separated itself from the
general blur of figures as Hardeen and Sonia approached
the end of the pier. In another few steps it became visible
as the glowing bowl of a pipe.

The briar belonged to a gray-haired man in dark
clothing. He advanced and shook hands with Hardeen.

'Sonia.' The magician took her arm. 'My friend Commander Jones, Mrs Lovecraft.' The officer removed his
pipe from his mouth and shook Sonia's hand.

Hardeen excused himself and walked to the end of the
pier, checked a wooden ladder fixed there with heavy
bolts, then returned to the others. With two assistants he
entered a canvas lean-to, emerged a few minutes later
wearing a bulky diving suit and weighted boots.

Sonia, watching Hardeen's every move, ran to his side.
She kissed him once on the cheek.

The magician lumbered heavily to the rude ladder, his
air hose and lifeline stretching behind him. At the head
of the ladder he turned and climbed slowly toward the
water.

He leaned back and tilted his head – and helmet – as
far as he could. He was able to see the edge of the pier
above him. His helpers stood at the brink, the portable

noctovisor ready to lower on its own power cable and lifeline.

Hardeen braced his elbow against the ladder, held up his hand, and waited for his helpers to lower the noctovisor. He grasped it in both hands, hoisted it before his face and clicked its switches carefully, examining the miniature viewing orthiconoscope that the Scots inventor had fixed to the camera gear. As if it were a tiny motion-picture screen hardly larger than a matchbox, he could see a faint image of the wooden underpilings he had noticed beneath the pier.

He balanced the noctovisor on his shoulder, held it steadily with one hand, and – using the other hand to keep his balance – made his way to the bottom of the ladder. Then he pushed himself away from the pier.

He slid backward and feet first into the black river. He sank quickly, accelerating downward with the weight of his heavy boots and the bulky noctovisor resting on his shoulder.

He turned around and walked carefully away from the pier as soon as he had his footing on the riverbed. He knew the length of the cables, felt the slight drag backward and upward as his crew paid out the lines.

He reached around to the front of the noctovisor and groped for the lens housing. The orthiconoscope screen dimmed slightly, and a vague shadow appeared at its center.

On the rectangular orthiconoscope the fuzzy shape he had seen resolved itself into a clear picture of his left hand, smaller than a silver dollar and lacking in color but perfectly defined. Hardeen let go a cry of exultation that echoed eerily inside his copper helmet.

With confidence he walked as far out onto the riverbed as his cables permitted. The noctovisor revealed to him every hole, every rock, every bit of jetsam that lay on the bottom. He circled back and, at the foot of the pilings that supported Coenties Pier, halted and gave the tugs on his lifeline that signaled his helpers to raise him and the noctovisor from the river.

An hour later he drove off in his Rickenbacker, Sonia Lovecraft again at his side. Hardeen's assistants were carefully stowing the diving gear and noctovisor for their removal from Coenties Pier.

'I'm famished after that,' Hardeen said to Sonia. 'I hope you can face an early breakfast.'

'I'd love it. I think some of Howard's odd notions of timing have rubbed off on me. Why don't we try Chinatown?'

'Wonderful! An inspiration!'

He headed the Rickenbacker through the shimmering gray dawn and pulled to the curb before an all-night eatery on Pell Street. Shortly, with a cup of piping-hot perfumed tea in his hand, Hardeen thanked Sonia for accompanying him to the pier for his early-morning experiment.

The waiter arrived with a huge bowl of steaming wonton soup, and Hardeen, acting as *pater familias de facto,* ladled out two servings.

Sonia accepted her cup, asked, 'Were you satisfied with your dive this morning, Theo? I must confess, I don't quite understand what your purpose was. You weren't just studying the river for an escape stunt, were you?'

'Hardly,' the magician laughed. He scooped up a slippery dumpling on a painted porcelain spoon and devoured it carefully. 'No, I was really testing out the noctovisor. That television device that John Baird invented over in Scotland. Had a devil of a time getting a working model out of him, but the man finally came through. The machine worked beautifully.'

'But what is it *for*?' Sonia asked.

'Baird's idea,' Hardeen replied. 'Ah.' He swallowed half a cup of tea. 'Baird's idea, I think, is to use his device somewhat as a motion-picture camera is used. But *my* idea is to use it for undersea exploration. That's why I got him to hook up a little orthiconoscope right on the back of the 'visor. It was nearly perfect.

'I have a few more modifications in mind. I don't think I'll need to go back to Mr Baird to have them made, though. Commander Jones's fellows are pretty bright. I think they can handle it for me. One thing . . .'

He pulled a golden mechanical pencil and notepad from inside his jacket. Still talking, he began to sketch. 'I found it pretty clumsy, trying to balance that thing on my shoulder. We can bring that under control. Build a little bracket for the 'visor, put in a gimbal-joint so I can swing it around and up and down.

'And I don't like all those cables. It's a nuisance, trailing them around wherever I go.'

Hardeen stared at his own diagram, lost in thought.

While Weiss sketched and muttered, the waiter removed the soup bowls and brought their Cantonese dishes. Sonia sampled a bit of lobster, then lowered her chopsticks. 'Is this all for your escape shows, Theo? I somehow felt – '

He looked up and grinned at her, carefully replaced his pencil and notepad in his jacket and began to fill their plates with rice and other foods.

' – oh,' Sonia resumed, 'is there something more at stake here than circusing?'

Hardeen considered seriously while he occupied himself with the food before him. Finally he looked around the restaurant, saw no one paying any attention to them, and said, 'Well, yes there is.' He lifted a morsel with his chopsticks and chewed.

When Weiss volunteered no further information, Sonia said, 'That Commander Jones has something to do with it. Theo, you don't have to tell me, of course. But if you would . . . I really would like to know. I do care about you, and . . .'

He reached across the table and patted her hand. 'Yes, naturally you'd want to know.' He took a sip of tea and gathered his breath.

'Sonia, you know this funny crowd that your husband's been mixing with lately.'

'Yes.' She lowered her eyes, then raised them again to meet Hardeen's. 'Certainly I know them – or know about them. Not that Howard's ever introduced me to any of them.'

Hardeen laughed grimly. 'What would you make of an opportunity to meet an Imperial Wizard, a couple of real if slightly shabby counts, and the bastard cousin of Kaiser Bill, all at one time?'

Now it was Sonia's turn to manage an uncertain smile. 'I'm afraid it's Howard's aristocratic yearnings getting the better of him. Well, who can blame him? If ten million American girls can fall into a nervous swoon at the thought of the Prince of Wales, I suppose Howard is entitled to go slightly ga-ga at the thought of a room full of fancy titles. You know he's always had a weakness for royalty and all its trappings.'

'But that's all show,' Theo said. 'What we're concerned over is the substance behind it. What those odd ones are really up to. Sonia, you saw conditions in Russia in the old days. You saw Europe as a child, and you know what America really means. Isn't it odd that people who've had all of this country's blessings like Howard, appreciate them the least because they don't know what other countries are really like!'

Sonia shook her head. 'Don't get so philosophical on me, Theo. If you're going to tell me what you're up to. And if you wouldn't mind telling me who the *we* is who are so concerned.'

Weiss twiddled with his food to delay his answer briefly. 'All right. You met Commander Jones back at Coenties Pier.'

'Oh, yes. What does he command? He wasn't in uniform.'

'Oh, he's Navy. Academy graduate, served in the war, had duty fighting U-boats, spent a while at Scapa Flow trying to salvage the German fleet.'

'You aren't going to tell me that he's interested in circusing your escape act.'

'No, he's interested in John Baird's machine. And he and I are part of the *we* I was talking about. Sonia, I can't tell you everything that's going on. Among other reasons I don't *know* everything that's going on. We're trying to find out, and if we can get your husband to help us instead of playing Sylvester Viereck's game, we might do it.

'Howard was a big help when we were up at Marblehead together. You remember he got that Burgess fellow to let us use his airplane. I'd really like to know what those Germans are doing with their ship *Der Traum* and their work near the harbor. So would Commander Jones, I can assure you!'

'Are you a spy?' Sonia asked incredulously.

'What?'

'You heard me, Theo.'

He grunted. 'Sure I did. I don't know what you think a spy *is*, Sonia.'

'Well, you travel all over the world and you spend a lot of time walking around the bottom of harbors in other countries. Then you come home and tell Commander Jones everything you've seen. Is that right?'

'Sonia, Sylvester Viereck has ties to the National Socialists in Germany. Thaon di Revel is in regular communication with Oswald Moseley in England and Benito

Mussolini in Rome. You know about Count Vonsiatsky. And as for our own homegrown demagogues . . .'

'You are a spy,' she said softly.

He frowned and reached for a red-shelled claw.

18
Providence

'What concerns us,' Pagnanelli said earnestly, 'is a sort of unholy alliance of foreigners and Americans. Some of 'em, for sure, are just clowns. I don't think your Count Vonsiatsky even takes himself seriously. He gets to live high on the hog. If he couldn't put his snout in the trough like he does, the poor simp'd have to find an honest job! And his wife's rolling in greenbacks anyhow, so she can afford to bankroll his funny game and she gets to put on airs and playact at being a countess.'

Howard Lovecraft slumped comfortably down in his high-backed armchair. Here at home he felt more at ease and in control of the situation than he had in Morelli's house on Federal Hill. The Italian had sent Lovecraft and Pagnanelli off in the Pierce at the end of their meeting; the two men had had more matters to discuss, and Lovecraft had invited Pagnanelli to visit him at Barnes Street.

'You contradict yourself,' Lovecraft accused. 'You sound the tocsin one moment, and the next, you discount your own cries of alarm.'

Pagnanelli clamped his teeth together, bounded from his own seat, and assumed an oddly personal posture, half-squatting opposite Lovecraft's chair and pointing his finger at the taller man. '*Some* of these people are harmless loonies. But others aren't. The Klan – '

'I'm afraid that the modern Klan does not live up to the principles of its forerunner,' Lovecraft put in. 'But I have the impression that Dr Evans is engaged mainly in the sale of membership cards and satin regalia for the purpose of filling his personal coffers. Hardly an admirable pursuit, but surely not a menace to the health and survival of the commonweal.'

'That's one side of the Klan, all right.' Pagnanelli ruminated for a moment. 'What's your source for that info?'

'A friend.'

'Huh! I don't suppose your friend knows how many niggers the Klan has lynched. Or how many mayors and governors and congressmen it has in its satin pockets. We don't much care if Doc Evans wants to sit there on Peachtree Street and take the suckers for fancy bedsheets. But he goes out killing people; you must have heard about the Fox lynching in Mississippi.'

'Of course. The niggers had murdered a white man. They deserved to die.'

'They were never tried, Lovecraft. They were *accused* of shooting Nichols! The Klan seized them from the sheriff and burned them alive!'

'And how much better is your patron Mr Morelli?'

Pagnanelli pushed himself back up and landed with a thump in his chair. 'Now you're the one reversing himself. Did you say you didn't give a hoot if mobsters knock off other mobsters?'

'I did indeed! But I did not suggest that we make league with them.'

'Ah. Fair enough. Okay. We ain't too comfortable with that angle ourselves. But you know about war and politics making strange bedfellows.'

Lovecraft turned a sour face.

'And as for some of those other characters, Lovecraft, you didn't give me a chance to get to them. We're really pretty upset over this Mussolini guy.'

'Italian politics are of no interest to me, Pagnanelli. Nor, I should hope, would they be of interest to the United States. Let the dagoes stew in their own juice.

Besides, Il Duce has restored discipline to a decadent and disordered nation. If his methods have been hard, his problems have been equally so – and his results have been most admirable.'

'But don't you see, don't you see?' Pagnanelli squeezed his eyes shut, then opened them again. 'Mussolini has followers *here*. You've met Count di Revel.'

'A cultured gentleman.'

'And Il Duce's satrap over every Italian enclave in the US. That's why we're cultivating Morelli and his ilk. Do you think we enjoy dealing with the likes of that?'

'He is a killer.'

'I know he's a killer. And if he can fight off Mussolini the law will look the other way, as long as he keeps his killing inside the underworld. It's a dirty business, Lovecraft, we know that.

'And if Mussolini's boys are trouble for us, we're even more worried about their pals. If they can really hammer out a front with Coughlin and Curran and that mob, and with Viereck and Heinz Spanknoebel and that Freunde bunch, and if the National Socialists take over when President Hindenburg croaks . . .'

'We are going around and around.' Lovecraft flushed slightly with embarrassment. He was about to commit an act of discourtesy. 'Will you excuse me for a few minutes,' he said, 'while I read this letter? It is from Clark Ashton Smith – I suppose the name will be unfamiliar to you, but he is one of the leading poets and fantastic dreamers of the day.'

'I'll go use the can,' Pagnanelli muttered.

He returned to find Howard Lovecraft pale and shaken. The taller man stood, his face more gray than white, the unfolded letter in his hands. He trembled visibly, the sheet of paper making an audible rattling sound. Lovecraft was staring at the page as if unable to believe what he saw on it; as Pagnanelli entered the room, Lovecraft raised his eyes to those of his guest.

'You are right, Mr Pagnanelli,' Lovecraft said.

The Armenian stood facing him, uncertain how to respond.

Lovecraft held the letter at arm's length, toward Pagnanelli. 'Not merely Smith,' Lovecraft said. 'That would suffice, but the old man. And children. A room full of children!' His eyes glistened as if with tears.

'A classroom of children, come to study Judaism,' Lovecraft said. 'Here, here.' He shook the letter at Pagnanelli until the smaller man took it from him.

With a look, Pagnanelli asked if he should read the letter, and with a gesture, Lovecraft told him that he should. Pagnanelli slumped into a chair, took note of the *Auburn Journal* letterhead, pored over the tightly packed paragraphs of typewriting. When he finished reading he folded the letter carefully and handed it back to Lovecraft, who slid it into its envelope and laid it carefully beside his own Remington typewriter on the old wooden desk.

'Heinz Spanknoebel,' Pagnanelli muttered. 'He's one of Sylvester's close chums, of course. This Martin Larrabee sounds like a passive sympathizer but not an actor. But this Thor Hotel operation, phew!' He held his forehead with one hand. 'Would it be rubbing it in, Lovecraft, to say . . .'

Pagnanelli let his voice trail off.

Howard Lovecraft ground one fist into the palm of his other hand. 'How could they – ? Sailors, ordinary merchant seamen on leave from their duties. How could they do that to those young girls, just children? I was right all along. I was seduced by this smooth Viereck. I know it now, I understand it. Yes, George, I was dazzled by the glitter of titles and the phraseology of Herr Hitler's book.

'And I was tempted.' His voice dropped to a whisper.

'I was taken to the mountaintop and shown the glory of my own name on the spine of a volume.' He raised a fist and spun on one heel, striking a bitter backhanded blow against the spines of a row of books on his own shelf.

'Like the veriest helot, I was tempted and I yielded and I was brought to heel by these vile beasts. I should have known better,' his voice rose to its normal volume, 'I should have learned a lesson when I was beaten and imprisoned by Kurt Lüdecke's men in Marblehead. But I was a crass fool! I let myself be bought off for thirty pieces of silver. I outdid Judas, for he betrayed another while I betrayed myself!'

There was a knock at the study door, and in a moment it opened to show the round face of Howard's aunt Annie. 'Is everything all right, Howard? I don't mean to interrupt you and Mr – ah, your guest. But I heard you sounding so upset, you were almost shouting. Are you all right?'

Lovecraft drew a deep breath, held it, let it hiss slowly between clenched teeth. 'Everything is all right, aunt, thank you. We're almost finished anyway. Mr Pagnanelli will be on his way shortly. Thank you, aunt.'

She stood with her head cocked dubiously.

'Thank you, aunt,' Lovecraft repeated.

She withdrew and clicked the study door shut.

'Now,' Lovecraft said. Pagnanelli was still sitting in his chair. Lovecraft faced him. 'I will assuredly *not* lend my name or my talent to this scheme of Viereck's. The man barely escaped sedition charges during the World War, and he is apparently up to his old tricks again.'

'That he is!' Pagnanelli agreed.

'Then you believe that his purpose is to coordinate the efforts of the Freunde, the Blackshirts, and the others . . . But to what end, Pagnanelli?'

George drew a deep breath. 'Nothing less than the seizure of power in this country, Howard. And the end of the American experiment in freedom and democracy. Do I sound like a Fourth of July orator? I've seen tyranny and brutality in other places, either permitted by governments or actually committed by them. I can see it coming back to Germany. It's in Russia already.

'You may think that America is safe from this, but it isn't.'

Lovecraft shook his head in disbelief. 'I've learned of dreadful acts. I have even experienced some. But you do not seriously believe that our government is to be seized by the likes of George Sylvester Viereck.'

'Dream on, dreamer,' Pagnanelli said.

'Eh?'

Pagnanelli drew his fists in before his body, raised his knees and shoulders so that he seemed to become a ball of energy ready to fly off in any direction. 'Don't think that America is safe forever. Conquest comes from within, these days, more often than from without. And by the quick blow more often than the long struggle. The Russians rid themselves of the Tsar after so many centuries and set up a free nation for themselves, and how long did it last? Five months! The other nations of Europe are walking on tightropes. Italy has already fallen off hers. Germany won't last sixty days once the old President goes . . .'

'But they're across the ocean.'

'The ocean is no barrier. It's a highway.'

Lovecraft sighed. 'I suppose,' he said softly, 'that I had already decided not to assist Sylvester Viereck. I had not spoken on the topic, but I may as well announce my intention. Although it involves the sacrifice, as well, of the prospect of the Jackson Press bringing out a volume of my tales, I could no longer in good conscience lend my name or my talents to Viereck's enterprise.'

'Is that all?'

'What more do you wish?'

Pagnanelli smiled grimly. 'We have to ask for your active help, Howard. Just not writing Viereck's book isn't enough.'

A strange little smile played around the edges of Lovecraft's thin mouth. For one moment he permitted his eyes to exhibit a whimsical attitude. Then he took himself in hand and asked, 'Do I understand correctly, Mr Pagnanelli? Am I being recruited?'

Pagnanelli wiggled the fingers of one hand in the air. 'If you wish to think of it that way. Yes.'

'Well,' Lovecraft rose from his chair. 'I think it would be appropriate for us to take a little stroll and discuss this further.'

Outside, bundled against the chilly Rhode Island night, Lovecraft guided Pagnanelli through the streets and past the buildings where he had spent his childhood. College Hill was more than Lovecraft's home – it was the environment to which he had attuned his whole organism and state of mind. This was his natural habitat, as Brooklyn had never been and so no other locale could ever be.

He stopped beside a half-rotted board fence closing off a weedgrown lot on Benevolent Street, near the main gate of Bryant College. 'Look at this, Pagnanelli.' He bent and pushed on the bottom of a loose board. It swung freely. Too narrow for a man, it would easily have admitted the form of a youngster to the vacant lot.

'One of the great jewel robberies of all time was solved, back during the McKinley regime, by the chief operative of the Providence Detective Agency, who discovered the glittering loot secreted in that lot. You see the tall maple near those boysenberries? I concealed myself in a fork and watched the malefactors burying their ill-gotten goods.'

He dropped the board back into place, and they walked away.

'Howard,' Pagnanelli said, 'we're going to need your help.'

'You are,' Lovecraft echoed noncommittally. 'You call upon oddly selected persons to aid in your schemes. I will admit that I found Signor Morelli a more worthy personage than I had anticipated. Nonetheless, we should make a very oddly yoked team.'

'You don't have to work with Morelli,' Pagnanelli replied. 'I'm asking you to do something for us on your own.'

'And what is that? I have already withdrawn from my participation in Sylvester Viereck's project.'

'That's what I don't want you to do.'

'At the risk of impoliteness, Pagnanelli, I must say that you make no sense. After all your efforts to have me withdraw cooperation from Viereck, you now wish me *not* to do so?'

'That's right,' Pagnanelli said. They passed the corner of Governor Street and continued along the cold sidewalk, their footsteps echoing in the stillness. No windows showed lights, and the streetlamps were few.

'What I'd like you to do,' Pagnanelli continued, 'is to keep up your contact with Viereck. Pal it up with him and the people around him. You're in a perfect position to ask questions without making him suspicious.

'I worked for years to get into that closed circle, and Viereck puts me off at the level of Spanknoebel and Hiram Evans. You just walk in, Howard, and you're chumming with Sylvester himself and Dr Kiep and the other big shots. It just ain't fair. But it's a lucky break for us.'

'But why? Why?' Lovecraft halted under a streetlamp, its yellow light held off his long face by the brim of his gray fedora. He looked down at the smaller Pagnanelli, the latter's face illuminated as he turned it upward. 'You want me to work with Viereck – why?'

'Because we don't know what the bozo is up to! Oh, we know *generally* what that whole crowd are after.' He turned his back to the light as the twin headlamps of an automobile appeared on Benefit Street and swept toward them. The two men resumed walking, putting the pool of light beneath the streetlamp well behind them.

The car moved past. Despite the cold night its top had been lowered and a crowd of young men and women – students from Brown and Pembroke out on a lark, in all likelihood – waved and cheered as the two men were picked up by the roadster's lamps.

'We know their general operation,' Pagnanelli resumed. 'They're after taking power in this country, by setting up secret societies like the Klan, by building their own little armies and enforcement squads like the Blackshirts, by plain and fancy rabble-rousing like Father Curran's . . .'

'Yes, yes,' Lovecraft prompted. 'That is nothing new, is it? You've still to give me a good reason for my continuing to mix with the Viereck circle, Pagnanelli.'

Pagnanelli pursed his lips and exhaled heavily, a pale cloud of breath condensing in the cold atmosphere. 'Is there some overt objective, some specific scheme, that we haven't yet stumbled onto? I can't see all of these odd ones mixing and mingling without some central plan, some definite goal. Even if they don't all know it themselves. Sylvester and Otto and – whoever their real sponsor is, most likely the National Socialist leaders in Europe – are certainly not above playing the rest of their fellows, the Evanses and Vonsiatskys and Dillings and Currans and Spanknoebels – as puppets.

'But if Viereck is the puppet master – is there a higher puppet master pulling *his* strings – perhaps without his knowing it? And what is the script for their puppet show?'

Lovecraft grunted. 'So, now I see what you wish me to do.'

'I suppose you do. You have to play double agent, Howard. You have to continue to fall in with Viereck's schemes, in order to find out their object.'

'And provide you with that information,' Lovecraft added.

Pagnanelli nodded.

A short laugh escaped Lovecraft's lips. 'Well, I had taken you for an uncouth monger of hate literature yourself, Pagnanelli. I suppose we are all playing double and triple games in this eccentrically woven fabric.'

'I suppose we all are,' the smaller man conceded. 'There's still plenty that we don't know, that I want to find out. When Mr Viereck travels to the Continent, for instance, I'd like to know more about his real purposes. He has a perfectly good excuse, of course. He's an interviewer, off to see this or that celebrity, a psychologist in Vienna, a deposed emperor in Doorn, a bunch of bureaucrats and apparatchiks in Moscow, Il Duce himself in Rome.

'He comes back and turns out a series of magazine pieces for *Liberty* and the Hearst supplements. Is that all he's up to?' He barked a short laugh.

'He travels up to Massachusetts and spends a few days at Marblehead with Otto Kiep. Are they just vacationing and talking over mutual friends in the old country? I doubt it.'

Lovecraft halted and raised his hands as if to stop the flow of Pagnanelli's words. 'I should guess that he was visiting his friend Lüdecke in Marblehead.'

Now it was Pagnanelli's turn to show startlement. 'Lüdecke? Is Kurt Lüdecke in Marblehead?'

Lovecraft frowned. 'I don't recall whether he mentioned his given name. A slim man, fair of color. Very Nordic, in fact. And given to dapper, military-looking apparel.'

Pagnanelli all but leapt into the air. 'Damn! Kurt

Lüdecke in Massachusetts. Do you know who Kurt Lüdecke is, Howard? Do you know what he was doing there? Are you certain that he was meeting with Viereck and Kiep?'

'What – why is the man so important to you?' Lovecraft asked. 'I'm not sure that I quite take your meaning. Know who he is? Why, he's a rather cold-natured fellow who made amends altogether unsatisfactorily when a couple of his henchmen attacked me one night, quite without provocation.' Reminiscently, Lovecraft fingered a spot on his forehead where he had received a kick from one of Lüdecke's men.

'I'll tell you who Kurt Lüdecke is,' Pagnanelli said. 'He's Adolf Hitler's right-hand man and roving trouble-shooter with special responsibility for the US. And as far as I know, he isn't supposed to be in this country right now. When did you see him? And what was he up to?'

Lovecraft rubbed his jaw. 'It was quite a while ago. The height of summer, in fact. And he was associated with an international research project, something to do with developing new materials for underwater construction of heavy piers. Very prosaic stuff, I assure you.'

'I wouldn't be so easily assured! And you can definitely tie him to Sylvester Viereck?'

'Well – well,' Lovecraft ruminated briefly. 'It is getting cold Pagnanelli. Suppose we turn back toward Barnes Street.'

'What about Viereck and Lüdecke? We can link them indirectly, through NSDAP headquarters in Europe. Can you link them for us in this country?'

'I was merely studying the architectural details of the building where Herr Lüdecke has an office,' Lovecraft said. 'Two of his men, seamen by their garb, beat and captured me and dragged me before Herr Lüdecke. As soon as he discovered my identity, he became suitably apologetic, I give the man credit for that. But I was not wholly satisfied. Especially when he offered me money in exchange for my withholding official action against him.'

'Yes, sure. Then – ?'

'Why, when the fellow saw that his explanation was insufficient and that his offer of money was an affront to a true gentleman, he appealed to me to consult Sylvester Viereck with regard to his own bona fides.'

'Okay,' Pagnanelli nodded vigorously. 'I just want to make sure of this. It wasn't your idea, right? Lüdecke said, something like, *Call Sylvester if you think I'm fishy?* Was that it? He said to call Viereck, you didn't?'

'But of course. Why should I suggest calling in a third party to a dispute between Lüdecke and myself?'

'No, no reason. I just want to make sure. And you did? You called Viereck?'

'I did.'

'And – what? What did he have to say?'

Lovecraft felt himself growing flush and felt relief that beneath the pale illumination his color would be concealed from Pagnanelli. 'He was at his most ingratiating. Apologized profusely for Lüdecke. Explained that the fellow was accustomed to a more authoritarian society than our own and not really adept at dealing with his social equals. Or betters, I should add.'

'Viereck showed no surprise that Lüdecke was in this country, then? That's what I need to find out.'

'Not the least,' Lovecraft shook his head. 'He clearly knew that Lüdecke was in Marblehead. Even mentioned having visited him there. And Sylvester was most regretful over the whole affair. Assured me that he would take it up with Lüdecke tête-à-tête at his earliest opportunity. I can assure you, Pagnanelli, that I was in no way pleased at the outcome of the incident. But I concluded that the gentlemanly procedure was to accept Lüdecke's apology and dismiss the matter, which I allowed Sylvester Viereck to understand would be my course.'

'Okay, okay.' Pagnanelli reached out one hand as if to take Lovecraft's overcoated forearm, but the taller man drew away. 'Now, please, Howard, this really needs to be followed up. Will you keep up your work with Viereck? You've got to get back to New York. Take up with Viereck and Kiep again. Tell him you're doing the book, whatever. We have to get more information.'

'You must understand,' Lovecraft said, 'New York has become distasteful to me. My home is here – ' He gestured. There was an uncomfortable silence, then he sighed in resignation. 'Very well, then. I shall phone Mrs Lovecraft in the morning and ask her to prepare lodging for me in Brooklyn. But I do not intend to remain there any longer than necessary!'

'That's all I'd ask for. I'll get a train out of Providence in the morning and head back for the city.'

19
Marblehead

The powerful long-hooded Horch automobile skidded on the hard ice and slid to a stop as it fetched up against the snowbank. The driver, Dr Otto Kiep himself, sat unmoving behind the wheel, his foot pressed futilely on the brake pedal. The engine, still engaged in high gear, lugged a few times, the heavy wheels of the Horch spinning on the ice, then stalled.

Dr Kiep blinked owlishly, opened and shut his mouth, then turned his jowly face toward the taller man seated beside him and made a helpless shrug.

His companion, George Sylvester Viereck, pulled his dark brown hat firmly onto his head and shoved open the door. The passenger side of the car was in the clear. He climbed down from the Horch, stepping carefully to keep his feet on the slippery surface, and walked around the car to the front fender. There was no visible damage, but the driver's door was jammed by the snowbank.

Viereck returned to the open door and leaned into the car. He told Dr Kiep that the vehicle would have to be abandoned. But they were already at the bottom of Water Street. They could walk the short remaining distance on Front Street, then down Ferry Lane to the wharf.

Dr Kiep grumbled about Viereck's going, instead, to summon help – a team to pull the Horch from its predicament, or another car to carry them to their destination – but Viereck remonstrated with him. The Horch itself was unfortunately conspicuous in Marblehead, but that could not be helped; there was no point in drawing further attention to themselves.

Muttering under his breath, Dr Kiep reached one arm

across the front seat and permitted Viereck to assist him.
As soon as both feet were planted on the frozen ground,
he muttered a low *Danke* and told Viereck that he would
please stay close by and offer his help to the doctor,
whose sense of balance was no match for this damned
ice.

Viereck nodded and mumbled assent.

They started out along Front Street.

Halfway to Ferry Lane Viereck uttered an oath and
left Dr Kiep clutching a leafless birch tree for dear life,
while Viereck ran back to the car. He returned, pink-
cheeked and panting, his breath suspended in the
December air in tiny white cloudlets, the stack of newspapers with New York and Boston headings clasped
under one tweed-coated arm.

'I apologize, Doctor.'

Kiep was shivering visibly with the cold.

'Herr Lüdecke, I know, will want to see the papers. I
forgot and left them in the auto.'

Dr Kiep made a sour face. 'Ja, ja, richtig. Das ist
selbstverstandlich. Aber komm jetzt.'

Viereck helped him the rest of the way, holding Dr
Kiep's black-coated elbow with his free hand, keeping his
grip on the accumulated dailies with the other. They
reached the end of Hooper's Wharf and hammered on
the front door of a shuttered store. A dark-jowled man in
ribbed sweater and dungarees admitted Kiep and Viereck.
They brushed past the sailor and marched directly
upstairs, Viereck stomping his feet to clear his shoes of
slush, Kiep scraping his polished high-tops carefully on
the angles of the stairs.

In the upper room they found Kurt Lüdecke sitting
alone behind his desk. He looked up when they entered,
gestured curtly. Viereck and Kiep stood uncertainly for a
few seconds, then Dr Kiep poked the taller man with his
elbow and muttered a word to him.

'Ah, we have the newspapers, mein Herr.'

Lüdecke crooked one hand.

Viereck advanced and held out the stack of dailies. 'They aren't so . . .'

Lüdecke repeated the motion.

'I think we can still – '

'Herr Viereck!'

Viereck reached the other's desk in a single quick stride and laid the newspapers before him, face up, turned so the headlines were glaringly evident.

Lüdecke raised one blond eyebrow toward Viereck. 'Vielen Dank.' He concentrated on the newspapers, scanning the headlines and a few paragraphs of one, shuffling it to bring another on top, repeating the action until he'd read parts of half a dozen dailies. 'The others, Viereck – all the same? Need I continue?'

Viereck cleared his throat. 'No, mein Herr. Ah, I mean, they are the same, you need not continue unless you wish. All have the same story. About the *S-4*.' He ran one hand through his wavy hair. 'And the *Paulding*. The *Paulding* is safe in port. The *Paulding* is a surface ship anyway, she probably knows nothing important. But I think we will be all right. I mean, it was the submarine we were so worried about. Our ship got her, and then when the *S-4* tried to surface and the *Paulding* was just – '

'Genug! I know everything that happened. Alles, Herr Sylvester Viereck. Danken Sie. I was in the *Unterwasserprojekt* when the first contact was made.'

'Jawohl, mein Herr. I am sorry.'

Lüdecke looked up, fixed a cold glance on Dr Kiep. 'What word from Germany, Doctor?'

The pink-faced diplomat, appearing pale instead of rosy, stammered. 'There was not. Auf dem Dienstwege . . . Sylvester?' He turned, pleading.

Viereck seemed distracted. 'Ah, official word. Officially.'

'Ja, danke. Officially word there was none.'

'Naturally. But unofficially? Have we word von München?'

'Ja. The Führer says that you in charge are completely, mein Herr. Berlin knows nothing, but the Party demands information.'

'Of course.' Lüdecke struck the stack of newspapers with his fist. 'Everything is happening at once. Well, if the rescue attempt fails – what do you think, Viereck?'

'Sir, I telephoned to Continental Laboratories. In New York.'

Lüdecke smiled. 'Yes, we have control of that.'

'The Navy has asked them for help. They are going to send up the resuscitator from Germany. But they told me, it will fail.'

'Gut.'

'Will we go to the *Unterwasserprojekt*?' Viereck asked.

Lüdecke smiled coldly. 'Where is your memory, Viereck? Back in New York. Or in Doorn?'

'If you please, mein Herr! If my connections with Doorn are offensive to you, I ask you – '

'Stop, stop, stop.' Lüdecke rose from his seat and paced around the room. 'Oh, sit down, you two!'

Viereck and Kiep obeyed.

'Spanknoebel arrived earlier today,' Lüdecke said. 'He is already at the unterseeisch project.' The trim, fair man stood at a window, his hands clasped in the small of his back and his feet spread on the wooden floor. Outside the early dusk of New England winter had already fallen. In the town above Hooper's Wharf a number of houses were decorated with Christmas candles and lights. Out to sea, the darkness was total save for an occasional pale streamer when a break in the heavy clouds admitted a weak reflection of watery moonlight.

'No response from the others?' Viereck asked nervously.

Lüdecke spun round to face his colleagues. 'Herr Spanknoebel came to us with the highest recommendations, and he has performed most correctly. He will travel to Germany to receive his instructions, I have no concern with Heinz.

'As for Herr and Frau Lovecraft, Viereck – your protégés.'

Viereck nodded.

'A foolish scribbler, this Lovecraft. A dreamer. But his wife! How could you make such a selection, Viereck?'

'They are not living together.'

'Ah, Viereck. You brought this man among us, and now he knows what we are doing. If he proves unreliable . . .'

'I'm sure he'll turn up, sir. After the telegrams that we sent. They will both arrive.'

'Even though they are not living together?'

'Herr Lovecraft is a very strange man. In some ways, a very cold man. But he has a strong sense of loyalty, of chivalry. Die Ritterschaft, verstehen Sie? And although they live separately, he is still married to his wife.'

'Mm. So?'

'So, when he receives a message from her, saying she is in trouble, he will come. She is the lady in distress. He is the knight in armor. He will come, mein Herr.'

'Well, our men are at the station. If he arrives, all good. If he stays away, then to pursue him will be not so good. And the woman?'

'I doubt that she knows, mein Herr. He would not tell her, I think.'

'But do you know, Viereck?' Lüdecke pounded an elegant fist onto the stack of newspapers.

'I cannot be sure, mein Herr. But I'm sure she will come, too. That was why I sent her a telegram, also.'

'Will she arrive by means of Ritterschaft also, Viereck?'

'She loves him. It is clear, Herr Lüdecke. Even though

he does not bring her with him, everything that he tells of her makes it clear. He wishes to live with his aunties, but his wife wishes him to come back to her. When she receives the telegram, she too will respond.'

Lüdecke returned to the window and gazed out to sea, as if he could summon up the picture of the events recently past: the test cruise of the US Navy submarine *S-4*. Its accidental discovery of the *Unterwasserprojekt*. The frantic efforts of the German submarine docked at the sea-bottom structure, working with the support-ship above. The successful sinking of the *S-4* and its accidental collision with the Coast Guard destroyer *Paulding* before the submarine finally settled to the seabed – an accident as fortuitous for the project under Lüdecke's command as it was disastrous for the occupants of the *S-4*.

And now, while shoppers hurried to make their final Christmas purchases . . . while speakeasies stocked up in preparation for the following week's celebrations in welcome of the year 1928 . . . while tinny loudspeakers played recorded songs like 'Christmas Morning at Clancy's' . . . Lüdecke pressed to save the secret structure off Satan Rock and the others at strategic points along the Atlantic and Pacific coasts of North America.

At the tip of the Neck almost directly opposite Hooper's Wharf and far to the southwest of Satan Rock, the Marblehead Light flashed its steady beacon.

Kurt Lüdecke turned back to face Otto Kiep and Sylvester Viereck. 'I think you should get to the project, Viereck. Go down and have some of the men take you out there by launch. I do not want you here when Herr and Frau Lovecraft arrive. There is only one risk, now – what if they arrive together? Each can assure the other that they did not send the telegraph message. Have you thought of that, Viereck?'

Sylvester shook his head. 'No worry, mein Herr. I checked the railroad schedules and sent the telegrams carefully. Frau Lovecraft should arrive tonight. Her husband, I believe, not before morning.'

'You had better be right. Very well. Go now.'

Viereck rose and moved to take a set of diving equipment from the metal lockers.

Sonia Lovecraft sat in the Boston & Maine car as the train pulled out of North Station for its little spur trip to Marblehead. Her single light valise was stowed on the rack overhead, her heavy winter coat hung on a hook. She held a silly novel in one hand. Oppenheim's new *Miss Brown of XYO*. She'd been prompted to look at it solely by Howard's speculation that the author might be distantly related through the Phillips branch of the family, but in all the hours since leaving Brooklyn she had read the first page a hundred times and never got further than the second.

Folded inside the flyleaf was the telegram from her husband. She'd read that a hundred times, too. It revealed that he was in Marblehead, that it was urgent she join him there, that she would be met at the railroad depot and brought to him. The telegram had arrived as a shock to Sonia, changing her mood from one of pleased anticipation to one of cold apprehension.

First Howard had phoned her from Providence. She knew that he disliked telephones and almost never placed trunk calls; when he had announced his intention of returning to New York and resuming work on his book, she had been delighted. When he had asked if he might stay with her at Parkside Avenue for an indefinite time she had nearly wept.

Then the second message had come. Sonia had very nearly telephoned Howard's aunts in Providence when she received the telegram. They might know more of his situation. But then Sonia had decided that the two older women would only interfere. Whatever it was that

Howard needed from her, Sonia would provide – without the assistance of the aunts who had driven her from Providence and done so much to ruin her marriage to their nephew.

She held the blue-and-white Postal Telegraph form between numb fingers, staring out the window at the dark Massachusetts night, blinking at the occasional point of brightness that shone from some farmhouse or automobile near the Boston & Maine tracks.

Whatever Howard needed, she would provide. This much Sonia knew. His telegram had been waiting in her apartment when she arrived home from selling hats at Russeks: the delivery boy had slipped it under the front door of her apartment. She'd telephoned her friend Theo and canceled their engagement for dinner, then packed a few clothes and summoned a taxicab.

Now she saw the lighted buildings of Marblehead as the train neared the edge of town. There were few passengers in the car with her – the Boston & Maine cut its service to a single evening and a single morning train to Marblehead in the dead of winter. By spring there would be half a dozen a day, and at the height of the yachting and vacationing season the little railroad terminal would bustle with color and excitement.

But now, as the train pulled into the Marblehead terminal, Sonia had the full attention of the black porter, who assisted her into her coat, hefted her valise down from the overhead rack, and helped her to alight from the train.

In the terminal she saw a few crusty New Englanders waiting to greet relatives returning home for Christmas. She stood beside her valise, momentarily at a loss for what to do. Then two men in dark sailors' garb approached her.

One of them pulled off his black knitted cap and asked, 'Frau Lovecraft?'

She nodded.

He picked up her valise, asked her in broken but courteous English to accompany him and his companion. 'Herr Lovecraft, he awaits for you,' the sailor said.

They led her to a waiting automobile and helped her into it. They drove through the ice-filled streets of the town to the end of Ferry Lane, escorted her into a dingy storefront. There, a short, pudgy man in elegant clothing rose and greeted her. For an instant Sonia thought of Dash Weiss. This man was nearly a foot shorter than Theo, and softly fleshy where Theo was heavily muscular, but the style of the two was oddly alike.

The man introduced himself as Dr Kiep. He said he was a friend of Howard's and would take her to him.

A cold hand clutched Sonia's insides. 'You're a doctor! Is Howard ill?'

The pudgy man smiled unctuously. He spoke English badly and interpolated occasional German words, but Sonia's knowledge of Yiddish helped her to understand him.

No, Howard was not ill. Dr Kiep was not a physician but a philosophical doctor of the gymnasium and the university. If Frau Lovecraft would please come upstairs, special clothing would be needed to reach Herr Lovecraft.

Sonia found this difficult to understand. She accompanied the little man to the second floor. He reached barely higher than her shoulder, where Howard stood several inches taller than her own more-than-average height and Theo Weiss was as tall as Howard, or taller.

The upper room was outfitted as a barren office with clothing lockers along one wall. Diminutive Dr Kiep opened one of the lockers and produced from it a diving suit such as Sonia had seen Hardeen use in his recent East River excursion. She was more mystified than ever at the idea of having to wear diving costume to visit her husband, but Dr Kiep's broken English was inadequate to express the reason why she needed to adopt such attire.

He pattered downstairs gallantly while Sonia climbed into the diving gear; then she waited in the storefront while Dr Kiep returned upstairs and donned a similar outfit.

Finally they exited through the rear of the building and met waiting sailors who guided them to a motor launch. The sailors helped Sonia into the launch. Dr Kiep joined her, nearly tumbling from the wharf into the harbor's water as he climbed into the small boat.

One of the sailors cast off a line that held the launch to the piling of Hooper's Wharf. The engine was already running. Sonia and Dr Kiep sat stiffly in their canvas suits and weighted boots, copper-and-glass helmets held in their laps. There seemed to be no winches or compressors in the launch, nor even room for such equipment, and Sonia wondered how long one could survive underwater, even in a diving suit and helmet, with no supply of air or no line to haul oneself to the surface.

The launch proceeded northeast, toward the Marblehead Light, past old Azor Burgess's solitary shack, beyond the lighthouse itself, and into the coastal waters, headed toward Satan Rock.

Howard Lovecraft was sound asleep when the doorbell shrilled at Barnes Street. His aunt Annie had already left for the day, to perform her duties at the public library. She had had certain reservations, at first, about taking a job as librarian. She had been uncertain that it was proper behavior for a member of her social class and old American heritage to take employment at all.

But library work was suitably dignified and quite intellectual, she finally decided. The finer type of citizen had long been willing to serve the community in jobs such as university professor or clergy or judge, and the position of librarian was gratifyingly consonant with this tradition.

Lillian had cleaned and set the house to order after Annie's departure and was pursuing her own work, painting a small still-life near a well-lighted window, when the telegraph message arrived.

She accepted the blue-and-white envelope, reluctantly handed the delivery boy a dime, and read the address carefully. The telegram was definitely for Howard and for him alone. She held the envelope to the window but was unable to glean anything of its contents. She went to Howard's room and listened intently at the door. His steady breathing was audible with Lillian's ear pressed to the wood, and she sighed in disappointment and returned to the parlor, laying the envelope on the table for Howard to see when he arose.

Shortly after noon Howard Lovecraft opened his eyes, stretched and yawned, and climbed out of bed. For a moment he stood looking around his room, then remembered yesterday's bizarre occurrences: the blindfolded ride in the Pierce automobile, the curious interview at Morelli's house on Federal Hill, the tantalizing glance he'd had of young Miss Morelli, the strange revelations made by George Pagnanelli.

And then, the even stranger conversation he had held with Pagnanelli after they left Federal Hill and returned to Lovecraft's home on Barnes Street. It was all very unsettling. He found himself wishing that he'd never become involved in the whole convoluted affair with Viereck and Evans and Vonsiatsky and di Revel, Father Curran and George Pagnanelli and all the rest. He would have been far happier to remain in his comfortable rut of writing for *Weird Tales* and corresponding with Belknap Long, Bob Howard, Clark Smith, Vincent Starrett.

Shoemaker, stick to your last! he quoted to himself.

A little later, shaved and freshly dressed, he came out of his room. Aunt Lillian was waiting for him.

'Howard,' she said, 'there's a telegram for you. I haven't read it, of course. It's on the table, dear.'

Lovecraft picked up the envelope and slit it open. The message, surprisingly, was from his wife Sonia. Even more surprisingly, it had been dispatched from Marblehead, Massachusetts.

Howard's aunt Lillian hovered nearby, trying to read the message slip over his shoulder. He doubled it carefully to conceal its contents. His aunts had never approved of his wife, both because of her race and her profession; there was no need to distress the sensitive Lillian by letting her see that his message was from Sonia. Instead, Lovecraft folded the slip and replaced it carefully in its envelope.

It was most puzzling. Only this morning, after George Pagnanelli's departure for Union Station and before retiring to bed, Lovecraft had placed a telephone call to Brooklyn and reached Sonia before she left for work. He had told her briefly of his impending return to New York, and she had been most cordial in inviting him to use the Parkside apartment during his stay.

Now she had sent a telegram stating that she was in Massachusetts! Unthinkingly and to an inevitably futile end, Lovecraft had attempted to reach Sonia's apartment by trunk line. Of course she was not there. He placed a second call, this time to Russeks department store. On this occasion the call went through, and after much confusion he had managed to reach Sonia's superior in the millinery department. She had failed to report for work this morning. It was the last week before Christmas, the busiest days of the year, and Mrs Lovecraft was absent! Her superior had even tried to reach her at home by telephone, and failed.

Then it was true! Lovecraft replaced the earpiece on its

hook and stood over the telephone, swaying slightly. It was true! He turned toward Lillian, still hovering nervously at his elbow. 'Aunt!' Lovecraft exclaimed. 'I must leave at once! I shall be back as soon as possible, but that may not be for some time.'

Riding the electric streetcar down College Hill to Union Station, Lovecraft felt his mood changing from one of confusion and despair, to one of happy anticipation. He was setting out on an adventure again. This time he was not the great C. Auguste Dupin. He had to ponder briefly before he recognized his new persona, that of Mr William Legrand, resident of Sullivan's Island, South Carolina. And he was setting out to restore the lost grandeur of his house.

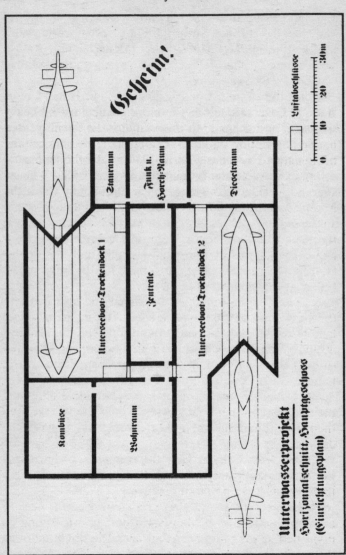

Geheim!

Raumraum

Tank u.
Vorrh=Raum

Dieselraum

Unterseeboot=Trockendock 1

Zentrale

Unterseeboot=Trockendock 2

Kombüse

Wohnraum

Luftabschlüsse

0 10 20 30m

Unterwasserprojekt
Horizontalschnitt, Hauptgeschoss
(Einrichtungsplan)

20

Marblehead Neck

Azor Burgess held on to the aiming wheel of the heavy
six-incher and shivered at the sound of the Spanish shore
batteries booming across Manila Harbor. He clutched the
firing lanyard in tense fingers, waiting for the command
of his gunnery officer to pull the cord and send a heavy
shell screeching through the clear Pacific sky, over the
bright sun-sprayed waters of the bay.

The shore batteries thumped out their steady barrage;
the American fleet under Admiral Dewey moved closer
and closer, ignoring the heavy shells and the shore-
launched torpedoes, positioning itself for the single greatest naval engagement of the war.

A Spanish shell screamed overhead and splashed into
the brine just beyond Azor's ship. The gunnery officer
held his command. Another round followed the identical
azimuth of the first, but at shortened range, and impacted
short of the ship with a spectacular flash. If the shore
battery got off another round, Azor thought, and if the
Spanish gunners were any good, they would be observing
their strikes through field glasses, would surely have seen
their over round and their short, would simply halve the
distance and fire for effect.

At last Azor's officer gave the command to fire. Azor
jerked the heavy lanyard, and the six-incher fired with a
thump that shook him to the marrow.

He blinked and found himself no longer on the deck of
his ship standing to in Manila Harbor; he was sitting up
in his bed, in his ramshackle cottage. The bright morning
in Manila Harbor was almost thirty years ago. Azor was
an old man, most of his teeth were gone, he hadn't

shaved in a week, and the bottle of cheap hooch that he'd used to help him sleep was lying empty on its side. That, he discovered when one gnarled hand trailed accidentally from his cold bed to his freezing wooden floor.

But the thumping of the big guns was still going on!

Or –

Burgess pushed himself to the side of his bed, shoved his feet into the doubled pair of heavy winter socks that made do as house slippers for him, and then stood unsteadily.

The banging at the wooden door of his shack continued, a loud voice now added to the thumps. 'Mr Burgess! Mr Burgess! Are you there?'

He yelled back, groped around his dark room to find a kerosene lamp and strike a match. Damned visitors, what time of night could it be? He woke with the sun each day, when its rays pierced the grime on his windows and lit up his room, and he could see now that it was still pitch-dark outside. 'Hold on there,' he grumbled. 'I'll be with ye in a minute.' Why didn't they just try the door-latch and come on in, he wondered. Did they think he had a lock on his door? What would he need one for, even if he had the money to afford one?

He shuffled across the room, kerosene lamp in hand, and pulled open the door. Two men stood there, one who looked vaguely familiar to Azor, the other a perfect stranger. 'Mr Burgess?' the larger of the men said.

Azor blinked sleep-crusted eyes. 'Yep. Who's there? What's goin' on?'

'It's Hardeen,' the big man said. 'Howard Lovecraft introduced us, sir. We've some very urgent business!'

Azor rubbed his face with his free hand, then backed away from the open doorway. 'Oh, yeh. You're that Weiss fella, Hardeen the Mysterious. Sure. Well, come on in and sit whilst I pull on some duds.'

The two men entered Azor's cabin. Hardeen introduced his companion as George Pagnanelli. Burgess waved a hand. He pulled on a pair of baggy trousers, tucking his flannel nightshirt into the waist. He felt under the bed for a pair of old boots and tugged them over his double woolen socks.

'All right, now. Say, you fellas have a seat and tell me what's the trouble. What time is it, anyhow?'

Hardeen held his watch to the yellow kerosene flame. 'Nearly four in the morning,' he said.

'Heh! Must be something urgent for sure, to bring you fellas all the way out to the Neck this time of night! Well, shoot, I'm done sleepin' for the night anyhow.'

Hardeen had lowered himself carefully onto a rickety chair that threatened to collapse beneath his weight. He leaned forward earnestly. 'Mr Burgess, can your seaplane fly now?'

Azor leaned back and scratched his head. 'You mean, can she get up in winter? Long as the harbor don't freeze, she can – and the harbor *don't* freeze, Mr Weiss. Or do you mean now, at four in the morning?'

'I mean both!'

'Ah, well, the answer's the same to both. Sure, she can fly. I built that ship with my own hands, ten years a-gone. I know every wire and bolt in her! Sure, she'll fly any time I ask her to, she's a solid ship!'

Hardeen was clenching and unclenching his fists nervously. 'Mr Burgess, I need a flight right now. I'd rent the aircraft from you and pilot her myself, but I don't know the waters here and I don't want to wait for morning.' He bunched his fists and rested them on his elegantly suited knees, as if he were working the controls of an airplane. 'It's a dark night outside. Mr Burgess, can you dead-reckon your plane to Satan Rock, land there, and wait for me?'

'Wait for you? Are you daffy? What are you after on Satan Rock in the middle of the night?'

'I don't want anything *on* Satan Rock. I have some underwater work to do. If you can get me there and land your plane, I'll just climb overboard, do what needs to be done, and come back aboard.'

'Come back aboard?' Azor shook his head. 'You don't make no sense, Mr Hardeen! What-all do you need to do out there? And why does it need doin' in the dark?'

Hardeen exchanged a glance with his traveling companion, then turned back toward Burgess. 'All right,' he said in a lowered tone. 'You know about *Der Traum* and the workers who've been out there these past months.'

Burgess grunted assent.

'I've got to do some checking up on those wiseacres,' Hardeen explained.

Azor Burgess snorted. 'Never did like them krauts. But they'll sure as heck hear us a-comin', even if they can't see us.'

Hardeen bit his lip for a moment. 'Mr Burgess, I don't want to ask too much of you. But do you think you could come in high over their ship and Satan Rock, and – '

'Nup.'

Hardeen was startled. 'What do you mean?'

'Can't come in over their ship 'cause their ship ain't there no more. Pulled up anchor and skedaddled back to the other side weeks ago. Just a few of them krauts left, see 'em around town when I hike in for groceries. Guess they're keepin' an office or something till springtime.'

'I still want to see what they're doing – or what they've done – down by Satan Rock. If their ship is gone, I suppose that will make things easier. What do you think, George?'

Pagnanelli nodded. 'No antiaircraft batteries, anyway.' He didn't laugh as he said it.

'Well,' Hardeen resumed, 'if you could fly me in with a

little equipment I've got, come down on the water and wait for me.'

'How long? Y'want me to just taxi in circles?'

Hardeen frowned. 'I don't think I can finish that quickly. Can you cut your engine and anchor your plane?'

'No self-starter.'

Hardeen moaned. 'Suppose I stand on the planing hull to throw the prop?'

Now Burgess began to pace the room. 'It'd work, I s'pose. Then how'd you get past the propeller and back to the cockpit?'

'I'd have to spin her, get the engine started, drop off the hull and let you taxi past me, then climb back onto the hull, over the lower wing and into the cockpit. Could the plane take that kind of treatment?'

'No doubt about it, Mr Hardeen. I told you, I built that ship, I know what she can do. Can *you* do what you said?' He sat.

'Oh, yes. I can do it.' He clapped his hands. 'Now, what about the dead-reckoning?'

Burgess stood up and walked to stand close to Hardeen. He picked up the kerosene lamp and held it between their faces, chin-high, so its swaying illumination lit fully on his features. 'Take a good look at my eyes.'

Hardeen obeyed. Burgess's eyes were covered by milky films. 'Cataracts,' the magician whispered.

'I'm not blind,' Burgess said. 'Not stone-blind, anyhow. Pebble-blind, mebbe. But I do a lot more dead-reckoning than anybody knows about. I know these waters like a baby knows its mother's teat. I can dead-reckon you anyplace in thutty miles. By day or by dark or by blindfold, don't make no difference to me.'

Outside Burgess's shack Pagnanelli helped Hardeen unload his gear from the luggage compartment of the

Rickenbacker and carry it to the tarpaulin-covered seaplane. Hardeen stripped off his elegant suit and handed it to Pagnanelli to carry carefully back inside. The magician stood wearing an unusual outfit, a sort of baggy shirt and pantaloons, the shirt drawn shut with a string at neck and wrists, the pantaloons tucked into a pair of odd-looking galoshes.

Hardeen and Pagnanelli helped Burgess start the seaplane, then Hardeen climbed into the passenger seat and the old man gunned the seaplane's Renault engine and the ship moved slowly away from the Neck, out into Marblehead Harbor.

Burgess turned the seaplane, and Hardeen felt the ship begin to accelerate. Hardeen raised his eyes and saw no stars. Dead-reckoning indeed! The old man had better know what he was talking about or they would be hopelessly lost within minutes. He glanced back and saw the speck of light near Burgess's shack that must be Pagnanelli still standing with kerosene lantern in hand. The seaplane's Renault engine showed flame and sparks in her exhaust – the plane would be visible to Pagnanelli longer than the kerosene flame would be visible to Hardeen. But even that would disappear as Burgess carried them into the night.

'Hold tight!' the old man shouted. Hardeen felt the seaplane surge forward, then rise clumsily and begin to bump as her float lifted above the sea, slapping and jouncing as it struck each wavelet.

The ship climbed above the water, headed straight on whatever course Azor Burgess held in his mind's eye. Neither man tried to shout above the roar of the engine. Hardeen scanned the sky and sea; neither showed any feature that was useful in guessing where the airplane was. He had no choice but to trust the old man.

The airplane tilted, and Hardeen clutched his equipment to keep it from tumbling from the passenger seat.

He felt Burgess put the seaplane into a long banking spiral, dropping slowly toward the Atlantic. The water below was a solid wall of blackness to Hardeen; if Burgess could see anything at all it would have to be in recollection. Hardeen peered ahead into the darkness, unable even to make out a horizon line.

The plane had leveled off and was flying on a steady horizontal course. Suddenly an obsidian pyramid loomed before them. The seeming blackness of sky and sea must have been a species of deep blue-gray, for the tall triangle gave new meaning to *black*.

Hardeen clutched the edge of the cockpit before him.

He thought he could hear Burgess grunt.

The seaplane bucked once, lumbering upward a few yards, then dropping suddenly into a power stall. The wings lost their purchase on the air. The ship started to nose over, but before it had dipped more than a few degrees there was the smack and thump of float kissing water, and Azor had cut the power.

'Satan Rock,' the old man announced. 'Whatever you've got to do, Mr Weiss, feel free to do it now. I'll cast my anchor.' The old man scrambled beneath his seat. 'Now, if you don't come back – '

'I'll come back!'

'Well, if you don't, I'll have to wait till morning and get a tow back in. Not much traffic on these waters in December, I'll tell you. We're mighty lucky to have clear air and a smooth sea as 'tis. And about my rent, now – '

'If I don't come back, Mr Pagnanelli will pay you.'

'Fair 'nough. You need a hand with that gear o' yours?'

Hardeen was already clambering over the edge of the cockpit. When his feet hit the seaplane's broad float, he said, 'Thanks, I can handle it.'

He hoisted the noctovisor from the cockpit, fitted it to the harness on his right shoulder, then reached back for the watertight Tungar power unit and adjusted it on his left. He needed all his skill as a contortionist to reach behind himself and connect the power cable from the Tungar to the noctovisor. He flicked the toggles on the noctovisor, tested the infrared light tube and the orthiconoscope screen, then snapped the toggles back to *off*.

'Just a few minutes more, Mr Burgess.' Hardeen stood balanced on the float, noctovisor and Tungar on his shoulders, and proceeded methodically through the series of breathing and concentration exercises he had developed with his dead brother. He slapped the old man on the shoulder as a farewell and stepped off the float.

He heard the splash of his galoshes entering the water, then felt it close over him. He was committed.

He sank quickly, borne down by the weight of the noctovisor and Tungar. He flexed his knees, preparatory to landing on the seabed. With eyes open he could see nothing – even before he reached a depth where daylight would fail to penetrate, there was complete darkness.

His ears rang with the sudden increase in pressure. That would be no problem. The body could adapt to varying pressure with astonishing speed. Returning to the surface was another matter. There would surely be nitrogen bubbles in the blood. The likelihood of rising slowly enough to permit them to dissolve safely was almost nonexistent, nor was there a pressure chamber available. The risk of bends would simply have to be accepted.

He felt his feet grind upon the sandy sea-bottom; here beyond the mouth of Marblehead Harbor there was no silt, and the Atlantic floor offered a firm footing. For an instant he had nearly buckled under the descending weight of the noctovisor and Tungar, but trained muscles responded and he righted himself at once.

His balloonlike outfit served as an insulator against the frigid ocean water, but his face and hands told him that he was in an ice-cold region. He switched on the infrared tube and noctovisor, concentrated on the orthiconoscope screen.

Straight ahead he could see nothing but clear water, but by tilting the noctovisor on its gimbal he could scan the seabed. Coarse-grained sand was littered with scraps of seaweed and with the jetsam of three centuries of commercial shipping, among which a great scuttling lobster paused to wave its antennae at him before disappearing into the murk. Except for blackened bottles and metal debris, no man-made object was to be seen.

Hardeen's ears felt the pressure of the depth, translating it into an illusory hissing. His lungs still held part of the air he had pumped into them before dropping from the surface, but most of his oxygen supply was distributed through his bloodstream and tissues; that, rather than simply overfilling the lungs, was the secret of long endurance without fresh air.

Hardeen paced in a slowly widening spiral. As he made his second turn there was a thump. He whirled, the move slowed to almost Chaplinesque grace by the drag of the water, and saw that Azor Burgess's anchor had landed a few yards away. It dragged, kicking up a small cloud of sand particles, then caught against a low rock outcrop on the seabed.

Matching Hardeen's confidence in his endurance was a prudent unwillingness to waste precious time. He did not look up in search of the aircraft but continued his steady spiral.

A ghostly light appeared, a wavering blue-green-white flare. Hardeen turned his infrared lamp toward it, but the light was too far distant for any effect. Hardeen thought of a ghostly presence, some revenant mariner of ancient times, even of his brother Houdini. Ehrich had promised to return, to contact his wife Bess if it were possible. Could this be Theo's dead brother?

He shook his head.

He lowered himself to his belly, feeling the gritty seabed through his rubberized suit. He pointed the noctovisor ahead like a soldier pointing a weapon as he crawled beneath a barbwire fence. He crept forward, wincing when a half-buried rock pressed against a rib or knee.

Now a second light appeared beside the first. This one was not as bright, yet it seemed to emanate from a larger source.

Hardeen calculated the time he had been submerged. His body was not yet at its limit of endurance, but despite all his care and conditioning he knew that the oxygen in his system was being used. Before it was exhausted he would have to find a new source or his mission was doomed – and, very likely, he with it.

He paused behind a large clump of seaweed. Without warning a ghoulish face plunged toward his own, great eyes blazing and murderous fangs exposed. Hardeen threw his free arm in front of himself as the demon-visage flashed past him. He shuddered, watching the heavy-bodied moray eel swim rapidly away, as terrified by this strange intruder into its domain as Hardeen was of it.

His body tried to heave a sigh of relief, but he checked the impulse. Instead he scrabbled in the sand until he had taken firm grasp on a heavy rock half again the size of a baseball. Dazzy Vance he was not, but accurate throwing was part of his stage skill and he might need it soon.

He crept forward again. His diaphragm made one of its spasmodic attempts to resume breathing, and he took a moment to calm it.

Now he could see the source of the two lights. A pair of human figures, bloated by glass-and-metal diving helmets and canvas suits, were standing on the seabed. Beyond them loomed the dark bulk that Hardeen knew

must be the *Unterwasserprojekt*. A long brutal shape
was merged to it; Hardeen recognized the characteristic
sharklike configuration of a German Unterseeboot. The
two men were working on the hull of the *Unterwasserprojekt*. The intensely flaring greenish light must be an
oxyacetylene torch; the other, a sealed tungsten work-
lamp.

Hoping to obtain a better look at the structure and to
find a means of ingress, Hardeen crept closer. He worked
on his belly, as silently and inconspicuously as he could,
but some clue of his presence must have made itself felt;
the two divers turned toward him.

He could see the glare of the tungsten lamp beaming
fully into the lens of his orthiconoscope.

The divers started toward him, gesturing clumsily to
each other in their heavy diving costumes. They moved
like monstrous robots in some film by Murnau or Lang,
their air cables playing slowly out behind them.

Hardeen rose in place and cautiously advanced. Now
there was no hope of entering the *Unterwasserprojekt*
undetected. He could not make his way by stealth; he
must do it by trickery or by force. He was willing to use
either.

He felt a flash of blackness rather than saw it; another
sign, he knew, of the slowly approaching limitation of his
body's oxygen supply.

They were within a few yards now. Hardeen cast a
quick glance at the silent Unterseeboot and the *Unterwasserprojekt*. Although the larger structure was outfitted
with heavily glassed portholes, there was no other figure
on the seabed and there appeared to be no observers
from within the heavy metal hull.

Hardeen attempted a placatory gesture to the two
divers, but at his first movement the man wielding the
tungsten lamp stepped aside, holding its glare full upon

him, while the torch-wielder adjusted the flame on his tool. It became a virtual lance of searing gases.

As the torch-wielder lunged at him, Hardeen stepped aside. He heaved his rock, muttering a subvocalized prayer to Uncle Wilbert Robinson and the sainted Charlie Ebbets. The rock moved with surrealistic slowness. The diver attempted, with equal slowness, to dodge.

The rock smashed into the glass lens sealing the tungsten lamp. The lamp flared for a fraction of a second, then faded to blackness.

There remained the oxyacetylene torch, its flaring gas a murderous spear still directed at Hardeen.

But Hardeen knew now that he was virtually invisible to his enemies, while he could perceive them clearly by the noctovisor's infrared tube as well as the glow of the oxyacetylene torch.

The torcher strode forward, lunging at Hardeen. There was apparently enough glare from the lance of flame itself to outline him as a shadowy target.

He backed slowly.

The two divers advanced after him, their cables trailing behind. No spoken message could pass between them, Hardeen knew, but they moved with coordinated strides, signaling to each other with hand-gestures.

Hardeen proceeded carefully toward the torch-bearer. The man canted forward, extending his lance of flame. With a leaning step, Hardeen changed his course toward the second diver. The torch-bearer wheeled, driving his lance of flame toward the magician, but Hardeen was not there: he had dodged aside.

The lance of flame swept in a murderous arc.

It seared a diagonal line across the second diver's canvas suit. There was a burbling escape of bubbles, then the diver collapsed as the rush of pressure jellied his body within the suit. He crumpled to the seabed and lay still, a dark cloud rising in the water above him, the bubbles of air dancing over his still form and ascending steadily toward the surface of the sea.

Enraged by this turn of events, the torch-bearer renewed his attack on Hardeen. He swept his flame-lance in arcs. Hardeen danced just beyond their range.

Hardeen moved sideways, then tried to dodge forward, past the torch-bearer. His oxygen supply was nearing its end. He must appear a terrifying creature to this German: a man walking around the floor of the harbor, weighted down with unexplained equipment, but unencumbered by diving gear.

How, the other must wonder, could he survive?

The black dots dancing in Hardeen's vision told him that he could not, in fact, survive very much longer.

The diver lunged forward like a soldier in a bayonet charge. The lance of flame swept across Hardeen's wrist a fraction of an inch below his own rubberized cuff.

The pain of its passage was intense. Hardeen opened his mouth in an involuntary gasp; he locked his throat shut in the split instant that it took the water to fill his mouth with its icy, briny taste. He spat it out at the expense of a portion of his precious remaining air.

But the German had extended his arms across Hardeen's front. Hardeen grasped his adversary, hand-to-wrist, and struggled to wrest the oxyacetylene torch from him. Working for Hardeen were his great strength and superb physical condition, and the German's heavy, bulky diving suit. Against him was the fact that his air now was virtually exhausted. He could see the black pinpoints expanding as they danced before his eyeballs. The ringing in his ears was growing louder, and his head was growing light.

The two men struggled for the torch.

Hardeen bent and tugged at his adversary, hoping to pull him forward and tumble him over his back, causing him to lose his grip on the torch. Instead the torch twisted in both pairs of hands as the German, at the end of his tether, was jerked suddenly backward.

The torch was yanked from both men's grasps and revolved, cutting an arc above Hardeen's head so close that it shriveled a tuft of his thick wavy hair. It continued to revolve, sweeping across the diver's faceplate.

The glass panel in the front of the diver's helmet, chilled to the near-freezing temperature of the harbor-brine, was suddenly heated to the temperature of white-hot gases. In a fleeting moment it blackened and cracked. Then the crushing pressure of the water shattered the glass and flooded the diver's suit.

Staggering and half-unconscious from oxygen starvation, Hardeen struggled past the two crushed bodies. The oxyacetylene torch lay beside the man who had used it, flaring its ghostly lance through the water. Hardeen collided with the hull of the *Unterwasserprojekt,* fell to his knees on the sandy harbor-floor, dragged himself into the structure's airlock and lay gratefully gasping in the dank, oily air within.

He knew that he might be discovered at any moment; he had to recover his strength, find Howard and Sonia – for he had collected the clues and combined them into a pattern that indicated that the Lovecrafts were almost certainly here – and get them out before a general alarm was sounded.

The bulk of his task still lay ahead of him, but even by getting this far he had accomplished more than most men would have dared hope to achieve.

Sonia clutched Howard's hands, intertwining her fingers with his. At first Lovecraft winced and tried to draw his hands away from Sonia's. It was an instinct to which he had been conditioned since childhood. His mother, the beautiful Susie, had truly loved him. This he believed. But she had herself been a touch-me-not and had withheld from her child almost any physical contact. Yet she had loved him: why else call him her little sunshine, and dress him in long curls, and keep him from the other children so she could have him to herself, all to herself, while her salesman-husband was on the road philandering with loose women and drinking with fellow drummers?

Howard tried to relax, tried to permit Sonia whatever comfort she could gain from holding his hands. He even returned a small squeeze.

'I was right from the start,' he said over his shoulder.

They were seated in aluminum chairs, tied in them back to back. The air in this storage room of *Unterwasserprojekt Elf* stank of staleness and of oil. And of brine. Howard hated the odor of brine. It reminded him of fish, of the sea, of everything formless and viscous and runny, from loose human excrement to semen to the primal protoplasmic ooze from which life had first sprung.

'There must be something we can do,' Sonia said. She twisted her hands and her shoulders, trying to work loose from the ropes that held her.

'I had Viereck properly assessed in 1915,' Howard said. 'A traitor he was then and a traitor he is now. My mistake was to doubt my own beliefs. If I had stuck to my convictions, we would be free now. You would be in Brooklyn and I would be in Providence, each of us pursuing his own affairs.'

'Howard!' Sonia's voice had dropped in volume and increased in urgency. 'There's nothing to gain from regrets now, Howard! That man, that Lüdecke man – '

'I mistrusted him from the first. His thugs assaulted me, and he bought my silence with his unctuous apologies and Sylvester Viereck's assistance. If I had risen above my own pride I should have ended this affair that night!'

'Never mind that night, Howard! He says they're going to take us to Germany. I don't believe him. I think they're going to kill us. Don't you see what they're building here? This is a secret naval base and barracks. They're getting ready for another war, once the National Socialists take power in Germany. And they don't want to fight it in Europe like last time. They're going to invade America!'

'The Navy must have found out,' Lovecraft said. 'That submarine, the S-4. I can't believe that Commander Jones would just surface right under a destroyer. No captain could be so incompetent. These men were responsible in some way.'

'Howard, do you see anything we could use to cut these ropes? There's a lot of equipment in this room. If we could move these chairs maybe we could get a tool.'

'To what end, Sonia? We are imprisoned by a force of enemies, trapped in a structure on the bottom of the ocean. If we should escape our bonds we would still be locked in this room. If we could escape the room we would still be surrounded by enemies. If we were to escape *them*, we would still be imprisoned in this steel shell, and if we could escape the shell we would find ourselves on the ocean floor far from land, in midwinter. We should surely die. Let us accept our doom with such dignity as we can muster, and show our inferiors that we can die without sacrificing our humanity and pride.'

Sonia exhaled furiously. 'No, Howard! No, no, no! For once in your life get *involved*! You can't stand back and watch this happen! I'm not going to die without a fight, Howard! I'm not going to die!' She drew a ragged breath. 'Right now, help me slide this way. To the left. Look over there – you see that wire cutter? We have to get to it!'

She began sliding her chair sideways, shoving against the iron deck with her feet, moving a fraction of an inch at each shove. At first her chair swung in a small arc, Howard's remaining stationary. Then he too began to push with his feet, and both chairs moved a short distance.

'Good!' Sonia grunted. 'Again – now!'

They moved another fraction of an inch.

'Again!'

'Again!'

'All right, Sylvester. At least immediate concerns seem to be under control. You sent a good driver to get Otto back to New York?'

'Ja, Herr Lüdecke.'

Lüdecke let out a long breath. 'Poor judgement, Sylvester. One poor choice and you see what we wind up with.' He nodded in the direction of the bulkhead that separated his own quarters from the storage room where the prisoners were tied. 'What are we going to do with them, Sylvester? Do you not feel a responsibility for them?'

'I thought he was fully in our camp, mein Herr. It was my error.'

'I know that, Viereck! I am asking your suggestion as to their disposal. Your guilt is already established.'

Viereck flushed and swallowed uncomfortably at the noun. 'I thought you planned to ship them to Deutschland.'

'*You* I am shipping to Deutschland. Not aboard your usual luxury liner, Sylvester. I do not know whether you will return to this country, and if you do not, I wish no trail to lead nach München. So you will return by Unterseeboot. Then, if you can convince the Party to offer you another opportunity for service, you may return to the United States.'

'I am an American citizen, you know!' Viereck's attempted bravado sounded unconvincing even to himself.

Lüdecke answered with a tiny downward tic at the corner of his mouth. 'No, Sylvester, I wonder only whether any purpose would be served by shippping Herr and Frau Lovecraft back to Europe. She is, I fear, a hopeless case. Jewish *and* Slavic *and* an enemy of the Party. Her husband, perhaps, we might reconvert to our cause, but a man who turns his coat so easily once, twice – is he ever to be trusted? Why not a third time, eh?'

The dapper blond man rose from his seat, walked to the porthole that looked out upon the Atlantic seabottom. Outside the thick double glass there was only blackness.

'No, I think a quicker and more definitive solution will be best.'

He returned to his desk, opened the center drawer, and pulled from it a ring of keys. With one of these he opened a locked drawer, lifted a blue-gray pistol from it, and placed it on his desk. From the same drawer he took out a rectangular cardboard box and set it beside the pistol. He opened the box and began to take bullets from it, examining the brass cartridge and lead slug of each as he slid them carefully into the pistol's metal clip.

'Is there no – no other way, mein Herr?' Despite the perpetually dank air of the *Unterwasserprojekt* Viereck was sweating.

Lüdecke looked up with surprise written on his face. 'Sylvester, you balk at destroying our enemies? After I read Dr Kiep's report on the disposal of Signor Carisi and Signor Amoroso?'

Viereck blanched.

'I think the red neckties were a very good touch, Sylvester. And I meant to ask, how is the food at Turin's restaurant? I hope you had time to finish your lamb chops and broccoli before you left for the elevated station. Dr Kiep always looks as if he has had a good meal, but you are a bit on the ascetic side, Sylvester. You look as if you might miss a meal now and then. Mortify the flesh and elevate the soul, eh?'

Viereck stepped backward as Lüdecke crossed the room, opened the door to the companionway, shut the door behind him. He held the ring of keys in one hand, the blue-gray pistol in the other.

Hardeen peered around the corner of the companionway, hoping to find it empty, and hoping even more to find a room both vacant and unlocked where he might set up a temporary base of operations. He'd already learned enough to set his head spinning and to send Yarnell and the rest of the naval group into frantic action. Of course *Der Traum* hadn't just been carrying out a test of construction materials. That story had been too thin to stand the simplest scrutiny.

But this – this – he didn't even know what to *call* what he'd found! A secret underwater submarine base? And what more than that? A virtual fortress, designed for what object? He could think of no reason less menacing than a blockage of Marblehead Harbor. And why would the Viereck group want to do that? Perhaps more than a blockade was the objective. But what then? Did the NSDAP plotters intend to smuggle saboteurs through the underwater fortress? Or did they plan to smuggle in a whole invading army, a few soldiers at a time, by means of Unterseeboot or merchant ships like *Der Traum* . . .

But why Marblehead?

Unless – this operation was only one of a series. What if there were similar concealed structures off Boston, New York, Chesapeake Bay, Hampton Roads . . . What if invading armies should rise simultaneously from the sea at ten, twenty, fifty locations all up and down the coastline? And was the operation limited to the Atlantic coastline?

He shivered, rubbed his hands on his cold cheeks to restore circulation, drew a deep breath of the chilled, oily air that pervaded this sinister place.

Hardeen was about to step into the empty companionway when he jerked his head back and waited. He pulled a small mirror from a slit in his odd rubber outfit and held it so he could see into the passage. A hatch had opened, and a man with blond hair and dapper clothing stepped out. He closed the hatch behind him. Hardeen could see that he carried a pistol.

The man walked a short distance, halted before a second hatchway, and fitted a key into its lock. He opened the hatch and stepped into the cabin, then there were sounds of violence.

Hardeen sprinted down the companionway, shoving his mirror into his pocket as he ran. He pushed the hatch farther open and took two steps into the cabin.

He saw the blond man lying on the steel deck, an ugly patch of red spreading through his light-colored hair. A figure was crouched over him, some heavy long-handled tool held at the ready. The figure straightened and pointed a blue-gray pistol at Hardeen.

'Sonia!' he gasped.

Recognition flashed into her face. She stepped across the motionless figure, arms spread. Hardeen embraced her. They stood, holding each other, exchanging kisses for a few seconds. Then the woman backed away. Hardeen looked around, saw another man standing against one wall, his face an ashen off-white contrasting with the somber black of his suit.

'Howard,' Hardeen said.

As the two men faced each other, Sonia crossed behind Hardeen and shoved the hatch quietly shut. 'Someone will come,' she said softly. 'We've got to get out of here. Thco, how did you get in?'

'I walked,' he answered simply, suppressing an impulse to burst into laughter. 'I knew you had to be here,' he said in a low voice. 'It was all obvious, and I was inexcusably slow to see it. If only I'd acted faster – but I couldn't be sure which side you were on. Which side your husband was on.'

'Howard was finished with Viereck,' Sonia said. 'He told me that Pagnanelli had convinced him to spy against Viereck – that was why he didn't break with him openly. But I didn't know that you were part of – *our* side, Theo.' She squeezed his hands and pressed her face against his shoulder. 'When I called you and canceled our dinner engagement – '

'I should have understood right then, Sonia. I should have acted then!'

'I had a telegram from Howard. Supposedly from Howard – summoning me to Marblehead. I was taken in, Theo.'

'And I,' Lovecraft put in, 'received a wire purportedly dispatched by Sonia, summoning *me*.'

Hardeen scanned the compartment. 'You two have got things well in hand, I can see.'

'Only for the moment.' Sonia controlled her sense of urgency. 'But there are more of them. Theo, how can we escape from this trap? And – Theo – really, how did you get here?'

'Oh. Old Burgess brought me in his airplane. He's waiting above.' He jerked a thumb toward the ceiling, indicating the ocean where Azor's plane was anchored. 'I used the noctovisor, you know, Baird's invention. It brought me down here by its weight. We have to get out now, you're right, before they discover us.'

An ashen-faced Howard Lovecraft spoke. 'Can we get diving costumes? What will we do for air?'

'Nothing like that.' Hardeen shook his head. 'We'll just have to hold our breath. We can exit through the airlock. I'll just have to abandon the noctovisor. Burgess can taxi back to his place with us all in the plane, or else standing on the float. We'll just have to risk nitrogen bubbles.'

Lovecraft grew even paler. 'Nitrogen bubbles?'

'Never mind, Howard,' Sonia whispered urgently. 'Never mind about that. Our lives are at stake.'

Hardeen slipped back through the hatchway, followed by Sonia and Lovecraft. They started softly toward the airlock.

There was a sound behind them. A voice called, strangely soft in tone, as if the speaker wanted not to arouse attention. 'Stop!' the voice came. 'Come back!'

Howard Lovecraft spun about. He saw his almost-patron George Sylvester Viereck trotting along the companionway toward the three fugitives. Without waiting for Hardeen or Sonia to act, Lovecraft ran back, full-speed, toward Viereck. He raised his right arm, balled his fist, and lunged for Viereck's jaw, putting all his strength into a single blow.

It landed with a loud thud. Viereck, a startled expression on his features, toppled slowly backward and crumpled onto the deck.

Lovecraft and Sonia and Hardeen made for the airlock.

21

Spite House

Even at noon the innkeeper fed the blaze with a steady supply of heavy logs so it warmed the old room and held the darkness and chill at bay. The sky and sea merged into a vista of unbroken gloom, the horizon line a vague blur to the east, the upper half of the prospect only slightly less dark than the lower.

Sonia had recovered quickly from the ordeal of imprisonment and escape. It was the latter that had nearly killed Lovecraft. The quick ascent from the airlock had been cold and frightening but otherwise simple. Theo Weiss, Sonia, and Howard had clasped hands, pushed off from the sea-bottom, and within seconds emerged gasping into the predawn Atlantic gray.

Azor Burgess had not seen them, but they spotted his anchored seaplane and swam to it. The old man had helped them out of the water, Theo and Sonia chilled but strong and alert, Howard Lovecraft nearly comatose with hypothermia. Sonia had ministered to him as best she could while Burgess and Weiss started the seaplane's engine. Then they had taxied back to Burgess's solitary home near the Marblehead Light.

They half carried the frigid Lovecraft into Burgess's shack, stripped his sopping clothes and rubbed him dry, bundled him into a make-do cocoon of spare clothing and woolen blankets, poured a mixture of hot coffee and cheap rum into him until he had revived. Then Hardeen and George Pagnanelli paid off old Burgess and conveyed Lovecraft into the rear seat of the magician's Rickenbacker, where Sonia massaged his face and hands all the way back to the Spite House.

Weiss and Pagnanelli had departed almost at once, telling Sonia that they would be back in a few hours. Meanwhile she worked over her husband, massaging him, coaxing him to consume hot soup and remain near the fireplace.

Now, hours later, Lovecraft seemed nearly to have regained his normal strength.

From outside the Spite House there came a steady droning, a sound like that of a huge flight of honeybees proceeding through a meadow. Sonia left Howard's side and crossed to the window, looking toward the harbor and the ocean. She wasn't sure, there might have been a few tiny black specks moving against the gray of the sky.

There was a series of distant thumps, so low that Sonia was uncertain that she was hearing them at all, and a shudder that made the building vibrate as if there had been a small earthquake. Sonia peered harder into the December air, but the specks – if she really saw them – grew no larger or more distinct.

She returned to her husband's side and took his hands in her own. For once, Howard didn't resist her efforts to touch him. 'Howard, did you hear that?'

He turned drowsy eyes to her. 'Hear what?'

'The droning, and the – other sounds. Like, oh, explosions.' She chafed one of his hands, then reached for the other. 'And the house seemed to move. The whole house.'

He looked a little more alert but offered no response.

From the open sea there came another series of deep thumps.

'There,' Sonia said, 'did you hear that? Feel it?'

Howard nodded.

'What can they be doing?' Sonia asked.

The droning continued, punctuated occasionally by new series of thumps and shudders. The innkeeper popped his head in the doorway and exchanged puzzled glances with

Sonia. After a while the droning grew fainter. In its place Sonia heard the sound of a car drawing up in front of the Spite House. She ran to see if it was Theo Weiss and George Pagnanelli, returned from their errand.

The two men walked into the room weary and unshaven, little Pagnanelli more rumpled than ever.

'Well, it looks like everything is getting cleaned up,' Theo said.

'What's everything?' Sonia asked. She took a few steps toward Hardeen, held out her hands to him. He accepted them for a moment, bent over to give her a tiny kiss on the cheek. 'You mean those gangsters under the ocean there? How did you clean them up, Theo? You and Mr Pagnanelli?'

Weiss shook his head. 'How's Howard doing?' he asked. 'I'd like to talk about this with both of you, if I can.'

Sonia made a cautionary gesture with the fingers of one hand. 'He's much better, Theo. For a little while I thought – ' She stopped with a catch in her voice, breathed deeply and continued. 'I thought it was the end for him. You know Howard could never stand cold. I think this was nearly his finish. But now I think he's almost all right. Almost all right.'

She walked around to face Howard. He sat low in a deep easy chair. Sonia knelt on the braid carpet beside his chair. She looked up into his face, took his hands again. 'Howard, dear! It's Theo! Theo and Mr Pagnanelli!'

Lovecraft lifted his chin from his chest and gazed at Sonia. 'Your good Jewish friend and my good Armenian friend.'

'Come, Howard.' Sonia tried to lift him to his feet, then Weiss came and helped her. They got him up and walked him around the room. 'Do you think he should be in the hospital?' Sonia asked Theo.

Hardeen looked closely into Lovecraft's face. 'Howard?'

The other responded.

'I think he's really all right. He's just had a terrible chill,' Sonia insisted.

'A terrible chill,' Lovecraft repeated. 'Thank you, Weiss. I've had a terrible chill. But I am all right, thank you very much.' He stopped walking, freed his arms from those of Hardeen and Sonia. He looked around. 'Is this the Spite House?'

They chorused that it was.

'How did we get back here? I – the last I remember – ' He stopped talking, a misty expression in his eyes. Then, slowly, a huge grin spread across his face. He raised his right hand, held it before his eyes, balled it into a fist and grinned even more broadly. 'Say, I really let that scoundrel have one right in the chops, didn't I? Did he get up?'

Weiss smiled. 'No, he didn't.'

'Why, I'm another Manassa Mauler,' Lovecraft said. 'I really floored the villain, didn't I?' He put an arm around his wife and the other around Hardeen. 'Well, the winner and new heavyweight champion of the colonies, eh? But what happened? What were you saying just now?'

Hardeen exchanged a relieved look with Sonia. 'Let's sit down, and George and I will deliver our reports, eh?'

Weiss lowered himself into a blondwood chair near the fireplace, facing the others. 'Now, you must have heard the explosions for the past hour or so,' Weiss said.

Sonia said she had.

'Those were government planes, at least that was the droning sound all along.'

'I saw some little specks,' Sonia said. 'That was all.' She inclined her head toward the window. 'They must have been well out at sea.'

'The installation down below is surely nothing but

wreckage by now,' Weiss said. 'Pagnanelli and I have been in Quincy. We met Captain Yarnell.'

'Who is that?'

'He's the naval commander. He's in charge of the aircraft carrier *Saratoga*. You know, we've been in touch with the military throughout this matter.'

'I didn't know,' Sonia answered.

Lovecraft shook his head. 'Nor I. What's your role been? Pagnanelli here gave me a long talk in Providence. But I didn't know you were involved, too, Weiss.'

'That isn't the word for it,' Pagnanelli put in. 'Theo is my chief.'

Lovecraft grunted.

'We needed bombers to make sure that rat's nest was cleaned out. The *Saratoga* carries only fighter planes and observation craft, but they steamed anyway and summoned Army bombers. Those thumps were explosives coming from the bombers. The government has already put out a covering story, it should be in the evening papers in Boston. Might be interesting to look at them. The Army's been holding a competition for a new, heavy bombing craft, and all the manufacturers want that contract, so they've built test models and they've been eager for a chance to show off their birds. Curtiss, Martin, Fokker, Sikorsky. It was quite a show.'

'And now they're all dead, I hope.' Sonia reached to squeeze Theo's hand.

The magician shook his head. 'I doubt it. We won't know for a while. The Navy is trying to salvage the *S-4*, and they'll have their divers look for wreckage of this too. But you know, they had a submarine in dock down there. Once we made good our escape . . .'

He leaned back in his chair and yawned hugely. 'Excuse me! I guess this is all catching up with me at once.' He rubbed his temples with his hands. 'As soon as the *S-4* stumbled on their base, they must have feared that the jig was all up with them, and been preparing to pull out. Abducting you and Howard, Sonia, was part of a rear-guard action. But they must have known it was really all over, when we got away.

'I'm sure they piled into that U-boat and headed for sea well before the bombers arrived.' Again he paused, then resumed. 'Strange, though. I don't mean to take anything away from you, Howard. But Mr Viereck seemed to go down awfully fast and awfully hard from a single punch. I wonder about that man.'

'You needn't,' Howard countered; 'he's a scoundrel of the first water.'

'Hmph. Well, you're probably right.'

'So it's all done with,' Sonia persisted. 'Isn't it? Isn't it?'

Hardeen shook his head. 'Not quite, but it will be. If they were building this one fortification, they were probably building more.'

'Captain Yarnell thinks so, anyhow,' Pagnanelli put in. 'He said that he'd cabled to the Navy Department in Washington, and they're going to search all up and down the coast. Even in the Gulf, and even in the Pacific. If there was one of these nests, he thinks there will be more. But we'll get them all. We'll clean them out, every one of them. No question about that!'

'And what about us, then?' Theo asked.

'What do you mean? We're finished with this. We can go home, go back to our lives.'

Theo said, 'Then – you and Howard . . .?'

'I think – ' George Pagnanelli interrupted them. 'I think I'd better go back over to the Neck. Over to Burgess's. When we settled up with him for the plane I forgot to bring away Mr Lovecraft's clothes. And we ought to pay Burgess for the old outfit of his and the blankets we took.'

He started toward the door. 'I'll take the Rickenbacker, is that all right, Mr Weiss?'

Theo grunted agreement.

Pagnanelli left.

Theo looked at Sonia and Howard. Lovecraft had returned to his seat near the fire and was staring into it drowsily. Theo reached for Sonia's hand and drew her to the far side of the room, near the great window overlooking the harbor. 'Do you really think he's going to come back? Do you really think that, Sonia?'

She looked past Theo, toward the drowsing Howard. 'No. No, I'm afraid not. I've competed with his aunts and I've lost out, I think. But I have to make one more try. I do, Theo.'

'And if you fail? I don't mean to be cruel, Sonia. But . . .' He shook his head.

She smiled at him and shrugged; for a woman so generously proportioned it was a surprisingly winsome gesture. Keeping Theo at her side, she returned to the fireplace and sat down beside her husband.

Weiss said, 'You know, you've performed a great service for the nation. You, Sonia – and Howard even more.'

Lovecraft responded, sitting taller in his chair. He rubbed his eyes with his knuckles. 'Service?'

'We had our eyes on this bunch for a long while,' Theo went on. 'If this were wartime we'd have those men up on treason charges, and you'd be wearing a medal.'

Lovecraft grinned. 'That's what I'd hoped for during the World War. I never even made it into a uniform.'

'But with the world as it is,' Weiss resumed, 'you'll probably get a letter from the White House thanking you for your services. Which will not be specified, of course. And no photo in the newspaper, no handshake from the President, no glory.'

Lovecraft shook his head. 'Those who most seek glory are often those who least deserve it, Weiss.'

Theo nodded his head. 'We can't quite apply that rule in my business. You remember Ehrich's notions about circusing.'

'I do.' There was a silence, then Lovecraft spoke again. 'Perhaps that is the difference between us, Weiss. For all that I could admire Houdini's achievements and respect his undoubted skill, there was a certain difference of – I do not wish to appear unkind – breeding.'

He gave the magician a kindly smile. 'I have always thought that you demonstrated a greater dignity of style than your brother. Your skill is doubtless the equal of his. And you have shown far more class. Yet, which of you is the more famous? Houdini is dead, Hardeen lives. But in a decade or a century, which name will the herd recall? Houdini or Hardeen?

'Perhaps we share more than we realize, you and I, despite the difference in our blood.'

When Lovecraft finished, there was a lengthy silence. Finally Hardeen cleared his throat self-consciously. 'Well, if you're sure you'll be all right. Howard, I think you ought to have a thorough medical checkup. Of course the government will cover all the expenses. And, ah, can we offer you transportation? Pagnanelli and I will be headed back toward New York in a little while. If we can give you a ride back to the city, or to Brooklyn? Or if you prefer, we could drop you in Providence . . .'

Lovecraft shook his head. 'I think I'd prefer to rest for another day. Then I can take the Boston and Maine from here. Thank you just the same.'

Hardeen said, 'Sonia?'

She shook her head. 'I'll stay with Howard. Maybe he'll change his mind. If not, we can ride together as far as Providence. Then I'll continue.'

Hardeen shook hands with each of them. 'Pagnanelli

should be back any minute. I'll wait in the foyer.' He left.

Sonia took Lovecraft's hands as soon as Hardeen had closed the door. 'Are you comfortable, Howard dear? Can I get you anything? Some soup? Tea?'

Lovecraft thought for a moment. 'No, I'm quite comfortable, thank you. But if you could – oh, my commonplace book and Waterman were in my suit. I suppose they're ruined by now. But if you could find me a writing pad and a pencil. Thank you.'

She located the requested articles and sat beside him.

For a little while the hiss and crackle of the fire was the only sound in the room. The droning aircraft, the shudders and the thumps that had marked the day, were ended. The naval planes had returned to the *Saratoga*. The experimental bombers had turned about and flown back to their own bases. The Army and Navy would be searching the harbors and coastal waters of the nation for weeks, seeking out other secret installations like the one destroyed near Satan Rock. Surely word would have reached all of the men in the structures, and they would be gone before the bombs arrived.

Sonia found that she was trembling slightly and leaned forward to press her cheek against her husband's. He held the yellow pad she'd brought him, in one hand, and a wooden pencil in the other. 'Howard, are you all right?'

His eyes had been closed, but he opened them and gazed upon her. 'Quite, thank you.'

'Howard darling, I was thinking about what Theo said. If you could see your way clear to come back to New York to live. You know, you have a lot of friends there. And most of the publishers are there. I know Henneberger's in Chicago, but most of the others are in New York. Mr Gernsback is.'

Lovecraft nodded absently.

'And – and, Howard.' Sonia hesitated. 'Howard, I'm

still your wife. I know that you're very attached to your aunts, and I was perfectly willing to live in Providence, you remember that, Howard. But they wouldn't have me. You understood that. They said I couldn't operate a shop in Providence, it was beneath the family's standing. So I had to leave.

'But we could live in New York again. You could visit Belknap Long whenever you wanted, and your other friends, and write whatever you wanted to. I'm making a good salary now, Howard.'

She drew back and looked at his face. His eyes were closed, but more as though in deep concentration than as in sleep.

This had been an astonishing experience, Lovecraft was thinking. From that first terrifying, yet exhilarating, encounter at the edge of the Seekonk River, when he'd discovered the drowning man Madeiros, through the whole adventure with Viereck and Lüdecke and all of the others in their strange conspiracy. There must be some way to make something of it all. Of course he couldn't just tell his story. The government would interfere if he tried to do that. And besides, as he'd told Hardeen, circusing might be all right for escape artists and magicians, but it was hardly suitable for a born aristocrat and serious artist like himself.

But he must be able to turn the experience to good use.

He opened his eyes and smiled distractedly at Sonia, made a few random jottings on the yellow pad she'd found for him, then shut his eyes again to think.

Of course he couldn't say anything about Marblehead. But in his own stories he'd already used the ancient town, altering its name but retaining its location and historic nature. And for the same reason he couldn't use a location like Satan Rock. He'd transform that, too. Let's see, instead of a simple conspiracy of politicians and traitors he would devise something more in keeping with the kind of story he preferred to write, and rather than Europe as the enemy's base of operations he would select a more exotic locale.

Sonia was still talking to him, something about taking him to see her doctor in Brooklyn. As if he needed a doctor, and as if there weren't perfectly competent physicians near his home in Providence-Plantations.

He opened his eyes and smiled benignly at his wife. 'If you please, Sonia, I should like to concentrate on my work. Perhaps we could continue our conversation over dinner.'

He turned his eyes back to the pad, balanced the lead pencil thoughtfully for a moment, and began to write: *During the winter of 1927–28 officials of the Federal government made a strange and secret investigation of certain conditions in the ancient Massachusetts seaport of Innsmouth. The public first learned of it . . .*

Postscriptum: March 14, 1928

The North German Lloyd liner *Bremen* moved majesti-
cally through the Narrows separating Brooklyn from
Staten Island, and into lower New York harbor. The
great ship swung to port, proceeded southward of the
Battery, and came up the Hudson River to be greeted by
hooting tugs and guided carefully to her berth at Pier 19
on the West Side of Manhattan.

The day was bright and seasonably warm, with the
promise of an early and pleasant spring already in the air.
Leaning against the railing of the *Bremen* in raglan tweed
topcoat and a cloth cap, George Sylvester Viereck peered
into the dark waters and the white foam stirred up by the
passage of the ship. There had been a setback; there
were always setbacks, but one resolutely put them behind
and turned to face the future. One resumed one's tasks.

He had been gone from America longer than he had
expected, but his business in Europe had not been unpro-
ductive. He had obtained interviews with any number of
lions and had conversed with William Randolph Hearst
by transatlantic telephone to establish a good market for
them upon his return. He had seen his correspondent-
friend Dr Freud in Vienna, and visited his cousins the old
Kaiser and the Kronprinz-pretender in Doorn.

And in Munich he had visited NSDAP headquarters
and squared himself with the Führer and other Party
leaders. One took risks in striking for grand objectives.
The alternative was to play safe, to proceed cautiously,
and to accomplish nothing. The bold stroke, that was the
Führer's philosophy, and he had praised rather than

condemned Lüdecke, Kiep, Spanknoebel, and Viereck himself.

As for the Lovecraft affair – that was hardly mentioned. It was the blind bad luck of the American submarine S-4 making her test runs off the Massachusetts coast that had led to the discovery of *Unterwasserprojekt Elf*, and to the destruction of the secret undersea installations.

Hitler had not blamed Viereck for the misfortune. In fact, as Sylvester was leaving, the Führer had given him another sheaf of manuscript sheets to translate and prepare for publication in the English language.

Viereck drew on his corona maduro, threw the stub of the cigar overboard, and watched it spin and tumble into the Hudson. He turned and began to make his way belowdecks, ready to return to his home.

At the customs shed on the pier there was a small delay. Nothing wrong with Viereck's luggage – a few changes of clothing, some toilet implements, a writing kit and papers. But there was an oddity involving his passport and visés. Yes, this was very odd. Certainly the passport itself was in order; Viereck was a citizen of the United States. But there seemed to be no record of his having *left* the country on his present journey. Every earlier departure and return was stamped – but this time only a return.

But a quick telephone call to the German Consulate, and a high officer there, a Dr Kiep, spoke with the immigration officials. It was all some sort of administrative error, of course. Mr Viereck an American citizen *was*, and his visé in order certainly *was*. Dr Kiep for Mr Viereck personally could *vouch*. He would even send an automobile from the Consulate to carry Mr Viereck to his home. Official conferred with official and Mr Viereck permitted to leave the pier *was*, with a somewhat puzzled apology for the confusion.

He lit a good Cuban cigar and made his way to the

street to await Dr Kiep in his Horch. A radio store nearby had set up a loud-speaker, and a recent show tune was squawking away. A newsboy hawked the early edition of Macfadden's *Daily Graphic*, where Viereck himself had worked for a time before returning to the Hearst fold.

He bought a *Graphic,* for old times' sake. He read the headlines as tinny music rattled in the background; the show tune was 'My Heart Stood Still'. Viereck read the lead story in the *Graphic:* a dam had burst in California killing almost five hundred persons and sweeping thousands of homes before the raging waters receded. The Saint Francis disaster was merely the latest in an uncanny series of violently destructive mishaps in American coastal waters since last December. From floods in Vermont to collapsed levees in Louisiana, the eastern sector of the country had been plagued with rampaging waters, and now the Pacific Coast had experienced its first such catastrophe.

Viereck was startled from his concentration on the paper. Two dark-suited men had approached him, and one now grasped him by the arm. 'Mr Viereck?' He nodded. 'We've sent your luggage on by taxi, sir. You're to come with us.'

Viereck tossed his cigar into the gutter, folded the newspaper under his raglan sleeve, and followed the two men. They reached the curb, and the men guided him toward the car. It wasn't Dr Kiep's familiar Horch, but a long sleek Pierce. 'Warten Sie!' Viereck exclaimed. The men ignored his command. 'Wait! This is wrong!' But he felt a hard object in his ribs. One of the men hissed at him, 'Just come along!'

He acceded.

Both men climbed into the rear seat of the Pierce with him. A third man was waiting in the driver's seat and guided the big Pierce across town and up Fifth Avenue to the Netherland Hotel. During the trip Viereck tried to get information from the others, but they ignored his questions and demands.

As the car approached the Netherland the man beside Viereck gave him instructions. 'We're not to hurt you, Mr Viereck, unless you start a row. Someone needs to speak with you. But don't shout or try to get away, you understand, sir? It's your life, you understand?'

Viereck nodded. 'Who is it? What do they want?'

The man did not answer.

At Fifty-ninth Street the car pulled to the curb. The hotel doorman held the Pierce's door while Viereck and his two companions climbed out; the driver pulled the car back into the stream of Fifth Avenue traffic. Viereck's companions stayed close as they crossed the lobby and hustled him into an elevator. When it reached its floor the two men guided him from the car, along a hallway, knocked at a door.

Still another well-dressed man checked them at the doorway and ushered Viereck into the sitting room of a suite.

A short dark-complexioned man with a black moustache sat on a Louis XIV sofa. 'Mr Viereck!' The man stood up and extended his hand. 'Welcome home! You must have missed America while you was away! How was Europe? I hope you got to visit Italy. Did you interview Signor Mussolini?'

Viereck frowned. 'What's this all about? Have I been kidnapped for ransom? What in hell do you want?'

The man dropped his hand to his side and looked disappointed. 'No, no, no. Please sit down. Make yourself comfortable. I only need to talk a little to you. Was my fellows hard on you? I'll scold them if they was hard on you. Would you like a glass of wine?' He called to one of his henchmen, and the man disappeared into a pantry. 'I guess you got no problems over drinks in Europe. Here in America, hah! Oh, well, I suppose you like something stronger.'

The henchman had brought in a tray with a bottle of dark red wine and two glasses. He stood waiting until the other waved him away. The man with the moustache said, 'I'm sorry, I didn't think. I should have got a bottle of schnapps for you, Mr Viereck. Oh, I'm sorry, I didn't introduce myself. My name's Morelli. I'm a stranger here myself. My home, it's in Rhode Island, in Providence.'

Viereck thought that Morelli pronounced schnapps as if it were spelled *shnop'sa* He was understandable, but his accent marked his every sentence.

'I'll pour us a glass, Mr Viereck,' the man went on. Viereck gazed suspiciously at the glasses. Morelli laughed loudly. 'No poison, Mr Viereck! No drugs! Such theater! Such – hah! – melodrama. I only got to talk to you, Mr Viereck, that's all!'

'Very well,' Sylvester growled. 'What have you to say?'

'Well, Mr Viereck, it's about your conduct. You're an American citizen, eh? I know, I know. I checked up a little. I hope you don't mind. You're a good American. Come!' Morelli picked up his glass, held it so the wine caught the light of the electric chandelier. 'Let's toast, to America!'

Viereck picked up his glass and sipped grudgingly. Well, at least Morelli served good wine. An Italian should! If Viereck could get to the telephone and call Dr Kiep . . . That would take too long. The police? Even the housephone, he could call the desk and – and what? Plead for help? Well, he was a legitimate citizen. He was being held prisoner, however gently. He had a right!

'Mr Viereck,' Morelli resumed. 'I understand you got some very odd friends. I understand you got some very odd hobbies, too. Like, yachting?'

'Yachting?' Viereck was startled.

Morelli grinned. 'Like yachting with submarines. Eh?'

Viereck felt his mouth drawing into a snarl. He picked up his wine glass and swallowed from it.

'And your strange friends,' Morelli resumed. 'You know, like those KKK people, and those funny Russians from Connecticut.' Morelli nodded earnestly. 'And your German friends. You should remember, Mr Viereck, you're a good American now, you're not German no more.

'Like *me*,' Morelli grinned. 'I used to be Italian. I'm an American now. We're both Americans, we're both good citizens, we understand each other, hey?'

Viereck said coldly, 'I don't think we do. Just what are you after? Is this some kind of shakedown?'

Morelli waved his hands in the air. 'Oh, no, no, no! Oh, Mr Viereck, you don't understand me. I'm a patriotic man, I want to talk to you about patriotism, that's all! You know about patriotism. Your friends, they talk about it all the time, eh? The flag, the law, all of that.'

He leaned forward seriously. He pointed a finger at Viereck's chest, and in an instant seemed to grow to twice his size. 'Mr Viereck, I'm gonna tell you this. I don't work for no government. I'm a businessman, you see? But I know what you been up to. You think I'm some criminal, but I care about my country.'

'I know who you are,' Viereck spat. 'I know you. I heard about you and your people in the Sacco matter. You're the Morelli gang. You're a killer! How dare you lecture me – '

Morelli's fist crashed on the table. 'And you're the same! You think we don't know who killed Carisi and Amoroso? We're the same, you and me, Mr Viereck! Yes, we're both killers! So we understand each other! Hey?'

Viereck remained silent.

'*Hey*?' Morelli insisted.

'Well then, what of it?'

'Okay.' Morelli took a breath. 'Okay, *this*. You want to play games, you want to write books, I don't care. You say anything you like to say. You love Il Duce, that's okay. I don't like him so much, but you can like him. You love your Hitler, that's okay too. I don't like him, you can like him.

'But we'll be watching you, Mr Viereck. No more funny navy games, hey? No little armies. You keep your step straight. Like they say, you keep your nose clean, amico mio. Hey, Sylvester?'

Viereck winced at the use of his familiar name.

'Or else, amico mio, you know what happened to poor Signor Madeiros?'

Viereck stared at Morelli.

'Not Madeiros what got burned,' Morelli said. 'That would be bad, eh? But we don't do that. I mean his brother. He got to go swimming, only he didn't come up. Maybe he was looking for submarines, do you think? What do you think, Sylvester, maybe he was looking for submarines!'

Bibliography

In addition to the correspondence and unpublished papers, sound recordings and personal recollections, and other primary material as indicated in the Compiler's Note, the following secondary sources proved helpful:

ALLEN, FREDERICK LEWIS. *Only Yesterday*. New York: Harper & Brothers, 1931.

ALLSOP, KENNETH. *The Bootleggers: The Story of Prohibition*. New Rochelle: Arlington House, 1961.

ALSBERG, H. G., ed. *The American Guide*. New York: Hastings House, 1949.

[ANONYMOUS]. *Magic and Mystery: The Incredible Psychic Investigations of Houdini and Dunninger*. New York: Weathervane Books, 1967.

BECKWITH, HENRY L.P. JR. *Lovecraft's Providence and Adjacent Parts*. West Kingston, Rhode Island: Donald M. Grant, 1979.

CARLSON, JOHN ROY. *Under Cover*. New York: E. P. Dutton & Co., 1943.

——. *The Plotters*. New York: E. P. Dutton & Co., 1946.

CARTER, LIN. *Lovecraft: A Look Behind the 'Cthulhu Mythos'*. New York: Ballantine Books, 1972.

CHRISTOPHER, MILBOURNE. *Houdini: The Untold Story*. New York: Thomas Y. Crowell, 1969.

DAVIS, MAC. *From Moses to Einstein: They Are All Jews*. New York: Jordan Publishing Co., 1937.

DILLING, ELIZABETH MAUDE. *The Red Network: A 'Who's Who' and Handbook for Patriots*. Kenilworth, Illinois: Privately printed, 1934.

– – . *The Roosevelt Red Record and Its Background.* Kenilworth, Illinois: Privately printed, 1936.

DE CAMP, L. SPRAGUE. *Lovecraft: A Biography.* Garden City, New York: Doubleday & Co., 1975.

– – .*Literary Swordsmen and Sorcerers.* Sauk City, Wisconsin: Arkham House, 1976.

– – , DE CAMP, CATHERINE CROOK, and GRIFFIN, JANE WHITTINGTON. *Dark Valley Destiny: The Life of Robert E. Howard.* New York: Bluejay Books, 1983.

DERLETH, AUGUST. H.P.L.: *A Memoir.* New York: Ben Abramson, 1945.

DOYLE, ARTHUR CONAN. *The Edge of the Unknown.* New York: G. P. Putnam's Sons, 1930.

[EDITORS OF TIME-LIFE BOOKS]. *The Fabulous Century, Volume III 1920/1930.* New York: Time-Life Books, 1969.

FURNAS, J. C. *Great Times.* New York: G. P. Putnam's Sons, 1974.

– – . *Stormy Weather.* New York: G. P. Putnam's Sons, 1977.

GERTZ, ELMER. *Odyssey of a Barbarian: The Biography of George Sylvester Viereck.* Buffalo, New York: Prometheus Books, 1978.

GIBSON, WALTER B. *The Original Houdini Scrapbook.* New York: Sterling Publishing Co., 1976.

GORES, JOSEPH N. *Marine Salvage: The Unforgiving Business of No Cure, No Pay.* Garden City, New York: Doubleday & Co., 1971.

HARDIN, NILS, ed. *Xenophile* 18 (October 1975).

HOUDINI, HARRY. *The Right Way To Do Wrong.* Boston: Privately printed, 1906.

JENKINS, ALAN. *The Twenties.* New York: Universe Books, 1974.

JOHNSON, NEIL M. *George Sylvester Viereck: German-American Propagandist.* Urbana, Illinois: University of Illinois Press, 1972.

JOSHI, S. T. *An Index to the Selected Letters of H. P. Lovecraft*. West Warwick, Rhode Island: Necronomicon Press, 1980.

– – . *H.P. Lovecraft and Lovecraft Criticism: An Annotated Bibliography*. Kent, Ohio: Kent State University Press, 1981.

LEIGHTON, ISABEL, ed. *The Aspirin Age 1919–1941*. New York: Simon & Schuster, 1949.

LONG, FRANK BELKNAP. *Howard Phillips Lovecraft: Dreamer on the Nightside*. Sauk City, Wisconsin: Arkham House, 1975.

LORD, GLENN, ed. *The Last Celt: A Bio-Bibliography of Robert Ervin Howard*. West Kingston, Rhode Island: Donald M. Grant, 1976.

LOVECRAFT, HOWARD PHILLIPS. *Supernatural Horror in Literature*. New York: Ben Abramson, 1945.

– – . *Selected Letters I-V*. Edited by August Derleth, Donald Wandrei, and James Turner. Sauk City, Wisconsin: Arkham House, 1965–76.

– – . *To Quebec and the Stars*. Edited by L. Sprague de Camp. West Kingston, Rhode Island: Donald M. Grant, 1976.

– – . *First Writings: Pawtuxet Valley Gleaner*. Edited by Marc A. Michaud. West Warwick, Rhode Island: Necronomicon Press, 1976.

– – and CONOVER, WILLIS. *Lovecraft at Last*. Arlington, Virginia: Carrollton-Clark, 1975.

MEIER, FRANK. *Men Under the Sea*. New York: E. P. Dutton & Co., 1948.

RUBER, PETER. *The Last Bookman*. New York: Candlelight Press, 1968.

SHREFFLER, PHILIP A. *The H. P. Lovecraft Companion*. Westport, Connecticut: Greenwood Press, 1977.

SIFAKIS, CARL. *The Encyclopedia of American Crime*. New York: Facts on File, 1982.

SILVER, NATHAN. *Lost New York*. New York: Weathervane Books, 1967.

SMITH, CLARK ASHTON. *Planets and Dimensions*. Edited by Charles K. Wolfe. Baltimore: Mirage Press, 1973.

— — . *The Black Book of Clark Ashton Smith*. Sauk City, Wisconsin: Arkham House, 1979.

ST ARMAND, BARTON LEVI. *The Roots of Horror in the Fiction of H. P. Lovecraft*. Elizabethtown, New York: Dragon Press, 1977.

ST GEORGE, MAXIMILIAN J. and DENNIS, LAWRENCE. *A Trial on Trial*. National Civil Rights Committee, 1946.

STARRETT, VINCENT. *Seaports in the Moon*. Garden City, New York: Doubleday, Doran & Co., 1928.

— — . *Books Alive*. New York: Random House, 1940.

— — . *Bookman's Holiday*. New York: Random House, 1942.

— — . *Books and Bipeds*. New York: Argus Books, 1947.

— — . *Born in a Bookshop: Chapters from the Chicago Renascence*. Norman, Oklahoma: University of Oklahoma Press, 1965.

STEPHAN, JOHN J. *The Russian Fascists: Tragedy and Farce in Exile, 1925–1945*. New York: Harper & Row, 1978.

SIDNEY-FRYER, DONALD, ed. *Emperor of Dreams: A Clark Ashton Smith Bibliography*. West Kingston, Rhode Island: Donald M. Grant, 1978.

THOMAS, LOWELL, *History As You Heard It*. Garden City, New York: Doubleday & Co., 1957.

VIERECK, GEORGE SYLVESTER. *The House of the Vampire*. New York: Moffat, Yard, 1907.

— — . *Glimpses of the Great*. New York: Macaulay Co., 1930.

— — . *Spreading Germs of Hate*. New York: Horace Liveright, 1930.

— — . *My Flesh and Blood: A Lyric Autobiography*. New York: Horace Liveright, 1931.

– – . *The Kaiser on Trial*. New York: Greystone Press, 1937.

WEINBERG, ROBERT, ed. *The Weird Tales Story*. West Linn, Oregon: Fax Collector's Editions, 1977.

WILLIAMS, BERYL, and EPSTEIN, SAMUEL. *The Great Houdini, Magician Extraordinary*. New York: Julian Messner, 1950.

WOODFORD, JACK. *The Loud Literary Lamas of New York*. New York: Vantage Press, 1950.